T0305125

Networks in the Innovation Process

Networks in the Innovation Process

Local and Regional Interactions

Holger Graf

Friedrich Schiller University,
Economics Department
Jena, Germany

Edward Elgar
Cheltenham, UK · Northhampton, MA, USA

Published by
Edward Elgar Publishing Limited
Glensanda House
Montpellier Parade
Cheltenham
Glos GL50 1UA
UK

Edward Elgar Publishing, Inc.
William Pratt House
9 Dewey Court
Northampton
Massachusetts 01060
USA

A catalogue record for this book
is available from the British Library

Library of Congress Cataloguing in Publication Data
Graf, Holger, 1973–
 Networks in the innovation process : local and regional interactions / Holger Graf.
  p. cm.
 Includes bibliographical references and index.
 1. Technological innovations—Economic aspects. 2. Diffusion of innovations—Economic aspects. 3. Business networks. 4. Strategic alliances (Business) 5. Economic development. 6. Knowledge management. I. Title.
 HC79.T4G6785 2007
 338'.064—dc22

                    2006021905

ISBN-10: 1 84542 930 3
ISBN-13: 978 1 84542 930 0

Printed and bound in Great Britain by MPG Books Ltd, Bodmin, Cornwall

Contents

Figures

Tables

Preface

In mainstream economics, all individual plans are coordinated ex ante by the invisible hand of the market. This assumption may hold in certain situations where uncertainty and information asymmetries are low, but certainly not in the process of innovation. As the price mechanism loses its potential and the repeated interaction between heterogeneous actors becomes central to the organization of the process, a different perspective has to be taken: the systemic view of innovation. The fact that innovative activity is neither uniformly nor randomly distributed across geographical space, provides the rationale to study innovation at a regional level.

Many scholars have learned from these major insights and analyze innovation processes at the regional level. Most studies in this field are either case studies of specific regions or comparative studies which employ a production function approach. While the former approach is able to identify important historical events and specific ties between important actors it is difficult or even impossible to reproduce the results or to apply it to a number of localities. On the other hand, the latter approach can easily be applied to different regions at different points in time, but does not account for specificities in the modes of interaction. This book is an attempt to combine the merits of both approaches by treating processes of knowledge generation and diffusion as specific interactions within an empirical approach which is applicable to a variety of regional entities. As a consequence, this work is rather heterogenous with respect to the empirical methodology.

This book was written as my PhD thesis at the Friedrich Schiller University in Jena. I am indebted to Uwe Cantner who raised my interest in the topic and provided a perfect working environment. Our joint articles provided the basis for chapters 4 and 6. Besides, the book would not have been written without the stimulating discussions and the cooperative atmosphere at his chair. In recognizing the risk of 'technological lock-in' he encouraged me to present my work at workshops and conferences throughout Europe and thereby absorb novel approaches. My work was also inspired by attending workshops and presentations at the nearby Max-Planck Institute for economics, which led to the fruitful cooperation with Dirk Fornahl in chapter 5.

I am deeply grateful to have Jens Krüger as a colleague who is especially helpful in questions about testing hypothesis and clearly sharpened my sense of empirical research. Support by Wolfgang Ziegler from the patent information center of the university in Jena was invaluable in gathering patent information for Germany on a regional level. I would generally like to thank my colleagues at the university of Jena for the frequent discussions and our students for their research assistance.

Finally, I want to thank my wife Judith and my three daughters Leonie, Luciana and Johanna who always provided a welcome distraction from the demanding research and cheered me up when things went different than expected.

1. Introduction

> When the process of innovation is regarded as the outcome of a complex interaction, it is obvious that the whole system might be more than a sum of its parts. (Lundvall, 1988, p. 361)

Innovation and technological progress are fundamental to economic growth. The question regarding the essential determinants of successful innovation is at the center of research on innovation in economics. A key concept to answer this question is the systems of innovation approach (SI).

The SI approach is largely based on the idea that abilities and incentives of firms and individuals to innovate cannot be analyzed in isolation. On the contrary, they are embedded within a more or less broadly defined system of actors and institutions. The diffusion of new information and knowledge is accelerated by the exchange of knowledge and experiences between the actors within the system. Thereby knowledge is accumulated and capabilities are broadened, which, if economically useful, might lead to more innovation.

The notion of an *innovation system* integrates this systemic and interaction-based view of processes that generate novelty. Properties of and mechanisms within innovation systems are identified on several levels of aggregation. Concepts of regional or local innovation systems (see Braczyk et al., 1998; Breschi and Lissoni, 2001a) assume a higher propensity of interaction between individuals that are close in geographical space. Cognitive proximity, on the other hand, might be higher between individuals working on similar problems with similar methods within technological or sectoral systems (Carlsson and Stankiewicz, 1991; Carlsson, 1995; Nelson and Mowery, 1999; Malerba, 2002). Both views are present in the literature on national innovation systems, which is more focussed on institutional and political aspects (Lundvall, 1992; Nelson, 1993).

The idea of thinking in terms of innovation systems is anything but new. A first systematic theoretical approach dates back to the German economist Friedrich List (1798–1846) (Freeman, 1995). In contrast to the rather cosmopolitan attitude of Adam Smith, where economic welfare arises through adequate allocation of resources and the division of labor, List (1841) had a rather

1

national view of economic development. He emphasized the relevance of own, i.e. national, productive forces, with the national government having important duties in fostering industrial development by providing infrastructure and a functioning education system, amongst others. Even though he did not explicitly speak of a system where the linkages between the actors and feedback mechanisms are of critical importance, he suggested policies that were aiming at learning about new technologies and their application (Freeman, 2002).

One might view the return to List as a sheer anecdote and see the focus on nations as irrelevant in a world characterized by increasing globalization. But recent history provides us with the Japanese model as an example of a national innovation system shaped and managed by the national government with a coordinator MITI and numerous linkages between firms and other public and private actors. The success of this model, at least in the 1970s and 1980s, has definitely led economists to acknowledge the systemic dimension of innovation and to start dealing with the analysis of innovation systems.

Relating the work on national innovation systems to regional economics, a vast and growing literature on regional innovation systems (RIS) emerged during the last two decades. Two facts provide the rationale for studying innovation on a regional level (see Asheim and Gertler, 2004):

i) Innovative activity is neither uniformly nor randomly distributed across geographical space. In particular, the more knowledge-intensive the economic activity, the more geographically clustered it tends to be.

ii) The tendency towards spatial concentration has been increasing over time (Leyshon and Thrift, 1997; Feldman, 2001). These observations contradict the view that the merits of information and communication technologies will lead to the dispersal of innovative activity over time.

The argument that geographical or spatial proximity of actors in such a system is beneficial to the establishment of relationships and the subsequent exchange of know-how and information is at the heart of this research. Also, other factors relevant to the exchange of knowledge such as technological proximity, culture, language, or institutional arrangements are frequently put forward. The prime example of a regional innovation system is Silicon Valley, a birthplace of modern information and communication technology (Saxenian, 1994). Silicon Valley today is a large agglomeration of high-technology firms that emerged in a self-organizing manner in the desert of California. The success story of Silicon Valley has led politicians to foster and support such systems. While there are some examples of the success of such policies, such as the 'Wissenschaftsstadt Ulm' or the BioRegio contest in Germany (Boucke et al., 1994; Dohse, 2000), there are also negative examples of such political efforts, especially in those cases where planned science parks have failed to develop innovative networks of cooperation and interactive learning (Asheim and Cooke, 1998; Asheim and Gertler, 2004). Cooke (2001) notes that, 'a lack of systemic network development' is observed, and, 'these [government research laboratories] stood like cathedrals in the desert, often in agglomeration but not clustering and not creating synergies through spin-off and subcontracting activities' (Cooke, 2001, p. 950). The problems of planning such a complex system are also highlighted by Edquist (2004, p. 191) in the following quotation:

> The systematic approach to SIs suggested here does not imply that they are or can be consciously designed or planned. On the contrary, just as innovation processes are evolutionary, SIs evolve over time in a largely unplanned manner. Even if we knew all the determinants of innovations processes in detail (which we certainly do not now, and perhaps never will), we would not be able to control them and design or 'build' SIs on the basis of this knowledge. Centralized control over SIs is impossible and innovation policy can only influence the spontaneous development of SIs to a limited extent.

A common conceptual mistake is to merely rely on the benefits of agglomeration which might arise as localized knowledge spillovers. The idea behind this concept is that some elements of knowledge are 'in the air' and might be absorbed by co-location. While the geographical effects of knowledge spillovers have frequently been tested (Jaffe, 1986; Jaffe et al., 1993), studies, like the one by Breschi and Lissoni (2003), provide a deeper analysis of the issue. Breschi and Lissoni (2003) find that it is social rather than geographical proximity that leads to interaction and therefore geographical proximity is only observed to be responsible for knowledge spillovers as it raises the probability of social proximity. Social contacts between the actors in such a system need a common basis and seemingly more time for interaction to become established than often expected.

Contrasting the sole reliance on the benefits of knowledge spillovers within local networks, only recently, several authors have pronounced the importance of interaction with actors external to the local system (Gertler, 1997; Bathelt, 2003; Bathelt et al., 2004). The benefits of dense local networks are higher if external knowledge can diffuse quickly within the system and the risks of technological lock-in by losing connections to new developments diminish.

These issues of internal and external interaction in local innovation systems motivate the present study on interaction in local innovation systems. We present our application of the concept of innovation systems to the case of Jena. The research objective is twofold. First, we will provide a comprehensive and detailed analysis of the actors in the local innovation system and their interaction in the process of knowledge generation. Second, we present novel methodological approaches to this issue by applying social network analysis to the system of innovating actors in Jena and to the technological knowledge-base of the innovation system.

The book has the following structure: chapters 2 and 3 provide an overview of the literature and give the theoretical background for the remaining, empirical chapters 4 to 7. In chapter 2, we discuss the economic properties of know-how and introduce the idea of invention and innovation as processes of experimenting and learning. These ideas merge into aspects of the organization of the innovation process in networks, which, as a whole, provide the basis for a systemic view of innovation. After the presentation of a stylized innovation system, we discuss the functionality and the boundaries of such systems, and provide a typology of innovation systems with respect to the system level of aggregation.

Following this rather abstract view of innovation systems as an adequate approach to analyzing innovative activities, chapter 3 shifts the focus to geographical aspects of economic activity in general and innovative activity in particular. The discussion of localized knowledge spillovers as a centripetal force in the process of agglomeration of innovative activity is of major importance, as it establishes empirical facts which are analyzed in greater depth by subsequent research. Aspects of the structure of these agglomerations, like technological specialization and diversification, supplement that discussion, while the mobility of labor is highlighted as a major mechanism for knowledge spillovers to arise. Besides, studies in that line of inquiry have been able to post some criticism on the naive view of knowledge spillovers, which calls for a more complex approach to the relationship between geography and innovation. The specificities of interaction between different types of actors, in particular local private firms, local public research, and external actors are discussed in the presentation of regional and local systems of innovation. To round off the theoretical part, we widen the view and establish linkages between geography, technological and sectoral innovation systems, and the integrative aspects of the innovation systems approach as a whole.

The empirical part of this study is covered in chapters 4 to 7. Starting with a characterization of Jena within the whole of Germany, we proceed with a detailed description of the innovation system in Jena by means of survey data (chapter 5) and social network analysis (chapter 6) and end this part with a detailed comparison of Jena with other successful regions in chapter 7.

Chapter 4 presents a study of the relationship between the structure of regions as well as the degree and types of interaction in these regions. Data on patents are aggregated to the level of technologies in regions. It shows that those technology regions which are moderately specialized have the highest propensity to cooperate and the share of internal cooperation is increasing with tech-regions' technological specialization. Within this chapter, the focus is shifted from a more general view of the matter to the specific case of Jena.

We focus on the local innovation system of Jena, because it stands out of the mass of communities in the East of Germany as a technologically and economically successful region (OECD, 2001; Cantner et al., 2003). Since the unification of Germany in 1989, Jena is often named as an outstanding example for prospering economic development in the eastern part of Germany. Comments like 'Silicon Valley des Ostens' or 'Boomtown des Ostens' are found in the press (e.g. Bott, 2000) and a recent series in the German newspaper *Handelsblatt* included Jena as one of nine 'Stille Stars' (silent stars).

For Jena we find a highly interactive structure, with the number of cooperations, internal as well as external to the system, being significantly above average. It also becomes apparent that the local technological trajectories are subject to a dominating influence of internal actors.

The observations of Jena as a successful and interacting innovation system provided the motivations for conducting a survey of high-technology firms in Jena. Chapter 5 presents the descriptive results of this survey. According to the literature, regional clusters or industrial districts are characterized by strong user–producer relationships within the value chain. However, the innovation system of Jena is rather characterized as a region with a stronger focus on external relations with respect to material and product flows and where most firms are specialized producers competing on international markets. It turns out that the internal relations within the processes of learning and innovation are of major importance for the local innovation system.

While the survey provides some quantitative evidence on the structure of local and external interaction, we deepen the quest for interactive structures and their evolution in chapter 6. By applying the methodology of social network analysis, we are able to generate graphical representations of these interactions and to perform statistical analyses on the networks, which are identified on three different layers: interaction based on a common technological knowledge-base, on the job mobility of scientists, and on cooperations between innovators. We find the dynamics of the system to be directed towards an increasing focus on core competencies of the local innovation system. It also shows that the local innovation system is clearly dominated by the local university and public research institutes, while, as a consequence of economic transformation in Jena, the dominating firms, the successors of the Carl-Zeiss combine, lose their central position.

Chapter 7 aims at questioning the favorable statements about Jena by evaluating the technological and economic performance of the local innovation system. Jena is compared to Ulm, Dresden, and Heidelberg with respect to innovative performance, modes of interaction in the process of innovation, and the structure and evolution of the technological knowledge-base. The regions are then compared according to their economic development as indicated by figures on regional GDP and employment. In the concluding chapter 8, the main results of the research project are summarized and related to each other.

There, we also make some suggestions for further research in this vital and promising field.

2. The Systemic View of Innovation

2.1 TOWARDS A SYSTEMIC VIEW OF INNOVATION

Three major insights provide the foundation for a systemic view of innovation: (1) technological know-how is the basis for successful innovation; (2) this know-how is developed through processes of experimenting and learning; (3) these processes are interactive, within social networks, and different phases of these processes are connected through feedback mechanisms.

These propositions provide the structure for this section. Section 2.1.1 deals with the characterization of technological knowledge and its properties. Section 2.1.2 then summarizes the main findings about the innovation process and the role of learning and feedback mechanisms therein, which leads to the organizational form of networks that co-ordinate these interaction and feedback loops in section 2.1.3.

2.1.1 The economic properties of know-how

What is innovative activity at the core? To answer this question we have to distinguish between invention on the one hand and innovation on the other. The term *invention* refers to the generation of new technological knowledge, whereas *innovation* refers to the first economic exploitation of this knowledge. The new knowledge with the potential to become an innovation constitutes an intangible economic good. If it is possible to codify this knowledge, i.e. to physically write it down in publications, patents or manuals, the term information is used to describe these parts of knowledge which are easily transferrable. If knowledge is incorporated in the final product, it is not always possible to imitate the product by reverse engineering or to infer to the whole process of production. Tacit knowledge, a concept developed by Polany (1967), captures these difficulties in the transfer of knowledge. Dosi (1988b) refers to this as being related to 'those elements of knowledge, insight, and so on that individuals have which are ill defined, uncodified, unpublished, which they themselves cannot fully express and which differ from person to person, but which may to some significant degree be shared by collaborators and

7

colleagues who have a common experience' (Dosi, 1988b, p. 1126).[1] All kinds of materializations of information and knowledge, e.g. in form of a CD-ROM with software stored on it or in form of a new production process, serve the marketing of this knowledge to realize profits.

An interesting aspect regards the circumstances and conditions under which these profits are appropriable by the inventor. These depend on the properties of the output of the process of invention, which is, as noted above, intangible. Intangible assets are characterized by two properties: They can be used endlessly by an infinite number of users (nonrivalry) and the economic utilization cannot be governed by the price mechanism of the market, i.e. individuals cannot be prevented from using the good (nonexcludability) or at least the profits from utilization cannot be appropriated completely by the provider of the good (nonappropriability). If these properties are fulfilled, the good is called a public good.

In a rather traditional view, technological know-how has been considered to have these properties of a public good. This implies that imitators could use the new knowledge without devaluating it, so that it consequently would have to be considered nonrival. These transfers of knowledge are called technological spillovers, which are strongly dependent on the public good property of knowledge. Since these spillovers are, by definition, nonmarket transactions, knowledge would not have a price, which in the case of a public good is 0 anyhow since an additional user faces marginal costs of 0 and therefore no profits could be appropriated by the inventor.

This view of technological knowledge leads to the need for a patent system that provides incentives to invest in the generation of knowledge. Intellectual property rights allow innovators to appropriate the profits from their investment. Without such property rights, competitors could costlessly imitate the innovation, which reduces the incentives to innovate. A patent system does not prevent the flow of knowledge from the innovator to the imitator since it has to be published in the patent, but it prevents imitators from using this knowledge during the duration of the patent and for the specified coverage.

It has to be questioned whether the public good properties of technological knowledge and the resulting incentive problems adequately describe reality. Empirical studies about firms' means to appropriate the returns from R&D support a different view. Based on results from the Yale Survey, Levin et al. (1987) show that besides patent protection, secrecy, learning curve effects, lead time, and sales or service efforts are more effective means of appropriating profits. Based on a closely related survey conducted in

---

[1] For a debate on the usefulness and conceptual problems in the distinction between codified and tacit knowledge see Cowan et al. (2000) and the following critique of their work in Johnson et al. (2002).

1994 among manufacturing firms, Cohen et al. (2000) confirm these results. Compared to the earlier results patents increased in importance. However, they are not the major mechanism in most industries, while secrecy has increased dramatically. These findings indicate that imitation is not as easy as suggested by theory. Consequently, technological knowledge cannot be classified as a pure public good. This argument is also supported by studies on the efforts of imitators to absorb the knowledge generated by the innovator. Mansfield et al. (1981) show that imitating costs are at least 50% of the original investment in R&D and sometimes even lie above 100%. Imitators need to dedicate resources – R&D expenditures, time – to absorb and understand the new knowledge. Cohen and Levinthal (1990) introduce the notion of absorptive capacity, which is a function of its level of prior related knowledge. They characterize firms' capabilities as historical- and path-dependent, greatly influencing firms' ability to innovate themselves but also to adopt novelties.

In the light of these findings, Nelson (1990) speaks of technological knowledge as a latent public good: know-how is only transferrable if the imitator also expends resources, meaning that nonexcludability and nonappropriability are not present and the innovator has incentives to invest in R&D even without full patent protection. In the case of tacit technological know-how (Polany, 1967), i.e. know-how which is tied to a specific person and its talents and cannot be articulated, it can even be considered as a pure private good.

Summarizing this discussion, we can state that technological knowledge cannot normally be considered a pure public good as a general rule. It rather has to be considered a latent public good or even private in the case of tacit knowledge. Therefore, the transfer of knowledge from one actor to the other is not costless but requires resources for absorbing, understanding, learning, using, etc. by the recipient.

So far, technological spillovers seem to pose a problem only for the innovator as the outflow of knowledge deteriorates appropriability conditions and reduces the incentives to innovate. However, there is another, additional view on spillovers. Technological spillovers are considered a main driving force of per capita growth in the new growth theory because they are a crucial mechanism for the diffusion of knowledge, thereby accelerating external learning (Romer, 1986, 1990; Lucas, 1988; Aghion and Howitt, 1992). Instead of decreasing the incentives to perform R&D, they are necessary for the accumulation of knowledge and further technological progress. Griliches (1992), Mohnen (1996), and David et al. (2000) provide reviews of the literature on R&D spillovers, their impact and measurement issues. Summarizing the reviewed studies, Mohnen (1996) finds that the social rate of return on R&D exceeds the private rate of return by 50 to 100%.

Following this line of argument, the conditions under which technological spillovers are more likely to occur are even more of interest as they increase the diffusion of knowledge and do not hamper the incentives to innovate. They are not just to be discussed as a side effect of R&D but might serve as a strategic option for firms and politicians, e.g. as firms locate close to competitors to absorb these spillovers, or as politicians try to attract firms active in a certain industry.

2.1.2   Innovation as a process of experimenting and learning

There are two main questions that drive the scholars of the economics of innovation and technological change: the first one deals with the determinants of successful innovative activities, the second one asks for the impact of new technologies on the economy. This section is about the first question of the two: how do actors learn and how are the ideas generated that lead to new products and processes.

But what is innovation? According to Dosi, 'innovation concerns the search for, and the discovery, experimentation, development, imitation, and adoption of new products, new production processes and new organizational set-ups' (Dosi, 1988a, p. 222).

Within the neoclassical approach it is the incentives to innovate that drive the actors to invest in R&D in order to generate more knowledge or to increase their knowledge-stock, which leads to economic success. Underlying these models is an idea of the innovation process which is linear and where technology is treated as a black box.[2] Increasing inputs to the inventive phase strictly leads to an increase in knowledge and innovations. Scholars within this tradition try to explain different levels of innovative activity (inputs) under different market settings (Arrow, 1962b; Dasgupta and Stiglitz, 1980; Reinganum, 1989).

Contrasting this technology-push model, Schmookler (1962) derives another linear model of technical change, the so-called demand-pull model. He finds that inventive effort is lagging slightly behind output, which suggests a relationship running from economic growth to innovation. In a review of empirical studies on this topic, Mowery and Rosenberg (1979) reveal the importance of demand in successful innovation but find no causal relationship between the two. According to Dosi (1984), the review by Mowery and Rosenberg (1979) demonstrates that the perception of a potential market is a necessary condition for innovation, but not a sufficient one.

Building on these linear models, Rosenberg (1982) and Kline and Rosenberg (1986) introduce the chain-linked model of innovation. In the graphical

---

[2]This linear model has also been proposed by Schumpeter (1912) and has been described as being of a science- (and technology-) push type (Cimoli and della Giusta, 1998). In his later work (1942), Schumpeter emphasized the role of corporate R&D, so that a feedback from successful innovation to increased R&D was introduced in his model. The fact that large corporations had an influence on market demand was also recognized (Freeman et al., 1982).

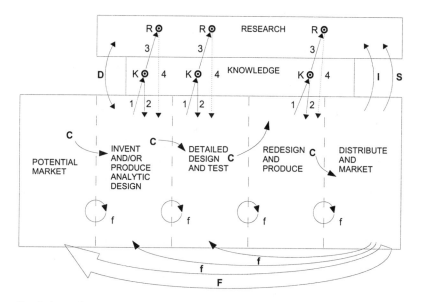

Symbols used on arrows:
C: central chain of innovation
f: feedback loops
F: particularly important feedback
K-R: Links through knowledge to research and return paths. If problem solved at node K, link 3 to R not activated. Return from research (link 4) is problematic – therefore dashed line.
D: Direct link to and from research to problems in invention and design.
I: Support of scientific research by instruments, machines, tools and procedures of technology.
S: Support of research in sciences underlying product area to gain information directly and monitoring outside work. The information obtained may apply anywhere along the chain.

Source: adapted from Kline and Rosenberg (1986, p. 290).

Figure 2.1: The chain-linked model of the innovation process

representation of their model (see figure 2.1), there are five major paths of activity. Arrows, labelled C, indicate the first path which is called the central-chain-of-innovation and corresponds to the linear model. The feedback links f and F connect back from perceived market needs and users to potentials for improvement of products and services in the next round. The systemic character of the innovation process is pointed out even more by the inclusion of a research sector which is linked to the firm by three types of interactions. D denotes the radical innovations that are made possible by new scientific results, whereas I is the feedback from innovation to science, e.g. in the form of new instruments. The linkages K-R indicate that science is lying alongside the development process and not just at the beginning of the process.

In this model, the economic incentives to innovate, i.e. the profits that can be yielded by an innovation, are still important, but the focus shifts towards the different sources of knowledge and their interaction. Potential innovators need the capabilities and the know-how to accomplish these innovations, i.e. they have to learn by investment and external knowledge sourcing. Without doubt, chance is a non-negligible player in the act of generating novelty, which cannot be dealt with analytically. But some statements about the circumstances under which innovations are more likely can be made: regularly innovations build on previously existing knowledge and are often 'constructed' through the combination or recombination of different knowledge and know-how components (Cantner and Graf, 2003b).

In this sense, the generation of technological know-how is to be seen as a cumulative learning process that essentially consists of two elements: within the idiosyncratic part each creative actor learns from his own experiences and accumulated knowledge. The second part takes the form of an outward orientation where the actors learn through communication with other actors and their experiences (Lundvall and Johnson, 1994). Technological spillovers are then the knowledge flows between actors that lead to cross-fertilization effects in contrast to sheer imitation which might diminish the economic rents of the sending actor (Cantner and Graf, 2003b).

This view of the innovation process is summarized in the five stylized facts about innovation (Dosi, 1988a, pp. 222–223):

i) *uncertainty*, which is not simply the lack of all relevant information about the occurrence of known events but also the existence of techno-economic problems whose solution procedures are unknown and the inability to predict precisely the consequences of one's actions;

ii) *increasing reliance* of major new technological opportunities on advances in scientific knowledge;

iii) *increasing complexity* of research and development activities which causes such activities to be more formally organized rather than carried out by individual innovators;

iv) *increasing role of experimentation* in the form of learning-by-doing and learning-by-using; and the

v) *cumulative character* of innovative activity.

The combination of these core components leads to the dynamics of knowledge accumulation, which is based on the knowledge and competencies of the single actors but also characterized by collective progress (Lawson, 1999; Lawson and Lorenz, 1999). Regarding innovation activities, the following can be deduced: even though innovations, i.e. new products, processes, or organizational forms, are ascribed to a single innovator or a small group of innovators, the whole environment and the system of relationships actors are embedded in are also crucial for the success of an innovative project. This idea is also referred to as *collective invention* (Allen, 1983) and processes of collective innovation. Thus, processes of collective innovation are based on the conscious and unconscious exchange of know-how.

2.1.3 Collective invention and coordinating networks

The sources of innovation are often found rather between firms, universities, research laboratories, suppliers, and customers than inside them (Powell, 1990). Firms commit resources to grasp these sources of innovation. Subsequent to Penrose's (1959) work on a resource-based view of the firm, the development of organizational routines (Nelson and Winter, 1982; Shane, 1996) and access to capital (Martin and Justis, 1993) have been shown to have positive effects on organizational growth rates. To overcome resource scarcities and to benefit from partner's resources, firms engage in interfirm cooperation (Combs and Ketchen, 1999). Since cooperation opens up possibilities to perform activities which a single firm could not perform on its own, resource sharing is considered a primary explanation for interfirm cooperation (Borys and Jemison, 1989; Hamel, 1991). Besides this cost-economizing argument, i.e. sharing the costs of research activities, risk sharing, obtaining access to new markets and technologies, and pooling of complementary skills are more strategic rationales for collaboration in research and development (Kogut, 1989; Hagedoorn, 1993; Eisenhardt and Schoonhoven, 1996; Mowery et al., 1998). In rapidly developing industries, where competition might be seen as a learning race, it is almost inevitable to engage in interfirm collaboration to identify new opportunities and learn about new technology (Powell, 1998). Accordingly, Teece (1992) argues that complex forms of cooperation are necessary for competition on a level of high technological sophistication especially in fragmented industries. With respect to welfare effects of cooperation in R&D, the theoretical discussion suggests that cooperation is beneficial if high technological spillovers are generated without threatening market competition (see Katz and Ordover, 1990, for an overview of this literature).

The conscious exchange of technological knowledge between actors can be organized in different types of arrangements. The normative basis for a market organization is a contract between the parties which relies on well defined property rights and actors largely communicate via the price mechanism. An employment relationship between the owner of a firm and research related personnel is present in hierarchies (firms, research institutes, but also joint ventures (Hagedoorn, 2002)), while interfirm cooperations and networks are based on complementary strengths, reciprocity and trust (Powell, 1990; Teece, 1996).

Certainly, there are markets for technologies where licences for patents, etc. can be traded.[3] In functioning markets, the licensee pays the price for using the technology developed by the licenser who is protected by intellectual property rights.[4] Contracts between the parties allow for the settling of conflicts before court. The transfer of knowledge can also be organized hierarchically, i.e. within firms where the researcher is obliged to leave the inventions to the employer. Here, the contractual obligations form the basis for a hierarchical structure of coordination.

These two cases, just illustrated, leave open the question whether the transfer of knowledge is complete, meaning if the receiver of knowledge is able to use the knowledge in the same way the inventor does or would do.[5] Leaving this aspect aside, we consider a third mode of organizing the knowledge transfer which has little or no underlying contractual relationships and therefore lies between the two extremes of market (price mechanism) and hierarchy (contractual arrangements). This mode of transfer is based on bilateral information trading on an informal or less formal basis (von Hippel, 1987; Schrader, 1991). The notion of *informal know-how transfer* comprises the transfer of knowledge between scientists, researchers or engineers on trade fairs, conferences or during informal meetings. These arrangements are based on trust and reciprocity and need time to develop.[6] Formalized research cooperations or collaborations can also be counted if contracts are incomplete due to the uncertainties of the innovation process. Cooperations might then provide the benefits of integration while avoiding some of the costs (Teece, 1996). Powell et al. (1996) argue that, especially in industries where the knowledge-base is complex and expanding, learning takes place in networks of interacting firms instead of individual firms.

The coordination pattern which underlies these bilateral informal or weak formal cooperative relations is called a network organization. The functionality of networks is based on the principles of complementarity and reciprocity. This means that firms will only participate in these networks, if they expect to learn from other network members (complementarity) and if the transfer of knowledge is bi- or multilateral (reciprocity) (DeBresson and Amesse, 1991).

---

[3] See Arora et al. (2001a) and Arora et al. (2001b) for strategic aspects and the overview article of Geroski (1995) for different aspects of failures in markets for technology.

[4] Cohen and Klepper (1996), in a study not directly related to this topic, consider only one out of 31 high-tech industries as an industry where licensing of new technology is a relevant means of appropriating returns from R&D.

[5] The literature on spin-offs tells us that this transfer is not complete, since many firm founders certified that the employers did not appreciate the invention the same way the inventors did, so that they were 'forced' to found their own enterprize to pursue their innovation.

[6] Fehr and Gächter (2000) give an overview of experimental studies that reject the pure self-interest model of neoclassical economics in many situations and circumstances.

In contrast to enforceable market contracts, networks are often more stable, in the presence of interdependent preferences, than market relations but more flexible than labor contracts.

Networks of innovating firms are identified in different configurations: supplier – user networks, networks of pioneers and adopters, regional inter-industrial networks, international strategic technological alliances, and professional inter-organizational networks (DeBresson and Amesse, 1991). Despite these organizational arrangements, the physical interaction takes place between people. Interpersonal networks are considered an important channel for the diffusion of knowledge and information (Zander and Kogut, 1995; Zucker et al., 1998b; Sorenson, 2003). Sorenson (2004) shows that the importance of these transmission channels depends on the complexity of the underlying knowledge-base, and in particular, that knowledge complexity limits the rate at which knowledge diffuses across geographic boundaries. Following the sociological literature (e.g. Granovetter, 1973, 1983), only recently an economic literature assessing the properties of knowledge networks and its influence on the rate of knowledge diffusion has emerged (see for example Bala and Goyal, 1998; Cowan and Jonard, 2003; Morone and Taylor, 2004). In performing simulations, these studies show that the rate of knowledge diffusion is highest in networks that exhibit small world properties, i.e. networks with short average path length and high degree of clustering (Watts and Strogatz, 1998). The empirical literature is not yet rich enough to confirm these propositions, but there are some examples of interpersonal networks with such properties.[7] Implications for local innovation systems arise as policies which only encourage dense local clustering might miss an important channel of knowledge diffusion. The findings suggest that the establishment of external linkages is necessary to link the different clusters and reduce the risk of technological lock-in.

Since the processes through which technological innovations emerge are extremely complex, characterized by complicated feedback mechanisms and interactive relations involving science, technology, learning, production, policy, and demand, Edquist (1997) argues that innovation processes have to be analyzed within a systemic approach. Investigations following the neoclassical paradigm of the profit-maximizing firm are not appropriate when studying processes of innovation and diffusion. Many actors are not even led by profit seeking motives as they work for governmental or private non-profit organizations such as universities or public research institutes as well as public administrations.

---

[7]Watts and Strogatz (1998) show that the network of film co-stars have small world structural features. Cowan and Jonard (2004) find these properties in knowledge networks of innovating Dutch firms, research institutes involved in the EU's TSER programme, and in a network of firms participating in the BRITE/EURAM programme. A review of this literature is given in Cowan (2004).

2.2   CHARACTERIZING INNOVATION SYSTEMS

2.2.1   Definition

The discussion about the systemic character of innovation, collective invention processes, and the network structure of the know-how exchange allows us to bring forward the concept of innovation systems. For these purposes we characterize and classify innovation systems, illuminate their functionality from a business and political perspective, discuss the boundaries of the system, and present the different levels on which they are analyzed. To provide a first overview, the main contributions of this approach to our understanding of the innovation process are summarized in Edquist (2001, pp. 2–3):

> ...[I]nnovations are normally seen as based on learning that is interactive between organisations in the SI approach; firms do not generally innovate in isolation.... [I]nstitutions are considered to be crucial elements in all versions of the SI approach.... [I]nstitutions shape (and are shaped by) the actions of the organizations and the relations between them.... [A]ll versions of the SI approach consider innovation processes to be evolutionary.

But what exactly is a system? Three characteristics are mentioned by Edquist (2004, p. 187):

    i)   A system consists of two kinds of constituents: there are, first, some kinds of components and, second, relations among them. The components and relations should form a coherent whole (which has properties different from the properties of the constituents).

    ii) The system has a function, i.e. it is performing or achieving something.

    iii) It must be possible to discriminate between the system and the rest of the world; i.e. it must be possible to identify the boundaries of the system. If we, for example, want to make empirical studies of specific systems, we must, of course, know their extent.[8]

An innovation system is then defined as a network of actors who interact in the processes of the generation, diffusion, and utilization of new, economically useful knowledge under a distinct institutional framework (Cantner and Graf, 2003b). Institutions are understood as 'sets of common habits, norms, routines, established practices, rules or laws that regulate the relations and interactions between individuals, groups and organizations' (Edquist and Johnson, 1997, p. 46). Thus, an innovation system is a group of actors who are related by know-how flows subject to the institutional environment. These linkages can be

---

[8]Only in exceptional cases is the system closed in the sense that it has nothing to do with the rest of the world (or because it encompasses the whole world). Like the SI approach, 'general systems theory' might rather be considered to be an approach than a theory.

built on purpose or emerge unintendedly; they can be incorporated in materials, products or persons or they can develop disembodiedly through informal knowledge exchange between the actors. In contrast to market exchange, the reciprocity in such a system of informal contacts is less strict, meaning that there is no direct payment for every bit of information, but if someone is free-riding, there are punishments such as exclusion from information channels.

2.2.2 A stylized innovation system

Actors in innovation systems can be assigned to different elements of the system which are either poles of the system or intermediary elements (OECD, 1992; Callon, 1992; Hull et al., 1999).[9] Figure 2.2 depicts a stylized innovation system with the three core elements:

i) **Scientific pole:** universities and public and private independent research centers which produce empirical knowledge.
ii) **Technical pole:** technical labs in firms, cooperative research centers and pilot plants which design, develop, and transform artefacts for specific purposes (e.g. models, prototypes, pilot projects, patents, tests, standards).
iii) **Market pole:** firms (customers, suppliers, competitors), professionals and practitioners who market the innovations.

Intermediaries link the various poles in the network: text (patents, journals, software), technical objects (telephones, fax machines, computers), skills (ability to mobilize a social network) and money (research grants, venture capital) (Callon, 1992).

The system poles and intermediaries are embedded in a framework of institutions that are either formed by the government (e.g. education, legislation or jurisdiction) or by the system actors themselves, such as technology-transfer institutions, conferences, trade fairs, or the culture of workers mobility within and between poles. All these aspects influence the frequency and modes of interaction and knowledge flows of the innovation system.

Every single pole can be understood as a (sub)system of actors who are connected by information and knowledge flows. Within the market pole there are market transactions and cooperative agreements between firms of the same or different industries. Research cooperations and informal know-how exchange between technical labs or research joint ventures are found within

---

[9]Callon (1992) provides the notion of techno-economic networks to link the economic and sociological literature on the innovation process. De Laat (1996) has produced a model with a fourth pole, adding government agencies and other public authorities. Here, these actors are included in the institutional framework, since they are not an active part of the innovation process but rather shape the environment.

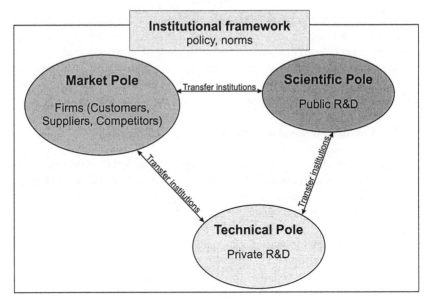

Figure 2.2: Stylized innovation system

the technical pole and universities and other research institutes interact through scientific publications or face-to-face on conferences. Besides, one should take into account the relations to actors external to the system (not included in figure 2.2). Local relations are believed to be reinforced by external relations, which increase variety and provide new impulses and ideas for the system (Bathelt, 2003; Bathelt et al., 2004). Also, the risk of technological lock-in can be decreased by connections to actors outside the system (Gertler, 1997).

2.2.3 Proximity

The functioning of innovation systems is based on the information and know-how exchange between actors. The success of the exchange depends on the frequency of interaction, the compatibility of know-how components, and the degree of mutual understanding. These criteria highlight the specific types of *proximity* between actors and constitute the different concepts of innovation systems. Proximity covers a number of dimensions and not just geographical closeness (Torre and Gilly, 2000). In a recent study Boschma (2005) provides an overview of the different concepts of proximity and its impact on innovation, which will be helpful for further discussion. Besides the positive effects of proximity, special attention is paid to the dangers of too much proximity, as the risk of lock-in rises with neglect of knowledge inputs from outside the system.

In the following, we describe the different types of proximity along the arguments in Boschma (2005). An overview of different forms of proximity is provided in table 2.1.

Cognitive proximity refers to the notion of unwritten codes where actors, capable of understanding these codes, are close in the cognitive dimension. Clusters are said to retrieve their competitive strength, as these capabilities are specific to a location and constitute cognitive and uncodifiable assets (Maskell and Malmberg, 1999). Firms usually search for new knowledge in close proximity to their existing knowledge-base. In following different trajectories, they develop specific capabilities, which makes them different from other firms. Knowledge from external sources can thus only be absorbed if the cognitive gap is not too large. Boschma (2005) brings forward three points why actors wanting to learn from each other should not be too close in knowledge space: first, the generation of knowledge requires dissimilar but complementary bodies of knowledge in order to trigger creativity and new ideas. Second, too much cognitive proximity might lead to a cognitive lock-in as routines obscure the view on new technologies and opportunities. The third reason is related to involuntary spillovers, as direct competitors with no specific capabilities are very reluctant to share knowledge or learn from each other and would rather not co-locate (Cantwell and Santangelo, 2002).

Organizational proximity refers to the organization of production. It is based on similarity and adherence, which means that actors are close if they belong to the same relational framework (i.e. the way interaction and coordination is organized) or share common knowledge and capacities (Torre and Gilly, 2000). Often, this type of proximity is associated with networks of reciprocal and trust-based relationships (Boschma, 2005). Organizational arrangements, like networks, reduce uncertainty in the transfer and exchange of knowledge but differ in the extent to which the related actors are autonomous or the degree of control that can be exerted on each other. Low organizational proximity then refers to independent actors on spot markets while high organizational proximity refers to hierarchical relationships within a firm. With respect to the effects on learning and knowledge creation, Boschma (2005) summarizes that organizational proximity is required to control uncertainty and opportunistic behavior, but that too much proximity is often not sufficiently flexible to allow for novelty.

Social proximity might be defined, '[...]in terms of socially embedded relations between agents at the micro-level. Relations between actors are socially embedded when they involve trust, that is based on friendship, kinship and experience' (Boschma, 2005, p. 66). This type of proximity draws on the embeddedness literature which states that economic relations are embedded in social context and these social ties influence economic action (Granovetter, 1985). While social relations positively influence the degree of knowledge

Table 2.1: Five forms of proximity

	Key dimension	Too little proximity	Too much proximity	Possible solutions
Cognitive	knowledge gap	misunderstanding	lack of sources of novelty	cluster built on shared knowledge-base with diverse complementary capabilities
Organizational	control	opportunism	bureaucracy	loosely coupled system
Social	trust (based on social relations)	opportunism	no economic rationale	mixture of embedded and market relations
Institutional	trust (based on common institutions)	opportunism	lock-in and inertia	institutional checks and balances
Geographical	distance	no spatial externalities	spatial lock-in	mix of local 'buzz' and extra-local linkages

Source: Boschma (2005).

exchange and interactive learning (Breschi and Lissoni, 2003), they might lead to a lock-in and an underestimated risk of opportunistic behavior (Uzzi, 1997; Boschma, 2005).

While social proximity describes relations on the micro-level, *institutional proximity* is associated with the institutional framework at the macro level (norms and values of conduct). Formal institutions, such as laws, rules and language are distinguished from informal institutions, like values, cultural norms or habits. Depending on the formulation of these institutions, they can support or hamper innovation, e.g. the pharmaceutical industry would clearly suffer if no effective patent system existed. While institutional proximity provides the basis for co-ordination and interactive learning, too much proximity can lead to inertia, and therefore provides insufficient opportunities for change.

Geographical proximity describes the spatial distance between economic actors. While this usually accounts for physical distance, it is influenced by transport and communication infrastructure which might decrease the costs for face-to-face interaction. Geographical proximity enhances innovation as it facilitates knowledge sharing while the institutions co-evolve during the frequency of interaction. However, geographic proximity cannot be considered a sufficient condition for the exchange of tacit knowledge. Blanc and Sierra (1999) describe how large multinationals face difficulties in getting access to the local networks when setting up subsidiaries in these locations. Locations which get too narrowly focussed on certain types of activities might run into a spatial lock-in, so that they are unable to follow new developments. To reduce the risk of such a type of lock-in, it is necessary to either diversify and profit from Jacobs externalities or establish and foster non-local linkages to get access to external knowledge.

Depending on the definition of an innovation systems, different types of proximity are pronounced. Within concepts of innovation systems, where the system boundaries are spatial, in terms of national, regional or local innovation systems, aspects of geographical proximity are highlighted. Geographical proximity allows frequent face-to-face contact to exchange information and build a stock of common knowledge. Regional agglomerations of economic activity, like clusters (Porter, 1990), industrial districts (Lazerson and Lorenzoni, 1999) or innovative milieu (Camagni, 1991, 1995a,b) are said to possess these conditions favorable to knowledge exchange. Focussing on a common culture, language and legislation (institutional proximity), one ends up at national systems of innovation (Freeman, 1987; Lundvall, 1988; Nelson, 1993).

The focus of technological systems (TS) (Carlsson and Stankiewicz, 1991) or sectoral innovation systems (SIS) (Breschi and Malerba, 1997; Malerba, 2002) is on the compatibility of the knowledge-stock. Here, the actors' cognitive proximity is highlighted, which fosters the successful exchange of knowledge. Depending on the type of the knowledge-base, spatial agglomeration of economic activities is not always necessary (Breschi and Malerba, 1997). The automobile industry might serve as an example which is made up of integrated producers of automobiles and specialized, heterogeneous suppliers, all working, technologically compatible, in the automotive technology.

2.2.4   The functionality of innovation systems

Functions in innovation systems

In the literature on innovation systems some relationships are frequently observed. In order to be able to focus on the more important ones, Johnson (2001) compares and summarizes the different approaches dealing with innovation systems with respect to the relevant functions to be served by the actors and institutions of the system. The different functions that are served by the innovation system are summarized in table 2.2. The broad approaches of these concepts show up in the breadth of these functions; from *problem identification* to *counteracting the resistance to change*.

The functions *directly concerned with the innovation process* are performed by the elements of the three poles mentioned above (scientific, technical and market) in interaction with each other. The interaction between actors is to be seen in light of the discussion of the feedback model of innovation described above. The function *create new knowledge* is of particular importance in the present study. It is served by the system poles by investments in R&D, processes of search and experimentation, learning-by-doing, learning-by-using, as well as imitation.

Functions that *support the innovation process indirectly* are served by the system poles but also by the politicians who influence the innovative environment for the actors. With our focus on interaction in local innovation systems, we analyze the diffusion of technology, co-ordination, and cooperation between the actors who thereby *facilitate the exchange of information and knowledge* within the system.

The actors within the system poles benefit from systems' achievements as they serve their functions. By participating they constitute and shape the institutional framework for the exchange of technological know-how. The variety and heterogeneity of actors leads to a more efficient way of identifying technological problems and bottlenecks. Competencies are not only built up at the level of the individual actor but also – through imitation or learning-by-doing – on the level of the system (Lawson, 1999). Being involved in the network provides possibilities to reduce the risks and uncertainties of research and innovation, but also of social uncertainties. The direct revenues of innovation systems for the firm are therefore availability of external knowledge, interaction of complementary competencies, accelerated learning through collective learning processes, and the improvement of cooperation competencies of the

Table 2.2: Functions in innovation system approaches

Function	How it is served
Directly concerned with the innovation process	
Identify problem	Identifying bottlenecks in the system (technical nature or with respect to the innovation system)
Create new knowledge	R&D, search and experimentation, learning-by-doing, learning-by-using, imitation
Support the innovation process indirectly	
Supply incentives for companies to engage in innovative work	Formal institutions that support appropriability conditions
Supply resources	Funding, competence, etc.
Guide the direction of search	Influence the direction in which actors deploy their resources; e.g. through standards and regulations
Recognize the potential for growth	Identifying technological opportunities; commercial viability; complementary resources
Facilitate the exchange of information and knowledge	Providing feedback between system performance and goals; diffusion of technology; co-ordination; cooperation between actors
Stimulate/create markets	Diffusion and the transfer of knowledge/technology
Reduce social uncertainty	Providing information, promotion of stable patterns of interaction and transactions
Counteract the resistance to change	Stimulate the enthusiasm for the new technology, clear political and legislative ground

Source: Elaboration on Johnson (2001).

actors (Drewello and Wurzel, 2002, pp. 20–21).

For politicians, innovation systems provide a mixture of direct and indirect research policies with the indirect character prevailing. By initiating, advising or even managing such innovation systems, politicians hope for an increase in innovative activities. On the national level, for example, legislation on property rights can influence the incentives to innovate and authorities setting standards for an industry can reduce uncertainties and guide the direction of the search process. Policies based on the concept of innovation systems focus on institutional failures. Due to frictions in the transfer of technological know-how between the system poles technological know-how may be insufficiently available or insufficiently used. These frictions often arise when actors within the system are not informed about where relevant knowledge might be available for them or how the knowledge they generated might be used in another application. Policies that are oriented towards innovation systems are not primarily focussed on the actors themselves but rather focus on the relations between the actors. Speaking in network terms, it is not about nodes, it is about edges. In serving the function 'supply resources', the government is obliged to strengthen the competencies through education policy or in the funding of basic research.

Problems within innovation systems

The functionality of innovation systems might also be restricted if some of the following problems are present.

Intermediation problems
It might be questioned whether and how the different system poles get into contact with each other. Should transfer institutions not exist or not act according to their purpose, knowledge flows might be hindered. Whenever such intermediation problems arise, these institutional failures call for political intervention.

Compatibility problems
Even if transfer institutions are present, other problems that hinder the flow of knowledge might arise if the actors in the system do not fit together. Several reasons might be responsible for this problem. We know that in some industries or firms basic or even applied research is not relevant and therefore not performed, rather external knowledge, incorporated in artefacts like process equipment, is purchased from other sectors. These industries, e.g. textiles, unlearn to innovate themselves and cannot benefit from knowledge generated elsewhere since they lack the absorptive capacities. But also when actors diverge in terms of technological directions, i.e. they follow different technological trajectories, the cognitive gap will become too large for knowledge to flow. The greater these gaps, the more difficult is becomes for the receiver to understand the knowledge to be transferred.

Reciprocity problem
Given that actors get into contact and are close in terms of their competencies, a lack of reciprocity might disturb the exchange of knowledge. If the trusting relationship (social proximity) between network or cooperation partners is undermined by some actors, these might be excluded from the knowledge network and thereby decrease the performance of the whole system. This problem arises when innovation systems are initiated and planned from outside and if the social proximity between the actors is too low for positive externalities to arise. The fear of opportunistic behavior prevents the voluntary exchange of knowledge.

2.2.5 Boundaries of the system

Following the presentation of the components and functions of innovation systems, the boundaries of these systems have to be discussed. Analyzing national innovation systems, the object of analysis is easy to identify: the country. The boundaries are less easy to identify within the sectoral approach but at least there are various industry classifications, which make it possible to identify the actors in such a system. But what is the appropriate definition of a region, when it comes to analyzing regional innovation systems? The problem is that the concept of a region itself is not clear. The scales at which regions are analyzed range from the Canadian provinces of Quebec (Latouche, 1998) or Ontario (Gertler and Wolfe, 2004) to industrial districts below the urban level of aggregation (Asheim and Isaksen, 2002). It makes a difference if the state level in the US or the level of 'Bundesländer' in Germany is analyzed in contrast to a city, or a region on the NUTS 3 level.[10] Therefore, we use the term *regional innovation system* for the larger entities, which usually have more political power, and *local innovation system*, whenever cities or rural areas on the NUTS 3 level are analyzed.[11] If only a specific industry within some locality (whether regional or local) is analyzed, it is usually referred to as *industrial district* or *cluster*.[12]

Edquist (2004) points out that no system – on which level whatsoever – has a clear cut boundary, where there is no interaction with the outside of that system. Consequently, the definition of the boundary in an empirical study depends upon the question one asks.

2.2.6 Levels of innovation systems

With this in mind, innovation systems can be identified on different levels and modes of aggregation. They all have the interactive element in common and foster joint research efforts. The observed networks might be classified according to their formal nature, their completeness (all poles present), the role and relevance of the different elements, and whether they are self-organized or initiated by public intervention.

---

[10]NUTS stands for 'Nomenclature of Statistical Territorial Units' and is the official division of the EU for regional statistics.

[11]Cooke (2001, p. 953) defines the region within the RIS approach as 'a meso-level political unit set between the national or federal and local levels of government that might have some cultural or historical homogeneity but which at least had some statutory powers to intervene and support economic development, particularly innovation.' We interpret this definition as excluding local levels, which are then termed *local innovation systems*.

[12]Porter (2000, p. 15) defines clusters as 'geographic concentrations of interconnected companies, specialized suppliers, service providers, firms in related industries, and associated institutions (e.g. universities, standards agencies, trade associations) in a particular field that compete, but also cooperate.'

Table 2.3: Overview of innovation systems

Innovation systems	Example
Incomplete forms of innovation systems	
Research cooperation	Intel-Microsoft
Research network	Bio-instruments Jena, OptoNet e.V.
Science parks, research centers	Sophia-Antipolis, Wissenschaftsstadt Ulm
Innovation systems in the narrow sense	
Technological, sectoral	Automobiles, biotechnology
Local	Jena, Cambridge, industrial districts
Regional	Baden-Württemberg, Silicon Valley
National	Japan, USA, Germany

Table 2.3 includes some examples for the different categories of innovation systems. The relevance of public authorities and government intervention increases from top to bottom of the list, while the formal nature of the contacts between the actors decreases. Innovation systems in the more narrow sense (local, regional, national) are complete in the sense above (see section 2.2.2), i.e. private and public organizations are interconnected by flows of information and knowledge, while these relations are guided by an institutional framework. Research cooperations, research networks, and science parks are rather to be seen as the formalized elements of these innovation systems. Here, the private actors are often initiators – except for the science parks – and central players in the network. While government policies are less relevant for the functioning of a science park,[13] research and technology policy might have a greater impact on the performance of national systems.

The most simple innovation system is the research cooperation between two organizations. More complex is the research network between firms and/or research institutes which perform basic or applied research (e.g. Bio-instruments Jena, OptoNet). Technological systems or sectoral innovation systems connect firms and other actors with a similar technological background (automobile industry, biotechnology). In that case, cognitive proximity is more relevant than geographical proximity (Breschi and Malerba, 1997; Carlsson and Stankiewicz, 1991). Science parks and research centers are usually planned institutions which aim at bringing together actors with a common technological background to profit from spatial externalities (Sophia-Antipolis, Wissenschaftsstadt Ulm) (Longhi, 1999). Local and regional innovation systems can be defined as, 'places where close interfirm communications, social struc-

---

[13]When comparing the performance of science parks, the macro-environment is often the same for the object of analysis.

tures, and institutional environment may stimulate socially and territorially embedded collective learning and continuous innovation' (Asheim and Isaksen, 2002, p. 83). So there is no clear distinction regarding the extension of local and regional innovation systems, but the institutional focus and the role of government intervention is more pronounced within the RIS approach as many examples are analyzed within their political boundaries such as Tuscany, Baden-Württemberg, or Québec. Other concepts, like regional innovation networks (RIN), innovation cluster and environment (innovative milieu), as well as technological/industrial districts, which are used in the innovation and regional literature, are all related to each other (see for example Camagni, 1991; Metcalfe, 1995; Braczyk et al., 1998; Lazerson and Lorenzoni, 1999). Finally, whole countries are analyzed within the concept of national innovation systems.[14]

2.3 SUMMARY

The purpose of this chapter was to introduce the concept of an innovation system, by outlining the basic building blocks of the approach. Describing the relevant dimensions and characteristics of technological knowledge and how it is generated in a processes of invention and innovation is essential for an understanding of knowledge exchange and learning in networks.

An innovation system comprises distinct poles, their interaction within and between the different poles and the guiding institutions, which all interact and serve the main function of creating knowledge. As these systems are identified within boundaries which are defined in accordance with the research question, the following chapter focusses on regional aspects.

---

[14]Recent surveys of NIS studies are for example, Edquist (1997), Edquist (2001), Lundvall et al. (2002), or Balzat and Hanusch (2004).

3. Proximity and Innovation

3.1 FOCUSSING ON THE REGION

In the previous chapter, we presented the concept of innovation systems and its foundations as it is discussed in evolutionary economics and the economics of innovation. Before we discuss the specific aspects of regional and local innovation systems in section 3.2, we present another strand of research which investigates geographical aspects of economic activity in general (section 3.1.1) and with a special focus on innovative activities (section 3.1.2). There, localized knowledge spillovers are the prime mechanism which explains differences in innovative activity over geographical space. These spillovers are subject to the composition of the respective localities, such as specialization, diversity, and local competition (section 3.1.3). Regarding the mechanisms, recent research suggests that social interaction and labor mobility are very important channels of knowledge transmission (section 3.1.4). These findings provide the rationale for an analysis of innovation systems at the local level.

3.1.1 Uneven distribution of economic activity

Economic activity is neither uniformly nor randomly distributed across the geographical landscape. There are metropolitan areas, large and small cities as well as rural areas. In some regions the manufacturing industry is dominant, in others the largest part of value added is generated in the service sector or in agriculture. Early approaches explaining the agglomeration of economic activity in some centers view the outcomes of firms' location decision as predetermined by geographical endowments, transportation infrastructure, and other firms' needs (von Thünen, 1826; Weber, 1909; Predöhl, 1925; Christaller, 1933; Lösch, 1941; Isard, 1956). According to Arthur (1994, p. 49), this view is very static because the equilibrium outcome is independent of historical decisions. Later works by the late Weber, Engländer (1926), Ritschl (1927), and Palander (1935) introduced the idea of agglomerative forces, which make it more profitable for firms to settle close to other firms.

Malmberg and Maskell (2002) review historical work on the origin and development of clusters. Three factors are held responsible for the emergence of spatial clusters of similar and related economic activity: 'they often originate in a series of events leading to the start of a new firm at the place of residence of the founder; they develop through spin-offs and imitation within the local milieu; and they are sustained by various forms of inertia, meaning that firms rarely relocate once they have been reproduced in a place' (Malmberg and Maskell, 2002, p. 431). Consequently, historical accident or chance influences the observed patterns rather than cost advantages, and Silicon Valley might be somewhere else if key people had not made their choice to settle in Santa Clara County (Arthur, 1994).

Marshall (1947) specifies three forces that give rise to what he calls industrial districts, i.e. agglomerations of firms that are specialized in a specific industry. These forces, called localization economies, explain the middle part of the genealogical approaches, i.e. why imitators might locate close to successful incumbent firms. First, a thick market for skilled labor is considered a major element of localization economies. The advantage for employers lies in the supply of skilled workers while employees seek locations where a large number of potential employers are located. Thus, the local labor markets function better for workers and employers, if similar and related firms are around (Krugman, 1991a). Second, backward and forward linkages associated with large local markets have the advantage of reduced costs for transactions and shipments. It is cheaper to discuss a deal with the partner next door than with a customer located far away. A local production chain has the advantages of lower overall shipment costs for the final products and is considered more flexible than a large integrated firm (Porter, 1998). Third, knowledge spillovers are facilitated in localized clusters of similar and related firms. If a local innovative milieu develops, new knowledge can diffuse faster as various forms of learning and adaptation are stimulated. Frequent relations and face-to-face interactions create trust among the actors as well as a culture (specific norms, values and institutions) which makes the transfer of tacit knowledge possible (Malmberg and Maskell, 2002).[1]

In tracing these localization economies, economic research pursues different directions. The new economic geography literature focusses on the increasing returns that arise in large local markets (Krugman, 1991b; Fujita et al., 1999; Fujita and Thisse, 2002), whereas others try to find empirical evidence on localized knowledge spillovers (LKS) (Jaffe et al., 1993) and the related learning processes (Cooke and Morgan, 1998; Maskell and Malmberg, 1999).

---

[1] In addition to these Marshallian externalities, Malmberg and Maskell (2002) mention that co-located firms in the same industry can share the costs for collective goods as the local education system, local infrastructure, and other collective goods can be focussed to fit the requirements of the industry.

3.1.2 Localized knowledge spillovers

While natural resource endowments and thick local markets can explain that economic activity is not evenly spread across geographical space, they cannot explain why innovation is even more clustered or why the pattern changes over the industry life cycle. A distinction between the activities with respect to the observed localization patterns is made in Feldman (1994, p. 15). She states that:

> [i]t is well known that as production processes standardize manufacturing industries, even high-tech manufacturing industries, become "footloose" – seeking out the lowest cost locations (Hymer, 1979; Bluestone and Harrison, 1982). In contrast, the non-routine production activities associated with innovation such as research and development, experimental and prototype manufacturing, and small volume production are increasingly spatially concentrated (Malecki, 1980).

To analyze this pattern in more detail, Audretsch and Feldman (1996a) relate the geographic patterns of production and innovation to the stage of the industry life cycle (cf. Klepper, 1996). They argue that at the beginning of an industry, tacit knowledge is relatively more important in generating innovations. But 'while the costs of information may be invariant to distance, presumably the cost of transmitting knowledge and especially tacit knowledge rises along with distance' (Audretsch and Feldman, 1996a, p. 254). This leads to a clustering of innovative activities in these industries. The geographic concentration of production, on the other hand, does not appear to be sensitive to the stage of the industry life cycle.

Jaffe (1989) employs a knowledge production function approach, using patents as an indicator for produced knowledge. Within this approach, R&D and other innovative inputs are related to the innovative output (patents or innovation counts). Besides own innovative effort, external inputs from the same location and more distant ones are included. Significant differences in the estimated coefficients for close and far away R&D are interpreted as evidence in favor of the existence and localization of knowledge spillovers. Jaffe (1989) finds that corporate patent activity responds positively to commercial spillovers from university research conducted in the same state. He only finds weak evidence that geographic proximity within the state matters as well. Commenting on Jaffe's (1989) work, Acs et al. (1992) find significant evidence in favor of the LKS hypothesis by using innovation counts instead of patents as an indicator for the output of knowledge production. The results obtained in Audretsch and Feldman (1996b) indicate that the relative importance of new knowledge in an industry is a key determinant of the clustering of production in that industry. And even after controlling for the concentration of production, they find innovative activities to be clustered more in industries where innovation related inputs like R&D, skilled labor, and university research are important. Ellison and Glaeser (1997) also show that industries are different with respect to their degree of clustering. In follow-up research the authors show that while in some industries these differences are explained by cost advantages due to natural resource endowments, in others LKS seem to be responsible for the clustering (Ellison and Glaeser, 1999).

Jaffe et al. (1993) provide more direct evidence for the existence of localized knowledge spillovers by analyzing patent citations. They assume to capture the direct flow of knowledge, which leaves a 'paper trail' as the user of previously generated knowledge has to cite the relevant sources. They calculate the frequency with which a citing patent and the cited patent match by location and compare it with the frequency of a locational match between the citing patent and a control patent with the same attributes in terms of time and technological field as the citing patent. The citations, excluding self-citations, are two to six times as likely to come from the same SMSA as the control patents. Further, they find a declining rate of localization over time.

In contrast to the review by Feldman (1999), Breschi and Lissoni (2001a) and Breschi and Lissoni (2001b) provide a more critical view of the empirical literature on localized knowledge spillovers. They criticize studies which employ the knowledge production function approach for drawing inferences from inadequate data bases (see for example Audretsch and Feldman, 1996b; Feldman and Audretsch, 1999). Spillovers from university labs might be overestimated in some studies since market transactions between firms and universities are not included in the respective data.

The main argument of the survey by Breschi and Lissoni (2001a) is that many studies that identify LKS actually observe localization effects that are based on contractual arrangements or other forms of market interaction. Empirical studies on spillovers should stick to the original definition of spillovers, i.e. an externality not mediated by market mechanisms. To be precise, they summarize that:

> [a]ll of these studies certainly strengthen the case for the existence of important localization effects in innovation activities, but do not prove, despite their authors' claims, the existence of LKSs. For example, there is no reason to believe that knowing about the local university's research results does not come from contractual arrangements with the latter (or with individual researchers therein), as indeed is suggested by many of the case studies.
> (Breschi and Lissoni, 2001a, p. 987)

The view that clusters are a special form of market organization where commodities and knowledge are traded in an especially efficient way is also put forward by Maskell and Lorenzen (2004).

Breschi and Lissoni (2001a, p. 1000) summarize their conclusions in the following three points:

1. What might appear as pure knowledge externalities are actually pecuniary externalities which are mediated by economic (market and non-market) mechanisms, such as the labor market, the market for technologies, and club or network agreements.
2. What might appear as involuntary knowledge spillovers are actually well-regulated knowledge flows between academic institutions (or individuals therein) and firms, or across firms, which are managed with deliberate appropriation purposes.
3. A large amount of the knowledge flowing in this way has much more to do with enhancing the innovation appropriation strategies of local companies (by speeding up the development phases of new products and processes) rather [than] their innovation opportunities (by providing them with new ideas).

With respect to the discussion of knowledge above, technological knowledge cannot be classified as public or private, but rather has two components: a public one – information, otherwise R&D spillovers could not be observed – and a tacit component which is costly or impossible to transfer, while the costs of transmission rise with geographical distance.[2] The fact that tacit knowledge is primarily embodied in individuals is particularly important and plays a major role in understanding the nature of the impact of science on technology (Pavitt, 1991).

3.1.3 Specialization, diversity and competition

A topic within the literature on agglomerations and LKS takes a closer look at the local environment and its influence on knowledge spillovers. In this body of research it is tested to what degree technological specialization of cities and/or regions and regional competition have an impact on the rate of growth or the rate of knowledge generation. The competing theoretical models are the so-called *MAR-model* (Marshall-Arrow-Romer),[3] which predicts a higher growth rate in a specialized and concentrated environment, the *urbanization* argument by Jacobs (1969), which emphasizes the positive effects of diversification and competition, and Porter's (1990) *cluster hypothesis*, which is in between the former two, as it suspects a specialized and competitive environment most conducive to regional innovation and growth.[4]

---

[2] Breschi and Lissoni (2001a) also name the intermediate cases, such as price-excludable public goods, common property and club goods.

[3] Based on Marshall (1947) and later formalized by Arrow (1962a) and Romer (1986).

[4] Other factors explaining how diversity and large size affect the level of output in a city are reviewed in Quigley (1998).

The argument put forward in the MAR hypothesis is that actors which are similar in terms of employed technology can communicate at lower costs and knowledge can spill over more easily. Marshall observed industrial districts with a business structure made up of small, locally owned firms that invest and produce locally. Research in his thinking focuses on intra-industry proximity effects, by concepts such as localization economies (local and regional specialization) and clustering of vertically integrated and flexible production systems. It is also assumed that local monopoly is superior to competition as the returns on investment in knowledge are better appropriated (Audretsch, 1998; van Oort, 2003).

In contrast, Jacobs (1969) thinks the most important sources of knowledge spillovers to be external to the industry in which the firm operates. Cities are the source of innovation because the diversity of these knowledge sources is greatest in cities. The exchange of complementary knowledge between diverse firms leads to more innovation and economic growth. Competition is seen as competition for new ideas embodied in people. A large number of firms facilitates entry of new firms specializing in niche markets, as complementary inputs and services are more easily acquired from specialized producers than from large integrated firms (Audretsch, 1998).

The cluster concept by Porter (1990) predicts higher success for regions that combine technological/industrial specialization within a local production chain and local competition. This model can be viewed as being in between the former two concepts. The three models (MAR, Jacobs, Porter) are frequently tested in empirical work, with a focus on the different effects of regional specialization, diversity, and competition on economic performance.

A frequently cited study on this issue is Glaeser et al. (1992). Using data on employment in US cities between 1956 and 1987, the authors find that local competition and urban variety and not regional specialization encourage employment growth, providing support for Jacob's model. Addressing a related problem, Feldman and Audretsch (1999) find evidence that diversity within a city rather than specialization is conducive to innovation. Using data on 3,969 US product innovations in 1982, they find that 96% of the innovations were made in metropolitan areas, which account for only 30% of the US population. In a Poisson regression of the number of innovations in an industry within a city on the degrees of specialization, diversity and competition,[5] controlling for city size and technological opportunity, the coefficient for specialization is significantly negative whereas the coefficients for diversity and competition

---

[5]The specialization of an industry in a city is measured by the share of industry employment within the city divided by the share of industry employment within the United States. Grouping related industries, they measure diversity by relating the share of employment in that cluster in a city to the share of employment of that industry in the United States. So the variable measures the presence of complementary industries. Competition is measured by firms per worker in a city industry divided by firms per worker in the US industry.

are positive. So the results are strongly in favor of the model by Jacobs. They also tested the impact of specialization and diversification on the firm level innovative output and conclude that, 'innovative activity tends to be lower when that innovation is specialized within a narrow industry than when it is diversified across a complementary set of industries sharing a common science base' (Feldman and Audretsch, 1999, p. 427). With respect to the effects of competition on innovative performance, their results indicate that local monopoly within a city is inferior to local competition for new ideas.

Supplemented by the results by Fujita and Ishii (1998), Duranton and Puga (2000) include the positive effect of diversity on innovation as a stylized fact about specialization and diversity in cities. Another finding in this review is that new plants are created in diversified cities, whereas plant relocation occurs from diversified regions to specialized ones. Duranton and Puga (2001) show how diversified metropolitan areas facilitate search and experimenting in innovation, while specialized environments are the preferred locations for mass production. Dumais et al. (2002) find that it is not the presence of up- and downstream firms which makes firms from different industries locate close to one another, but that knowledge spillovers and the composition of the local labor pool is of decisive influence. Firms from different industries co-locate if they use the same types of skilled workers.

Van Oort (2003) provides mixed evidence on the topic, depending on the econometric setup. Replicating the Glaeser et al. (1992) study, he concludes that, '[t]he regression results using data on Dutch municipalities provide general support for Jane Jacobs' (1969) hypothesis that knowledge spills over between sectors and that competition fosters growth because of the necessity to innovate and survive.' And further, when 'the research design focuses on aggregates of sectors, as in Henderson et al. (1995), outcomes are not as unambiguously "diversity-based" anymore' (van Oort, 2003, p. 28).

Duranton and Puga (2000) conclude that the disadvantages of regional specialization are less innovation and a greater exposure to risk, as industries and technologies rise or fall, while localization economies in the sense of Marshall externalities are an advantage of specialized regions, i.e. the advantages of specialization are of a static nature, while diversity might be necessary for dynamic efficiency. This research also shows that care has to be taken in specifying the econometric model and also in the data that is used.

3.1.4 Labor mobility

'Ideas in people' are identified as one of the most important mechanisms behind the rather abstract concept of local knowledge spillovers (Feldman, 1999). Breschi and Lissoni (2001a) take a critical point on that aspect as they state that, 'labour mobility generates "pure knowledge spillover" if and only if, as workers move from one firm to the another, they help in creating a common pool of knowledge from which *all* their previous employers are capable of drawing' (Breschi and Lissoni, 2001a, p. 990). This view is very restrictive though, as for knowledge spillovers not *all* the knowledge has to be available to the respective firms or organizations. And as (tacit) knowledge is not only incorporated in individuals, but can also be specific to organizations as well as geographic locations (Nelson and Winter, 1982; Amin and Wilkinson, 1999; Lawson, 1999; Lawson and Lorenz, 1999), there might well be a 'memory' of the firm where knowledge generated by former employees is stored and used (Kogut and Zander, 1992).

Recently, a number of studies, which build on the work of Jaffe et al. (1993), tried to trace knowledge flows through people. Johnson and Mareva (2002) perform their exercise on biotechnology patents in the US but in addition calculate measures on interpersonal networks. Their findings suggest a negative effect of distance on knowledge flows which decreases over time while the connectedness of actors is of growing importance. Using a a sample of highly cited, semiconductor-related patents, Almeida and Kogut (1999) also replicate the study by Jaffe et al. (1993). Focussing on mobility patterns of engineers, they find individual patent holders to be highly localized only in Silicon Valley. Breschi and Lissoni (2003), using Italian patent data, additionally control for the mobility of inventors across companies and space, as well as for the network ties established by this mobility, referred to as social proximity. In their interpretation, geographical proximity is not a sufficient condition for the flow of knowledge, as localization effects vanish for citing and cited patents that are not linked by network relationships. They conclude that the observations of localized knowledge spillovers are due to social proximity, which is higher between co-located firms or other organizations. These findings are supported by Singh (2003, 2004), who performs similar studies using US patent data.

The research by Zucker, Darby and co-authors also highlights the importance of contacts between people in the transfer of knowledge. In biotechnology, Zucker et al. (1998b) find localized effects through the connections of star scientists to local firms, which they cannot demonstrate to be spillovers. In another paper, the authors claim that these effects are largely mediated by market mechanisms like contractual cooperations or scientists who start their own firm (Zucker et al., 1998a).

These studies indicate that there is more to localized innovation, than an idea of localized knowledge 'in the air'. The circumstances under which the transfer of knowledge is facilitated and the patterns of regional development are central to the innovation systems approach which is analyzed on a regional and local level in the following section.

3.2   REGIONAL AND LOCAL INNOVATION SYSTEMS

So far we could show that the process of innovation is systemic, that innovative activities are not spread evenly in geographical space, and that localized knowledge spillovers are mediated by the mobility and interaction of people. All these aspects complement each other in the literature on regional and local systems of innovation. The central line of argument within this approach starts by acknowledging the crucial importance of learning in the innovation process. Learning is an interactive process which involves many actors from different types of organizations. Interaction is facilitated by geographical proximity and other forms of proximity as discussed above, especially when knowledge is largely tacit. Consequently, a sufficient degree of proximity is necessary for innovation.

Some authors argue that with the diffusion of ICTs geography will not only play a decreasing role in the transfer of knowledge but also in shaping the patterns of innovation and production (Kelly, 1998). While it might be true that the exchange of information does require fewer physical meetings of people, tacit knowledge still has to be exchanged by face-to-face interaction. Gaspar and Glaeser (1998) argue that telecommunication technologies are rather a complement – or at least not a strong substitute – to face-to-face contact and that the need for cities prevails. Knowledge relevant in the innovation process is only exchanged between people who trust each other, while face-to-face contact is decisive for the establishment of trusting relationships (Storper and Venables, 2004). The building of trust is facilitated by shared commonalities, such as the same language, common codes of communication, shared norms and conventions, and a history of past collaboration and informal interaction (Florida, 1995; Asheim, 1996, 2001; Morgan, 1997; Cooke and Morgan, 1998; Lundvall and Maskell, 2000). For a firm to become integrated in such a learning network it is required to interpret the local codes in a consistent way (Asheim and Gertler, 2004). Regions benefit from such localized capabilities and intangible assets, which are social assets; i.e. rather between than within firms (Maskell and Malmberg, 1999). Locations differ in the institutions which guide the local interaction. Saxenian (1994) describes how a culture of greater interdependence and exchange among individuals in the Silicon Valley region has led to a superior innovative performance compared to Boston's Route 128, where firms and individuals tend to be more isolated. The evolution of these assets explains the path-dependent development of regions and the difficulty of imitating successful regions (Maskell and Malmberg, 1999; Asheim and Gertler, 2004).

The system perspective provides a structure for the following discussion on knowledge transfer, interaction and learning on a local level. In the following section 3.2.1, we discuss the interaction within the market pole as covered in studies on local clusters. Moving to the scientific pole, we discuss the role of universities and public research infrastructure in local knowledge generation and transmission in section 3.2.2. Section 3.2.3 pays special attention to the establishment of local firms through spin-offs in driving the evolution of local innovation systems.

3.2.1   Clusters of local firms

Empirical evidence on the benefits of clustering is provided by Baptista and Swann (1998), who find that innovation, firm entry and growth are all stronger in clusters. In studying firms' location decisions, Aharonson et al. (2004) show that entrepreneurs in Canadian Biotechnology strategically locate in industrial clusters in order to reap the benefits from clustering.

The cluster approach largely focusses on the relationships between co-located firms in related industries. According to Porter (1990, 1998), firms in a cluster are more productive because of better access to employees and suppliers, access to specialized information, complementarities (product complements, co-ordination of activities, marketing), access to institutions and public goods (education, laboratories), and incentives by direct performance measurement. With respect to advantages in innovation he mentions the benefits of having a window on the market and facilitated learning. The ability of clusters to form new businesses is also highlighted. While the cluster and the RIS approach seem to have many ideas in common, Porter (1998) emphasizes the role of competition between co-located firms in the success of a cluster, whereas the RIS approach focusses on the cooperative interaction in the diffusion of knowledge and the underlying institutions.

Maskell (2001) distinguishes the benefits of clustering with respect to the relative position of localized firms, i.e. whether they are horizontally or vertically related. On the one hand, horizontally related firms need to compete on product markets to create variety and to be able to learn from each other by monitoring.

> The resulting enhanced knowledge creation following from the ongoing sequence of variation, monitoring, comparison, selection and imitation of identified superior solutions is in essence why N similar firms of size S are not equal to one firm of size $N \times S$ doing the same.
> (Maskell, 2001, p. 930)

This does not necessarily imply that co-located competitors need to interact with each other; localization economies are independent of the internal degree of interaction (Maskell, 2001). If the only way to learn from a competitor is through observing his actions and the consequences thereof, co-locating merely reduces to the costs for information.

Vertically related firms, on the other hand, do interact directly. Through input/output relations with specialized suppliers and critical customers, firms can improve their products. In increasing specialization, the division of labor accelerates the growth of knowledge in the cluster (Maskell, 2001). However, even though studies on industrial districts indicate the opposite (Pyke et al., 1990; Amin and Thrift, 1992), clusters and agglomerations are often characterized by weak internal input-output linkages in older industries (Pred, 1976) as well as in high-technology fields (Chapman and Walker, 1987; Oakey et al., 1988). The relatively modest relevance of local product transactions does not imply a similar relevance of knowledge exchange, though. Local lead users might be decisive in the development of new products, which are then sold globally (von Hippel, 1994).

Cooperations in R&D are also to be named as an important aspect of interaction between co-located firms. Access to external knowledge raises the innovative performance of cooperating firms (Palmberg et al., 1999; Czarnitzki and Fier, 2003). The partnering firms can learn from each other and accumulate a common knowledge-stock on the level of innovation systems (Pyka, 2002). Besides, firms can access larger spillover pools where knowledge is shared on a voluntary basis (e.g. Nelson, 1987).

Cooperation and monitoring are channels of knowledge transmission for actors to learn from each other. But the extent to which knowledge is utilized by the receiver is subject to cognitive abilities and absorptive capacity. The most direct way of transferring knowledge from one organization to another is by job mobility of the scientist who holds the knowledge. For example, the frequency of changing jobs turned out to be a major advantage of Silicon Valley compared to the Boston area (Saxenian, 1994).

3.2.2 Public research

Universities are considered the backbone of regional innovation systems. Universities are important for a region as they attract human capital to the local area and stimulate entrepreneurial talent in the region (Huffman and Quigley, 2002). But the main function of universities and public research institutes is to produce basic research and create human capital (Anselin et al., 1997; Lambooy, 2003). Research results and human capital spills into the economic sphere, as research labs collaborate with business firms, as scientists and engineers change positions, or as they start their own firm. These positive externalities that emanate from universities and research institutes have been shown to have the main effects on a local scale (Jaffe, 1989; Feldman, 1994; Acs et al., 1994; Acs, 2002).

R&D cooperations between public research and industry are a formal way to transfer knowledge from academia to practice. In chapter 7 it is shown that cooperations are rather internal to the region than external, if public research institutes or the university are involved in the partnership.

A qualified work force is especially important in knowledge intensive, high-technology industries. The supply of graduate students and well trained scientists and engineers represents important university–industry linkages. When scientists and engineers change their jobs, they are more likely to stay in the region (Almeida and Kogut, 1999), and university graduates search for their first jobs in proximity to their university (Jaffe, 1989).

3.2.3   Spin-offs

The establishment of new firms by former employees is another important, frictionless mode of knowledge transfer between firms (Audretsch and Keilbach, 2002): 'Thus, the mobility of economic agents across different contexts and their creation of trajectories becomes an important mechanism for the process by which knowledge spills over from one context and organization to another' (Audretsch and Keilbach, 2002, p. 23).

Four theoretical explanations for the formation of spin-offs are put forward in Klepper (2001a). The approach based on agency costs argues that due to asymmetric information the associated costs impede the employee from contracting the development of the innovation with the incumbent firm, leading to spin-offs. A second perspective holds organizational limitations responsible for spin-offs. As the incumbents have difficulties in developing the new product or implementing the new process, opportunities for the employees open up to start their own firm. The connection between spin-offs and learning is the focus of the third approach, where founders of spin-offs exploit the knowledge accumulated during their employment to compete with the incumbent. Analogies between the birth of children and the birth of spin-offs are drawn to make predictions about spin-off formation in the fourth theory.

Spin-offs are considered to promote the geographic agglomeration of an industry. Empirical work shows that spin-off firms locate close to their parent firm in automobiles (Klepper, 2001b), in lasers (Klepper and Sleeper, 2002), and in disk drives (Franco and Filson, 2000). Furthermore, successful firms spawn more spin-offs which themselves are more successful compared to other start-ups as the founders 'inherit' some of the organizational knowledge of the parent firm (Klepper, 2001a). These two characteristics, together with findings that spin-offs from successful firms are more successful than other start-ups (Klepper and Sleeper, 2002), form the basis for a virtuous circle that drives the evolution of an industry but also leads to path-dependent evolution and the success of the location where the first successful firms in an industry are located.

Academic start-ups from universities and public research institutes are considered a main mechanism in the commercialization of new scientific knowledge (Di Gregorio and Shane, 2003), but they also enhance local knowledge generation and learning processes (Lindholm Dahlstrand, 1999). Through spin-off processes, technological and managerial expertise diffuses within the region, regional industrial culture becomes more focussed, and inter-organizational linkages and personal networks are encouraged. Especially in the initial phase, local linkages between university spin-offs and the previous employer are important for their development. Only as firms grow, wider national relationships are becoming more important (Lindholm Dahlstrand, 1999). As all these transfer channels seem to be rather localized, it has to be questioned how local innovation systems reduce the risk of lock-in (as discussed in section 2.2).

3.3 EXTERNAL LINKAGES

3.3.1 Decreasing the risk of technological lock-in

As it is important for a firm to draw on knowledge generated by external actors, the same is true for local innovation systems. While the density of the local network is referred to as local 'buzz', some authors use the metaphor of global 'pipelines' to describe external relationships (Storper and Venables, 2004; Bathelt et al., 2004). So far, it has mostly been argued that tacit knowledge is transferred mainly by face-to-face contact, which is facilitated by geographical proximity. Knowledge, which is generated locally and quickly diffuses within the region increases the specific knowledge-stock of a region. While this – if it is best practice – might lead to a comparative advantage with respect to other localities, it might also lead to a lock-in situation, if local trajectories take the wrong direction (Gertler, 1997; Boschma, 2005). Especially highly specialized regions face the risk of a technological lock-in. While a dense local milieu generally enhances innovative activity it might also create situations where the actors become so narrowly focussed on a particular type of economic activity that a shift towards new developments is impossible (Camagni, 1991; Malmberg and Maskell, 1997).

Bathelt et al. (2004) argue that successful clusters are characterized by actors that are aware of these problems and generate novelty by drawing on specific local knowledge and combining it with external knowledge components. Even Silicon Valley, which is often regarded as the prototype of a dense local network (Saxenian, 1994), has been found to have important external channels of information and knowledge transmission (Gray et al., 1998; Markusen, 1999; Saxenian and Hsu, 2001). In a comparative study of ICT-related clusters, Bresnahan et al. (2001) find that access to external expertise and external markets are decisive for success of the cluster, especially in initial phases of its development.

Theoretical work as well as simulation studies which analyze the rate of knowledge diffusion under different network structures suggest that small world structures perform best with respect to diffusion rates (Cowan and Jonard, 2004). Networks that exhibit small world properties are characterized by a high degree of clustering (buzz) and a short average path length, which is accomplished if the clusters have long distance relations connecting each other (pipelines).

The establishment of external linkages is subject to investments in technological and management capabilities and need time to develop (Markusen, 1996; Lindholm Dahlstrand, 1999). While technological capabilities are important to absorb external knowledge, they are also an asset for the reciprocal aspects of cooperation. The prospective gains from external cooperation need to be based on the uniqueness of partners' capabilities and outweigh the costs of frequent communication. External relations also need an active management as these linkages are neither created automatically nor persist without substantial efforts in communication and interaction (Bathelt et al., 2004).

In opposition to the popular view of industrial districts as agglomerations of small, homogenous firms, Lazerson and Lorenzoni (1999) point out the relevance of large dominant firms in transferring skills and technology to the region through their external contacts. Large multinational corporations (MNC) surely have the capabilities to maintain these external relationships and increasingly do so (Cantwell and Iammarino, 2000). MNCs establish small-scale R&D units in locations with expertise in related fields of technology to broaden the MNCs' knowledge bases by monitoring regional knowledge bases (Patel and Vega, 1999). On the one hand, these subsidiaries establish linkages to local firms and amplify the advantages of geographical agglomeration and reinforce the technological specialization of local systems (Cantwell and Iammarino, 1998, 2001). On the other hand, they might only localize to exploit local competencies, while not being interested in or even prohibiting local interaction (Lorenzen and Mahnke, 2002).

Local innovation systems, however, do not have to rely on the advent of multinational players. Lindholm Dahlstrand (1999) points out that in later phases of development, spin-off firms become capable of maintaining external linkages themselves.

3.3.2   Geography, technological and sectoral systems

External linkages are supposedly formed between actors that are close in the cognitive dimension. To analyze the interdependencies between characteristics of technology and spatial patterns of innovative activity, we proceed with a review of concepts which deal with these issues. Within the SI approach, the organization and evolution of industries is analyzed in terms of technological

(TS) or sectoral innovation systems (SIS). These systems include actors that are involved in the development of certain technologies or innovate in related product markets. Both approaches (TS and SIS) investigate the spatial patterns of technological and sectoral development and are to a certain extent related to the study by Audretsch and Feldman (1996a), where the geographic clustering of innovation is analyzed over the industry life cycle.

Lundvall (1985, 1988) highlights the importance of user–producer relationships as critical features of an innovation system. In his view the importance of geographical as well as cultural distance between the actors depends on the type of innovative activity and the technology involved. If the relevant knowledge is codified, it will be easily transmitted over long distances at low cost so that users and producers will not have to be located close to one another. A common cultural background might be helpful though when the technology is complex and ever changing. While Lundvall pursued his ideas within the NIS-approach, others followed his emphasis on relationships between firms and organizations with a common technological or product background.

Carlsson and Stankiewicz (1991) introduced the notion of technological systems of innovation. It is defined:

> as a network of agents interacting in a specific *economic/industrial area* under a particular *institutional infrastructure* or set of infrastructures and involved in the generation, diffusion, and utilization of technology. Technological systems are defined in terms of knowledge/competence flows rather than in terms of flows of ordinary goods and services.
> (Carlsson and Stankiewicz, 1991, p. 111)

Within the technological system the institutional factors will be responsible for a balance of variety creating and selection mechanisms therefore assuring a high degree of system integration and stability. If this balance is achieved, the socio-economic system exhibits a high degree of adaptability and dynamic efficiency. The elements of the system are in most cases spatially correlated, whereas the systems might be regional, national, or even international (Carlsson and Stankiewicz, 1991). National technology policy should therefore encourage local technological agglomerations which have strong linkages to other centers of excellence spread all over the world (Carlsson and Stankiewicz, 1991).

In the sectoral innovation systems approach, Breschi and Malerba (1997) build on the concept of technological regimes (Nelson and Winter, 1982; Winter, 1984) and apply it to the systems of innovation approach. Less focussed on institutions and the connections of agents as the TS approach, the focus is on competition and the role of the selection environment.[6]

---

[6]This approach has recently been applied to a number of industries, including chemicals (Cesaroni et al., 2001), pharmaceuticals and biotechnology (McKelvey and Orsenigo, 2001; Owen-Smith

Breschi and Malerba (1997) provide a linkage between the characteristics of technology and the resulting geographical pattern of the innovative activity. With respect to the geographical boundaries and the nature of competition in such a system, they claim that, '[...] the forces that account for the dynamics of SIS and shape their spatial boundaries should be found in some specific features of technologies.' And further, they, 'determine the nature and intensity of competition and selection processes, the geographical distribution of innovative activities, and the relevant boundaries of the innovative process' (Breschi and Malerba, 1997, p. 132).

Some case studies are presented in Breschi and Malerba (1997), where the characteristics of the sectoral knowledge-base (opportunities, appropriability conditions and knowledge cumulativeness) are related to the number of innovators in the industry and the degree of geographical concentration of innovation (not consequently production).[7]

Traditional industries, which are characterized by low degrees of opportunity, appropriability and firms' cumulativeness, are composed of many innovators which are distributed randomly in space since knowledge has no specific spatial boundaries. Other sectors are found to be geographically concentrated, depending on the degree of market concentration:

First, they are localized if market concentration is high and only a few firms are active in that industry. Consequently, the sector is concentrated in few centers, which, at first sight, has nothing to do with a local innovation system. Two different cases might emerge though: if the supplier industry shows strong interaction with each other as well as with the large firm, a local system might emerge. A prime example would be automobiles with few innovators, local knowledge boundaries, characterized by high cumulativeness at the firm level and a system type of knowledge with some tacit components. On the other hand, if the industry is more dependent on formal R&D from universities, the larger firms might cluster themselves in some core areas as in the case of the computer mainframe industry.

Second, if market concentration is low due to low appropriability and low firm level cumulativeness, geographical concentration depends on the sources and nature of knowledge. If the industry depends on simple and codified knowledge, it will be geographically dispersed as in textile and other traditional sectors. If the knowledge-base is rather tacit and specific, one would expect a formation of industrial district type organization as in the case of the machinery industry where learning has a local character. Selection then takes place at the regional level. A rather ambiguous picture arises when looking

---

et al., 2002), software industry (Steinmueller, 2001), and in services (Tether and Metcalfe, 2001). For a review see Malerba (2002).

[7] The following is largely based on Breschi and Malerba (1997) but also in the overview articles by Malerba (2002, 2004).

at the software and microelectronics sector. Operating systems is probably the industry showing the strongest network externalities within the software industry which leads to an almost monopolistic market structure. A similar case is processors in microelectronics, where the reason for this kind of market structure lies in the cumulative nature of knowledge at the firm level. Other subsystems within those sectors show lower market concentration but a strong regional clustering. Here, both local and global knowledge boundaries are associated with very high opportunity conditions and a wide variety of potential technological approaches.

3.4 SUMMARY: SYSTEMS OF INNOVATION AS AN INTEGRATIVE FRAMEWORK

The previous sections show that the systems of innovation approach is applicable on various levels of aggregation. It also should have become clear that the different layers interact. Freeman (1995, p. 21) points out how substructures, such as regional innovation systems, clusters, and economies of agglomeration, 'have always under-pinned national systems from the beginnings of the industrial revolution,' and that the national system needs to interact with these subsystems and with transnational corporations 'as will be the role of international cooperation in sustaining a global regime favourable to catching-up and development.' If one wishes to understand how a national or technological system is organized, the embedded subsystems have to be accounted for.

Sectors are studied with respect to the scope of their geographic clustering and their dependence on the countries' institutional settings in which it is located (Breschi and Malerba, 1997). Sectoral systems, even though they rely on the same technologies, sometimes differ in structure depending on the country in which they operate. Malerba (2004) describes how in some cases national institutions (patent system, property rights, antitrust regulations) shape the sectoral systems but also affect the national sectoral composition. In certain cases countries provide an environment more suitable for certain types of sectors and constrain the development or innovation in others (examples are given in Dosi and Malerba, 1996). The interdependence and co-evolution becomes obvious when a sectoral system dominates the national system and is able to shape the national institutions according to the specific needs (Malerba, 2004).

In Porter's (1990; 1998) view, clusters have to be seen within a broader theory of competition and and competitive strategy in a global economy. Successful clusters are not only important for regional growth but also for the countries these clusters are situated in (Porter and Stern, 2004). This view is in line with Edquist (2004), who points out that the different variants of the SI approach (national, sectoral, regional) coexist, and complement each other.

Consequently, when analyzing regional or local innovation systems, the linkages to actors within the respective national and technological system have to be accounted for. Agents within local systems compete, cooperate, and interact with firms or other organizations on a national and on a global scale. So the regional perspective clearly has to recognize the market environment as well as the technological systems its members are operating in. Close relationships to the technological system foster intra-industry knowledge transfer, while knowledge might flow easier between actors of different industries when they are localized. Following from the discussion on the different types of proximity, it is clear that actors cannot be close in all dimensions, and if they were, they would face the risk of lock-in. Between actors that are co-located, a lack of cognitive proximity might be overcome by geographical proximity and the other related forms, while cognitive proximity is necessary for interactive learning between partners that lack geographical or institutional proximity.

4. Interaction in German Regions[*]

4.1 INTRODUCTION

The arguments summarized in the previous chapters strongly suggest that innovation is an interactive and highly systemic process involving many actors from different parts of the economy. The internal density of innovation systems, as well as the openness to external knowledge of the relevant actors, amongst other factors, have been identified as necessary conditions for a good performance of local innovation systems (Gertler, 1997; Breschi and Malerba, 2001; Bathelt, 2003; Bathelt et al., 2004). Linkages between actors from different localities are then the constituents of a national or technological system. Therefore, Jena is not analyzed in isolation, but within the wider scope of the national and technological systems.

Before we analyze the specific case of Jena, we focus on the general relationship between the technological knowledge of a region and the patterns of cooperative behavior of the actors within that region as a means of transferring this knowledge. Of course, there are many ways by which information between economic actors may be exchanged; one of the empirically more traceable is formal R&D cooperation. The theoretical literature on R&D cooperation has largely focussed on the social benefits as a means of internalizing positive spillovers generated through R&D (e.g. D'Aspremont and Jacquemin, 1988; Kamien et al., 1992). Since firms in those models are symmetric with respect to their technological capabilities, cooperation and its consequences are solely dependent on different product market and spillover conditions. These conditions are not questioned here. Rather, we build on those previous findings that cooperation is favorable to innovation. Assuming that firms are heterogeneous with respect to their technological capabilities, we investigate firms' decisions to cooperate and how this is related to patterns of cooperative activities on a regional level.

The main research question within this chapter is concerned with the relationship between the knowledge and/or the degree of specialization within

[*] A version of this chapter is published as Cantner and Graf (2004).

a region, the propensity to cooperate and the kind or pattern of this relationship. In particular, we are interested in whether the kind and level of sophistication of technologies applied in a region, the technological diversity of that region, as well as the relative technological position of that region with respect to other regions have a significant influence on the intensity and kind of cooperative behavior in research of the firms.

The two major results of our analysis are as follows: first, we find an inverted U-shaped relationship between the degree of technological specialization and the number of research cooperations; i.e. regions which are technologically moderately specialized show the highest number of research cooperations. Second, the higher a region's technological specialization, the more cooperation will take place with partners inside the same region compared to cooperation with partners outside that region.

The chapter proceeds as follows: first, in section 4.2 we present the theoretical background for the hypotheses we want to test empirically. Here we introduce our conceptions of technology gap, of technological diversity, of internal and external cooperations, and of the tech-region as main building-blocks. Section 4.3 is devoted to the description of our database and the construction of the various variables we use. Section 4.4 reports on our estimation results and gives appropriate interpretations. The focus of investigation is shifted towards the innovation system of Jena in section 4.5, where we compare the actual intensity and different forms of interaction with the predictions from our econometric model. Section 4.6 concludes the chapter by summarizing the main findings.

4.2   THEORETICAL BACKGROUND AND DERIVATION OF HYPOTHESES

In order to develop testable hypotheses about the specific regional pattern of firms' cooperative behavior, in this section we present the theoretical background. In particular, we first aim at the knowledge based incentives of firms for engaging in the exchange of know-how on a cooperative basis. In the second step, we extend the arguments from the firm level to the regional level. From this we derive – in the third step – three hypotheses about the relationship between a region's technological characteristics and the pattern of firm cooperation in research.

4.2.1   Collective invention

Theories of innovation networks, such as local innovation systems or technological systems, tell us that quite often new know-how is to be considered as the collective rather than the individual outcome of knowledge generating activities. This collective dimension is based on the conscious (but sometimes also unconscious) exchange of information and knowledge between specific actors that differ in the *kind* of knowledge and capabilities they hold and master as well as in the *level* of their respective technological competence. Knowledge exchange taking place among such heterogeneous agents may lead to a new combination or recombination of specific knowledge and competencies which then, via so-called cross-fertilization, leads to new know-how and new capabilities. Consequently, the resulting achievements are a collective outcome and would not have been possible by the knowledge generating activities of a single isolated actor (Allen, 1983).

4.2.2 Local innovation systems and technology systems

Whenever this exchange of knowledge takes place on frequent and even regular terms, whether formalized or not (von Hippel, 1987), the resulting structure of relationships can be described as a system or network of actors. Those systems reduce the cost of exchanging know-how and information and thus let the benefits of cross-fertilization be more easily reaped. Based on this aspect, networks for know-how exchange can be observed on different levels. Whenever geographical proximity enables and eases know-how exchange, a regional or local system of innovation (Saxenian, 1994; Cooke, 1998) may emerge, where a number of different technologies co-exist. If the ease of knowledge exchange is directly related to proximity in technological know-how, so-called technological or sectoral systems (Carlsson and Stankiewicz, 1991; Malerba, 2002) may be observed which are characterized by a nevertheless broadly defined core technology (such as automobiles, where a small number of sub-technologies, such as combustion engines, electronics, safety-technologies etc., come together). Of course, firms can be 'members' of both kinds of systems.

4.2.3 Know-how exchange and technology structure

So far, classifying network-based exchange of know-how has been based on the degree of accessibility and the related transaction costs. In addition to that, and maybe even more important than sheer (cost dependent) accessibility, is the degree to which exchange of knowledge is beneficial to both or all sides involved. As mentioned above, the knowledge-base of a firm at a certain point in time has at least two dimensions, the kind of knowledge on the one side, and its level or degree of sophistication, on the other side. For any two (or more) actors willing to exchange know-how, these two aspects are of importance.

Consider first the case in which the specific kinds of knowledge are substitutes rather than complements. Consequently, the actors will not get into exchanging know-how. Alternatively, in a situation where the specific knowledge endowments are neither substitutes nor complements, i.e. both parties have different capabilities, the combination of which may not be

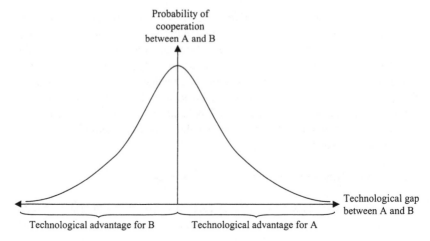

Figure 4.1: Probability of cooperation and technological gap

possible or sensible for the project in question, exchange of know-how will not benefit any of the parties. Third, of course, with complementary knowledge know-how exchange is likely to benefit all actors involved.[1]

With respect to the level of knowledge, consider actors whose knowledge by all means is complementary but who differ considerably in the level of technological sophistication, that is, there are high-tech actors as well as low-tech actors. In such cases, the difference in just these technology levels, the so-called technological gap,[2] may determine whether cooperation is beneficial for all exchanging parties. For two actors who are rather different, the technological gap between them is relatively large, and therefore the exchange of know-how may be beneficial for the technological laggard only. In that case, an exchange of know-how or cooperation will not be established.[3] Alternatively, when the technological gap between two actors is rather narrow, the exchange of know-how is beneficial to both, in which case a know-how exchange or cooperation is likely to become established.

This idea is graphically represented in figure 4.1, where the probability

[1] In their empirical study on interfirm cooperation, Mowery et al. (1998) find strong evidence in favor of their hypothesis that joint venture partners display a higher degree of technological overlap compared with non-collaborators.

[2] The technology gap here is to be considered as a multidimensional conception when different knowledge components make up the technology level of an actor. An appropriate measure should take account of differences in technological levels in the aggregate.

[3] We abstract from the possibility of financial compensation for the technological leader, even though we see cooperations between, for example, newly founded biotechnology firms (the leader) with large pharmaceutical companies (the laggard) where this compensation is taken to the extreme in the case of a merger.

of cooperation between two firms A and B is highest for a technological gap of zero, while the probability declines with the difference in the level of capabilities. Note that this holds for complementary knowledge only.

A consequence of this dependence of cooperation on technology gap structures is that technologically highly sophisticated firms might be unable to find appropriate cooperation partners. Take, for example, the only technology leader in a certain sector for whom the likelihood to find a partner is relatively low – in the case of a monopolistic situation, even zero.

In addition to these last arguments, one might also ask whether high-tech firms or rather low-tech actors are more interested or engaged in cooperation. On the assumption that low-tech know-how usually has diffused already and thus is public, it is high-tech knowledge which is supposed to be less easily accessible and will be only exchanged (and thus diffuses) in a cooperative arrangement. Consequently, high tech-firms tend to be more engaged in cooperation than low-tech actors.

4.2.4 Cooperation and relative technological position

Based on these arguments, we want to establish the following: assume that the actors considered are never identical with respect to their kind of knowledge and specific level of technological capabilities. The engagement of these actors in cooperation and know-how exchange then depends on their respective technological positions within the overall technology structure resulting from the specific knowledge endowments of the heterogeneous actors. The technological position is defined in a relative way, as an actor's technological gap with respect to other actors (lagging or leading), as well as the degree of complementarity of the specific knowledge endowments (complement, substitute or non-related).

4.2.5 Regional focus and tech-regions

Before we derive hypotheses that can be tested empirically, we want to switch the perspective and consider the actors as part of a certain geographical region. In order to take into account the various technologies performed in a certain region, we define so-called *tech-regions*. A tech-region ij consists of the firms located in region i and engaged in technology class j. For example, the optic firms Zeiss and Jenoptik belong to the technology class 'optics' and are located in the region of 'Jena'. This tech-region is potentially part of the local innovation system of Jena as well as potentially part of the technological system of the optics industry in Germany (or even world wide).

Looking at a specific tech-region ij, one may be interested in the following questions: (a) are firms that belong to tech-region ij engaged in know-how exchange or research cooperation?; (b) if there is cooperation observed for tech-region ij, what are the determinants for such cooperative arrangements on the tech-regional, regional, and technological level?; (c) what kind of network-relationships or know-how exchange relationships are the firms engaged in? That is, are they integrated in a local system of innovation and/or in a technological system? In the former case, the cooperation is called *internal* to the region; in the latter case we have cooperation which is *external* to the region.

In order to argue at the level of tech-regions, the above used concepts of *technology gap* and *kind of technology* have to be adjusted. For the former, we use the degree of technological specialization of a region i in technology j. The higher this degree, the more specialized is region i in generating new technological know-how and the higher the level of technological sophistication in technology j. For the latter, the degree of technological diversity describes an upper boundary for possible technological complementarities faced by the actors within region i.

4.2.6 Hypotheses

On the basis of this regional or local perspective, we can formulate hypotheses about the aggregate outcome of the cooperative endeavors of firms that constitute the tech-region:

Hypothesis 1. *Comparing different tech-regions, the number of cooperations is highest for an intermediate degree of specialization, implying that the number of cooperations is lowest for no specialization or complete specialization.*

This hypothesis follows directly from the idea that as long as two actors have complementary knowledge, the technological gap must not be too large for them to both benefit by cooperating.

Under the assumption that firms located within one specific tech-region are rather similar in technological level, we can formulate the next Hypothesis.

Hypothesis 2. *Tech-regions which are more specialized will show a higher number of internal cooperations relative to external cooperations.*

A tech-region being highly specialized implies that the knowledge generated therein makes up a large quantity of the new knowledge of the whole technological system. The probability of finding an appropriate partner for mutual beneficial knowledge exchange within the region rises compared to finding one outside.

For a third hypothesis, consider the following. Firms have closer contacts to other firms belonging to the same local or technological innovation system than to firms outside either system. Those existing contacts provide the basis for possible cooperations. On the one hand, diversity of the region provides easily accessible knowledge for diversifying or broadening firms' knowledge bases, an argument that has been put forward by Jacobs (1969). On the other hand, specific knowledge to the own field might be found within the technological system. Based on these considerations, we can now state:

Hypothesis 3. *Tech-regions within technologically more diverse regions show a higher level of internal cooperation, while those within less diverse regions cooperate more externally to their location.*

4.3 DATA

4.3.1 Patent level

For the empirical analysis, we use German patent data as provided by the German patent office (DPMA , Deutsches Patent- und Markenamt). The patents in the database were disclosed between 1995 and 2001 and were filed by at least one applicant located in Germany. We use information about the applicant(s), the inventor(s), and the IPC main classification of each patent.

Each patent is characterized according to its cooperative nature, technological class, location, and whether one of the applicants is a university or other public research institution. A patent is considered a cooperation (CO) if the number of applicants is greater than one (co-application). In our view, this assumption leads to an underestimation rather than an overestimation of cooperative research. Two organizations that decide to jointly apply for a patent, should in most cases have collaborated on that research project. On the other hand, not every research cooperation will lead to a co-applied patent if the partners find other ways to compensate each other.

A co-applied patent is counted as an *internal cooperation* (CO^{int}) if it is a cooperation in the sense above and all inventors are located in the same region. An *external cooperation* (CO^{ext}) is a cooperation where at least two of the inventors are not co-located. The reason for this classification scheme lies in the patenting conventions of organizations with more than one location. Large firms (e.g. Siemens) or research institutes like the Max-Planck or Fraunhofer society file patents in their headquarters no matter where the research leading to the patent was conducted. Therefore, cooperation between such large patentees and smaller ones in other regions will almost always be counted as external, even if they were actually within a region. Based on this procedure, 12,549 of the 231,720 patents in our sample are considered as cooperations with 3,421 internal and 9,128 external to regions.

Since this chapter is about interaction, network analysis seems to be a natural methodology for describing linkages between regions. The way internal and external links are calculated so far can only be an approximation to real connections of actors within and between regions, since it is a zero/one variable for each patent. Figure 4.2 shows how an alternative measure of internal and external interaction is computed. This figure gives a graphical representation of a network of innovators on one patent, with inventors 1 and 2 from region A and inventor 3 from region B. To get an account of cooperative research, we count the cooperative linkages each inventor of a particular patent has, distinguish by this external and internal linkages, and aggregate for the tech-regions with respect to the patent just considered. The variable $LINK^{int}$, taking account of cooperations internal to a region, will then have a value of 1 for region A and 0 for region B. The variable $LINK^{ext}$, measuring external cooperation, will be 2 for regions A and B. In the regressions below, we also use relative measures of external cooperation, i.e. $EXSHARE^{link} = \frac{LINK^{ext}}{LINK^{int}+LINK^{ext}}$ and $EXSHARE^{co} = \frac{CO^{ext}}{CO}$.

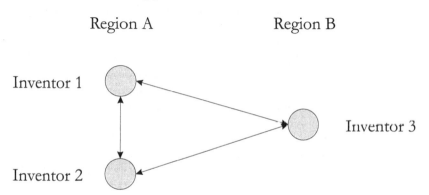

Figure 4.2: Construction of internal and external linkages

Note: *Three inventors from two different regions work together on one patent. For region A this constellation leads to one internal link and two external ones, whereas region B has no internal links but two external ones.*

4.3.2 Technology region level

Since our level of analysis is the tech-region, we aggregate the variables to the level of the technological region.[4] For the technological aggregation, patents have been classified according to a technology-oriented classification that distinguishes five industries and 30 technologies based on the International Patent classification (IPC). This classification has been elaborated jointly by the 'Fraunhofer-Institut für Systemtechnik und Innovationsforschung' (FhG-ISI), the 'Observatoire des Sciences et des Techniques' (OST), and the 'Science

---

[4]E.g. CO in the new dataset is the sum of CO on patent level for technology j in region i.

and Technology Research Policy Unit of the University of Sussex' (SPRU). Table A.2 in the Appendix lists the five industries and the 30 technologies that we use. The observation unit is then a technological class located in a region, according to the first five digits of the German 'Kreisgemeindeschlüssel' which make up the German 'Kreise',[5] of the first applicant mentioned on the patent. As a result of this procedure we end up with 9,648 observations consisting of 434 regions and 30 technological fields.[6]

To characterize the tech-regions, several variables as presented in table 4.1 are used.[7] As in Cantwell and Janne (1999), we measure, or rather approximate, the regional competence in a certain technology by the degree of specialization of that tech-region. We assume that in the long run a region will not follow a technological path if it is not successful in those technologies and therefore assume technological competence and specialization to be positively correlated. We follow Patel and Pavitt (1991) and Soete (1981) by employing the index of Technological Revealed Comparative Advantage (TRCA), originally used in a moderately different form in trade theory.[8] This *specialization* index uses the number of patents (P_{ij}) of region i in technology field j and is defined as a region's share of all patenting in a technological field, relative to its share in all patenting in all fields:

$$TRCA_{ij} = \frac{P_{ij}/\sum_i P_{ij}}{\sum_j P_{ij}/\sum_{ij} P_{ij}} \qquad (4.1)$$

A value above unity indicates a comparative advantage of region i in the technological field j. Calculated in this fashion, this index is not symmetric[9] and is therefore not an appropriate measure of specialization to be used in econometric models. Laursen (1998) suggests the following transformation to this measure:[10]

$$RSCA_{ij} = \frac{TRCA_{ij} - 1}{TRCA_{ij} + 1} \qquad (4.2)$$

The $RSCA$ is symmetric and bounded between -1 and $+1$, with no specialization indicated by a value of zero. Our expectations about the coefficients of this variable are discussed at length in section 4.2.

The role of diversity in cities or regions has been discussed in the literature. Glaeser et al. (1992) test three different models of knowledge spillovers

---

[5]This compares to the NUTS 3 level of territorial units for statistics by EUROSTAT.

[6]Of course, not all regions patent in all technological fields.

[7]Information about the relation between the data series can be obtained from the correlation matrix (table A.1) in the Appendix.

[8]Namely, Balassa's (1965) Index of Revealed Comparative Advantage.

[9]Its values range from zero to $max(\frac{\sum_{ij} P_{ij}}{\sum_j P_{ij}}, \forall i)$. In the extreme case, where one region only patents in one technological class, $P_{ij} = \sum_j P_{ij}$ and therefore cancel out.

[10]The $RSCA$ is similar to the hyperbolic version of the TRCA suggested by Grupp (1994) but discriminates better between high values of the $TRCA$.

Table 4.1: List of variables and descriptive statistics

	Description	Level	Mean	Std.Dev.	Minimum	Maximum	NumCases
Dependent variables							
CO	no. of co-applied patents	tech-region	1.30	4.19	0	147	9648
CO^{int}	no. of internal cooperations	tech-region	0.35	1.31	0	49	9648
CO^{ext}	no. of external cooperations	tech-region	0.95	3.47	0	142	9648
$EXSHARE^{co}$	share of external cooperations (CO^{ext}/CO)	tech-region	0.71	0.39	0	1	4098
$EXSHARE^{link}$	share of external linkages	tech-region	0.82	0.22	0	1	8721
Regressors							
$RSCA$	specialization index	tech-region	−0.08	0.41	0.98	0.97	9648
$RSCA2$	—"— squared		0.17	0.19	0.00	0.96	9648
UNI	no. of patents with at least one public R&D agency as applicant	tech-region	0.51	6.17	0.00	320	9648
POP	population of the region in 2000 (thousand)	region	213.41	244.98	40.20	3384.14	9648
$POP2$	—"— squared		105551.90	666898.16	1616.04	11452403.50	9648
DI	technological diversity of region i	region	10.58	3.45	1.99	19.39	9648
$DI2$	—"— squared		123.83	73.62	3.96	375.97	9648
$HERF$	concentration of innovators in a tech-region	tech-region	0.47	0.33	0.01	1.00	9648
$HERF2$	—"— squared		0.33	0.39	0.00	1.00	9648
$HERFTEC$	regional concentration of technology j	technology	0.05	0.05	0.01	0.27	9648
$HERFTEC2$	—"— squared		0.01	0.01	0.00	0.07	9648
$FIRMSIZE$	average size of business in year 1999 (workers per firm)	region	134.94	113.67	44.21	1615.06	9648
$SEC1-5$	dummies for the 5 major technological sectors						9648
NL	dummy for tech-regions located in the 'neue Bundesländer'						9648

according to their impact on the growth rate of cities. They find clear evidence in favor of the model by Jacobs (1969), where she argues that the most important sources of knowledge spillovers are external to the industry in which the firm operates and that cities are the source of innovation because diversity is greatest there. We therefore include a simple measure of *diversification* of the region. Duranton and Puga (2000) apply the inverse of a Hirshman-Herfindahl index, which translates for our purposes to summing the square of each technologies' share in local patents for each region over all technologies. Formally the Hirshman-Herfindahl index or diversity index is given by

$$DI_i = 1 / \sum_j p_{ij}^2 , \qquad (4.3)$$

where p_{ij} is the patent share of technology j in region i.

If patenting activity in the region under consideration is fully concentrated in a technology, we find $DI = 1$, and this index increases as activities in this region become more diverse. A positive coefficient of diversity would speak in favor of Jacob's (1969) argument.

To account for differences between tech-regions in terms of the *concentration of patentees*, we also calculate the Herfindahl Index for every observation unit ij as below:

$$HERF_{ij} = \sum_k \left(\frac{P_k}{\sum_k P_k} \right)^2 \qquad (4.4)$$

P_k is the number of patents filed by organization k in tech-region ij. The expected impact of the concentration of patentees on the number of internal cooperations is clear. In the extreme case of a single inventor of the tech-region, there is no possibility of internal cooperation, so the influence should be negative. For the number of external cooperations, this coefficient should be positive if we assume that the monopolist inventor searches for external partners if it does not find them locally.

The *regional concentration of technology* j is measured again with the Herfindahl index

$$HERFTEC_j = \sum_i \left(\frac{P_{ij}}{\sum_i P_{ij}} \right)^2 \qquad (4.5)$$

The *ideal type* local innovation system is specialized in a technology which is geographically concentrated with many local innovators (Porter, 1990; Saxenian, 1994; Bresnahan et al., 2001). We should therefore see more internal cooperations in those concentrated technologies, while for external cooperations there could be two effects, pushing in different directions. On the one hand, if there are complementary skills within the different regions performing in that technology, i.e. a regional division of labor, external cooperations could be expected to rise with concentration. On the other hand, in the extreme case of a single innovating region in that technology, we can – by definition – observe no external cooperation.

The regional statistics of the 'Statistisches Bundesamt' (as published in Statistische Ämter des Bundes und der Länder, 2002) provide further information to characterize the regions. POP represents the size of the region in terms of inhabitants in the year 2000, while $FIRMSIZE$ is the average working force of firms within the specific region (data from 1999). This variable indicates differences in industrial structure between the regions, but is only a very rough measure since it is only available on the regional and not the technological level, and it gives only one measure of the distribution of firm size within the region. One might also suggest that, for historical reasons, the culture of cooperation might differ between the eastern and the western part of Germany, and so we created the dummy NL ('Neue Bundesländer') which takes a value of 1 for communities located in the east.

With those variables at hand, we proceed with the regressions and their analysis in the following section.

4.4 EMPIRICAL ANALYSIS

4.4.1 The number of cooperations

The theoretical considerations predict that between tech-regions the number of cooperations is highest for some intermediate degree of specialization. Firms within a less specialized region lack the know-how to be a partner for other firms and, when they are too specialized, they have difficulties finding a partner from whom to benefit through cooperation. To test this hypothesis 1, we estimate the following model:

$$\ln CO_{ij} = \alpha \mathbf{D}_{ij} + \beta \mathbf{X}_{ij} + \gamma \mathbf{R}_i + \delta \mathbf{T}_j + \varepsilon_{ij}, \qquad (4.6)$$

where CO_{ij} is the number of cooperations performed by members of tech-region ij, $\mathbf{D}$ is the set of dummy variables, $\mathbf{X}$ includes the characteristics of the tech-region, $\mathbf{R}$ is a set of regional characteristics such as diversity, and $\mathbf{T}$ includes measures that are similar within technologies.

Since the dependent variable is a count variable, we specify a negative binomial regression (NB) to estimate the influence of technological specialization and the other variables on cooperation. Throughout all regressions in this chapter the test for overdispersion speaks in favor of the NB model.[11]

---

[11]The NB arises as an extension of the Poisson regression model, which is characterized by the equality of the conditional mean and variance (defined as equidispersion). The overdispersion parameter α indicates the degree of deviance of the variance from the mean. For the interpretation

In table 4.2, the results of four specifications, labelled A to D, are presented. In column A, the number of cooperations is regressed on the specialization index $RSCA$ and its square ($RSCA2$), the number of university patents (UNI) as well as dummies to control for sectoral and eastern Germany fixed effects (NL).[12] The coefficients of $RSCA$ and $RSCA2$ are significant and show the expected signs of an inverted-U relationship, so that hypothesis 1 cannot be rejected, i.e. an intermediate degree of specialization is favorable to a high level of cooperative research. As universities and public research laboratories might be more cooperative, since appropriability or secrecy is neither important to them nor wished for by the state[13] and joint projects with the industry serve as a way of financing university research, we included the number of patents in a tech-region, where at least one applicant is a public financed organization (UNI). The positive coefficient affirms our above argument. The negative coefficient of NL implies a lower degree of interaction in the eastern part of Germany.

In regression B of table 4.2, two additional variables with the respective squared terms are included. The population of the region embedding the tech-region (POP and $POP2$) is included to control for differences in size between the tech-regions. The diversity index DI (and $DI2$) is included to account for differences in the technological structure of the regions. If higher technological diversity of a region leads to more cross-fertilization of the actors with different technological backgrounds, this variable should show a positive coefficient. When cooperations take place between actors with the same kind of know-how (as assumed in the theoretical discussion), this coefficient should be negative. The size effect shows up positive, but decreasing, and the coefficients of the diversity index imply that the relationship between regional diversity and cooperation in patenting is U-shaped.[14] The qualitative interpretation of the other variables ($RSCA$, $RSCA2$, UNI,NL) remains unchanged, compared to model A. However, the inverted U-shape relationship

---

of the coefficients it is helpful to note that, in the NB model, the exponential conditional mean is

$$E[y_i|\mathbf{x}_i] = exp(\mathbf{x}'_i\beta)$$

and therefore

$$\frac{\partial E[y_i|\mathbf{x}_i]}{\partial x_{ij}} = \beta_j exp(\mathbf{x}'_i\beta).$$

The coefficient β_j equals the proportionate change in the conditional mean if the jth regressor changes by one unit. For example, if $\hat{\beta}_j = 0.2$ and $exp(\mathbf{x}'_i\hat{\beta}) = 2.5$, then a one-unit change in the jth regressor increases the expectation of y_i by 0.5 units. For a detailed discussion of count data regressions, see Cameron and Trivedi (1998).

[12] Cubic terms did not prove to be significant. Coefficients for the sectoral dummies are not reported since differences between sectors are not the focus of this chapter.

[13] Except perhaps defense related R&D and the like.

[14] For large values of DI, within the range of observed values, the positive coefficient of $DI2$ does not outweigh the negative coefficient of DI.

Networks in the Innovation Process

Table 4.2: Negative binomial regressions of the number of cooperations in patenting on regional and technological characteristics over all sectors

	Model			
	A	B	C	D
NL	−0.6093	−0.4275	−0.2824	−0.1150
	(0.0000)	(0.0000)	(0.0000)	(0.0142)
RSCA	1.1073	1.3025	1.3205	1.3426
	(0.0000)	(0.0000)	(0.0000)	(0.0000)
RSCA2	−0.7454	−0.3448	0.1907	0.1440
	(0.0000)	(0.0000)	(0.0077)	(0.0585)
UNI	0.1134	0.0256	0.0218	0.0199
	(0.0000)	(0.0000)	(0.0000)	(0.0000)
POP		0.0049	0.0038	0.0034
		(0.0000)	(0.0000)	(0.0000)
POP2		−0.0000	−0.0000	−0.0000
		(0.0000)	(0.0000)	(0.0000)
DI		−0.2330	−0.2415	−0.1507
		(0.0000)	(0.0000)	(0.0000)
DI2		0.0101	0.0094	0.0061
		(0.0000)	(0.0000)	(0.0000)
HERF			3.5050	−3.6153
			(0.0000)	(0.0000)
HERF2			1.6276	1.5744
			(0.0000)	(0.0000)
HERFTEC			7.1878	7.1191
			(0.0000)	(0.0000)
HERFTEC2			−31.9715	−31.2389
			(0.0000)	(0.0000)
FIRMSIZE				0.0021
				(0.0000)
ALPHA	2.0941	1.2814	1.0322	0.9578
LR-Index	0.0550	0.1193	0.1481	0.1574

Notes: N = 9648; Five sector-dummies are included; p-values in parentheses.

for specialization becomes less pronounced. This is due to the fact that, even though specialization and diversification are measured for different entities (tech-region and region respectively), there is obviously an interaction between those variables, leading to high regional diversity in regions with intermediate levels of specialization in the constituting tech-regions.

In models C and D, the path of our theoretical considerations is left in favor of more explanatory power of the econometric model. An important issue of the theoretical discussion above was the matching of cooperation partners when there is a sufficiently large number of possible partners, namely firms or organizations performing research in the same technology. The concentration of innovators within a tech-region ($HERF$ and $HERF2$) is a measure of the availability of local cooperation partners. If there is only one innovator in the respective technology, the possibility of – at least – internal cooperations is clearly lower than if there were several organizations involved in that technology. If this technology is, in addition, concentrated in few regions as measured by $HERFTEC$, the number of cooperations will have to be very low.

As expected, in models C and D, the concentration of innovators ($HERF$) affects the number of cooperations in a negative, while decreasing, way. Regarding the coefficients of the regional concentration terms ($HERFTEC$), we find the highest degree of cooperation in moderately concentrated technologies. Controlling for these concentration variables changes the picture we had about the relationship between specialization ($RSCA$) and cooperation (CO). While the other coefficients remain qualitatively unchanged, the square of the specialization term becomes insignificant. This could be explained by the relationship of specialization and regional concentration: highly specialized tech-regions imply that a great part of innovation of the technology takes place in that region. Therefore, the technology has to be concentrated rather than evenly spread across all regions. Consequently, if we control for regional concentration, the effect of specialization diminishes.

In model D, the average size of firms ($FIRMSIZE$) within regions positively affects the number of cooperations. This result might be due to the restrictions of our data. Cooperations in patenting only constitute a small part of the interaction between firms. Smaller firms might more often collaborate on an informal basis, which would not be captured by our data. Large firms, on the other hand, can devote more resources to formal R&D cooperations, and in screening the market for potential partners.[15]

4.4.2 Internal vs. external cooperation

While in section 4.4.1 we were interested in answering the question as to whether specialized tech-regions cooperate more than others in general, we now want to identify the characteristics influencing the pattern of cooperation, that is, we want to discriminate between factors related to overall cooperation

---

[15]One of the referees suggests, alternatively, that from a capabilities perspective, large size implies that more resources are available to conduct activities within the organization. If, however, firms 'know more than they make' (Brusoni et al., 2001), i.e. hold large stocks of knowledge but do not always execute the manufacturing process themselves, then large firms are likely to spend more time and resources on managerial control and coordination with networks of partners who use the large firm's knowledge.

and the ones related to internal or external cooperation. Assuming that the technological gap between any two firms within one specific tech-region is smaller than for firms from two distinct tech-regions, our model predicts a higher number of cooperations within tech-regions (internal cooperations) relative to external cooperations.

To analyze this hypothesis, we perform the same specifications as in equation 4.6 with internal and external cooperations as dependent variables.

The results are presented in table 4.3. We first find in any specification that the size of the region (POP) has a positive but declining influence on the number of internal as well as the external cooperations. In models E and F for internal cooperations as well as I and J for external ones, the specialization index ($RSCA$) is positive and significant, with the quadratic term ($RSCA2$) being negative and significant – again confirming hypothesis 1. Comparing regressions E (internal) and I (external), we do not find the influence of specialization being much different for external and internal cooperations. Since hypothesis 2 is about the relative importance of local partners, a direct test of this hypothesis is presented below in table 4.4. Small differences between internal and external cooperations appear for regional diversity ($DI, DI2$), where the (negative) coefficient is three times as high for external cooperations. This result indicates a relatively stronger use of local know-how for actors located in diverse regions compared to actors in regions which are focussed on few technologies. Comparing models G and H with K and L shows that the regional concentration of the technology ($HERFTEC$) does not seem to influence the degree of local interaction in a qualitatively different way from external cooperations. Another variable which shows a differentiated influence on the type of cooperation is the average business size ($FIRMSIZE$). Looking at model H compared with L, larger companies clearly raise the degree of external linkages. This is not surprising, since setting up and maintaining external channels of knowledge transfer require specific investments and complex capabilities (Bathelt et al., 2004), which are more possible for large firms than smaller ones.

The results in table 4.3 suggest a need to investigate the different influences on the density (internal) and openness (external) of tech-regions in more detail. As explained in section 4.3, we create two variables that represent the relative importance of external linkages in a tech-region: $EXSHARE^{co}$ as the share of external cooperations and $EXSHARE^{link}$ as the share of external linkages of a tech-region. Since these shares are bounded between 0 and 1, we transform them by $\theta = ln(s/(1-s))$, to be unbounded, where s is the original share. The following model is then estimated by OLS:

$$\theta_{ij} = \alpha \mathbf{D}_{ij} + \beta \mathbf{X}_{ij} + \gamma \mathbf{R}_i + \delta \mathbf{T}_j + \varepsilon_{ij}, \tag{4.7}$$

where $\mathbf{D}$, $\mathbf{X}$, $\mathbf{R}$ and $\mathbf{T}$ are defined as in equation 4.6 on page 58.

Table 4.3: Negative binomial regressions – internal and external cooperations

Dep. var.	Internal cooperations					External cooperations		
	E	F	G	H	I	J	K	L
NL	-0.2529	-0.3656	-0.0268	0.0252	-0.7591	-0.4481	-0.3334	-0.1366
	(0.0000)	(0.0000)	(0.6387)	(0.6691)	(0.0000)	(0.0000)	(0.0000)	(0.0116)
RSCA	0.9675	1.2384	1.1593	1.1830	1.1552	1.3179	1.3563	1.3811
	(0.0000)	(0.0000)	(0.0000)	(0.0000)	(0.0000)	(0.0000)	(0.0000)	(0.0000)
RSCA2	-1.1354	-0.5048	0.3726	0.3322	-0.5109	-0.2977	0.1506	0.0997
	(0.0000)	(0.0004)	(0.0014)	(0.0044)	(0.0003)	(0.0003)	(0.0574)	(0.2417)
UNI	0.0948	0.0165	0.0086	0.0082	0.1111	0.0261	0.0228	0.0207
	(0.0000)	(0.0000)	(0.0000)	(0.0000)	(0.0000)	(0.0000)	(0.0000)	(0.0000)
POP		0.0040	0.0022	0.0022		0.0051	0.0042	0.0038
		(0.0000)	(0.0000)	(0.0000)		(0.0000)	(0.0000)	(0.0000)
POP2		-0.0000	-0.0000	-0.0000		-0.0000	-0.0000	-0.0000
		(0.0000)	(0.0000)	(0.0000)		(0.0000)	(0.0000)	(0.0000)
DI		-0.0808	-0.0583	-0.0425		-0.2857	-0.2920	-0.1847
		(0.0195)	(0.0241)	(0.1045)		(0.0000)	(0.0000)	(0.0000)
DI2		0.0038	0.0014	0.0008		0.0123	0.0117	0.0078
		(0.0121)	(0.2128)	(0.4612)		(0.0000)	(0.0000)	(0.0000)
HERF			-5.8247	-5.8590			-2.7420	-2.8603
			(0.0000)	(0.0000)			(0.0000)	(0.0000)
HERF2			2.9780	2.9818			1.1707	1.0948
			(0.0000)	(0.0000)			(0.0000)	(0.0000)
HERFTEC			1.8301	1.8465			8.6394	8.6234
			(0.1092)	(0.1097)			(0.0000)	(0.0000)
HERFTEC2			-12.1204	-12.1811			-38.9848	-38.2814
			(0.0131)	(0.0132)			(0.0000)	(0.0000)
FIRMSIZE				0.0009				0.0024
				(0.0002)				(0.0000)
ALPHA	3.6433	2.0011	0.5423	0.5401	2.4281	1.5227	1.3249	1.2108
LR-Index	0.0490	0.1119	0.1509	0.1515	0.0562	0.1170	0.1367	0.1479

Notes: N = 9648; Five sector-dummies are included; p-values in parentheses.

63

Networks in the Innovation Process

In the first two regressions of table 4.4 (M and N), the dependent variable is $EXSHARE^{co}$. Since this variable can only be computed for tech-regions with at least one cooperative patent ($CO > 0$), the number of observations reduces to 4098, with only cooperating tech-regions left. In the last two columns (O and P), $EXSHARE^{link}$ is to be explained by our econometric model. In our view, this variable provides a better measure of the openness of tech-regions, since it distinguishes internal and external connections for every patent and not only for the ones classified as cooperations.

In the first two regressions, there is no linear relationship between specialization and the share of external cooperation as is put forward by hypothesis 2. For models O and P, the picture is somewhat different. There is a strong negative relationship between specialization and the share of external linkages, thereby confirming hypothesis 2.

Interpreting this result from a technological system point of view means that, in highly specialized tech-regions, a large quantity of research relevant for the technological system is performed in one tech-region, and the probability of finding capable partners inside this region rises.

Concerning the influence of regional diversity (DI) on the cooperative structure, the results reject our theoretical argument stated in hypothesis 3. There, we expect a negative coefficient for regional diversity, but the overall influence (models M and O) is insignificant and positive. Inclusion of the squared term leads to a U-shaped influence in regression N and a positive, linear influence is observed in regression P. This result is in contradiction to a previous version of this study (Cantner and Graf, 2003a), where we found evidence in favor of the hypothesis that technologically more diverse regions show more internal cooperations in relation to external ones.[16]

The finding that the concentration of local innovators ($HERF$) leads to a higher share of external connections (cooperations as well as linkages) is the most robust – and not very surprising – result from this exercise. The geographical concentration of technologies ($HERFTEC$) has no significant influence on either measure of external connections.

Technologies within large regions, in terms of population, show a higher share of internal connections, which makes sense, since the availability of human capital is thought of as a major agglomeration force in the literature. The importance of the university (UNI) does not influence the type of cooperation with either measure of openness, and average firm size ($FIRMSIZE$) influences both measures in different directions.

---

[16] In the previous version, the regions are defined according to the first three digits of the postal code. The only systematic difference between the two methods of aggregation is that very large cities are split into several (up to 29 in Berlin) regions compared to the aggregation to 'Kreisebene'. This means that some cooperations were considered as external to the region in the previous version, whereas here they are considered internal to the 'Kreis'. Since large cities are also more diversified, this might explain the difference.

Table 4.4: OLS regressions of the share of external connections through joint patenting on regional and technological characteristics over all sectors

Dep. var.	Share of **external cooperations**		Share of **external linkages**	
	M	N	O	P
NL	−0.005	0.024	−0.369	−0.451
	(0.983)	(0.920)	(0.000)	(0.000)
RSCA	0.040	0.052	−1.277	−1.410
	(0.860)	(0.822)	(0.000)	(0.000)
RSCA2		0.445		−0.634
		(0.394)		(0.000)
UNI	−0.003	−0.007	−0.006	−0.004
	(0.698)	(0.472)	(0.269)	(0.446)
POP	−0.001	0.000	−0.001	−0.002
	(0.007)	(0.514)	(0.000)	(0.000)
POP2		0.000		0.000
		(0.048)		(0.000)
DI	0.040	−0.308	0.012	0.081
	(0.126)	(0.009)	(0.226)	(0.077)
DI2		0.016		−0.003
		(0.002)		(0.181)
HERF	1.564	5.068	1.845	4.234
	(0.000)	(0.000)	(0.000)	(0.000)
HERF2		−3.299		−2.108
		(0.003)		(0.000)
HERFTEC	4.065	6.552	−0.317	1.098
	(0.057)	(0.207)	(0.668)	(0.554)
HERFTEC2		−17.102		−5.846
		(0.444)		(0.446)
FIRMSIZE	0.003	0.002	−0.001	−0.001
	(0.000)	(0.001)	(0.003)	(0.026)
R^2	0.027	0.032	0.091	0.098
Adj. R^2	0.025	0.028	0.089	0.096
F-Test	9.59	8.06	72.27	55.41
	(0.000)	(0.000)	(0.000)	(0.000)
N	4098	4098	8721	8721

Notes: Five sector-dummies are included; p-values in parentheses.

4.5 INTERACTION IN JENA

We now shift the focus towards a characterization of Jena in this setting. We question to what extent Jena is different from the picture of the 'average' region, drawn above. Or more precisely, is Jena more interactive than we would expect, given the characteristics that are included in our models.

A recent study provides the rationale for the hypothesis that Jena has a strong focus on internal relations in contrast to external linkages. In comparing six clusters within the opto-electronic industry, Hendry et al. (2000) find that Thuringia, with the major players located in Jena, has by far the most densely organized network, with local collaborations accounting for a third of all collaborations. These firms within the same region do not perceive their co-located firms as competitors though, but rather have user – producer relationships (Hendry et al., 2000).

To test our hypothesis, we retrieve the residuals concerning tech-regions in Jena from a selection of our econometric models. To test whether the difference between Jena and the 'average' region is significant, we include then a dummy for Jena. If this dummy is significantly different from zero, we propose that Jena is special.

Figure 4.3 provides residual plots for Jena in the 29 technologies that are covered by actors from Jena. The dependent variable and the respective econometric specification (model) are given as the title of each plot. The technologies are ranked in the order of specialization in Jena; i.e. we start with the technology with the highest score on the specialization index and end with the technology where Jena has the lowest comparative advantage.

The positive residuals in the first plot, suggest that Jena cooperates above average in 20 out of 29 classes. This tendency is especially pronounced in the most specialized technologies, with 8 out of 10 technologies above average and the actual values for cooperation (in these 8 classes) being between twice and seven times as large as the predicted values. To show that these observations for Jena are significant, the results from the same regression, additionally controlling for Jena, are presented in the first column of table 4.5. The coefficient for this dummy ($Jena$) is fairly large, and highly significant. Besides, when comparing this result with model D in table 4.2, it shows that the coefficient for tech-regions in the eastern part of Germany, NL, is lower and more significant, which supports the hypothesis that Jena is somewhat outstanding in the east. The other coefficients remain unchanged.

It has been argued above, that it is important to distinguish between internal and external interaction. The work of Hendry et al. (2000) shows a larger share of internal interaction in Jena compared to the other 5 clusters. This finding is not only supported by our results for optics (Technology 6), but for almost all technological classes (bottom-right plot in figure 4.3). Again, this is a robust finding as indicated by the negative and significant coefficient for Jena in the last column of table 4.5. If we only argue in shares of internal versus external knowledge sourcing or transfer, we would have to interpret this result as a lack of external knowledge in Jena with the risk of spatial lock-in. The analysis in absolute values indicates that this is not necessarily so. While internal cooperations in Jena are above average in 6 of the 10 most specialized

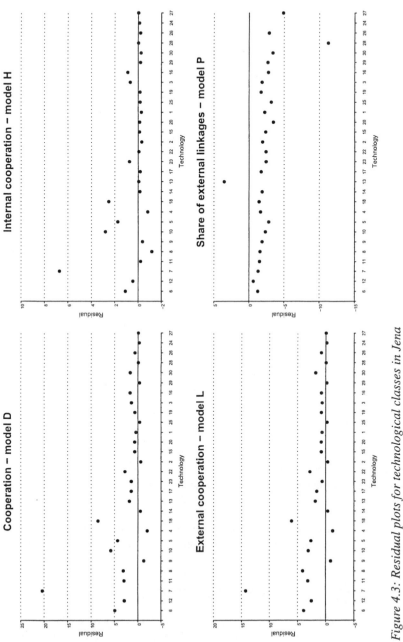

Figure 4.3: Residual plots for technological classes in Jena

Table 4.5: Interaction in Jena – regression results

	Negbin			OLS
	CO	CO^{int}	CO^{ext}	$Exshare^{link}$
JENA	1.2146	0.9038	1.4044	−2.4434
	(0.0003)	(0.0008)	(0.0009)	(0.0000)
NL	−0.1534	−0.0101	−0.1826	−0.4027
	(0.0013)	(0.8663)	(0.0009)	(0.0000)
RSCA	1.3497	1.1857	1.3898	−1.4238
	(0.0000)	(0.0000)	(0.0000)	(0.0000)
RSCA2	0.1325	0.3174	0.0850	−0.6105
	(0.0819)	(0.0066)	(0.3175)	(0.0008)
UNI	0.0169	0.0081	0.0173	−0.0022
	(0.0000)	(0.0000)	(0.0000)	(0.6586)
POP	0.0035	0.0022	0.0038	−0.0023
	(0.0000)	(0.0000)	(0.0000)	(0.0000)
POP2	−0.0000	−0.0000	−0.0000	0.0000
	(0.0000)	(0.0000)	(0.0000)	(0.0000)
DI	−0.1528	−0.0413	−0.1874	0.0831
	(0.0000)	(0.1137)	(0.0000)	(0.0697)
DI2	0.0062	0.0008	0.0080	−0.0030
	(0.0000)	(0.4550)	(0.0000)	(0.1544)
HERF	−3.5627	−5.8228	−2.8001	4.1369
	(0.0000)	(0.0000)	(0.0000)	(0.0000)
HERF2	1.5596	2.9737	1.0780	−2.0634
	(0.0000)	(0.0000)	(0.0000)	(0.0000)
HERFTECH	7.1077	1.8077	8.6220	1.0671
	(0.0000)	(0.1182)	(0.0000)	(0.5650)
HERFTECH2	−31.6896	−12.2114	−38.7819	−5.3957
	(0.0000)	(0.0135)	(0.0000)	(0.4812)
FIRMSIZE	0.0021	0.0009	0.0023	−0.0006
	(0.0000)	(0.0002)	(0.0000)	(0.0292)
ALPHA	0.9480	0.5388	1.1972	−
LR-Index / R^2	0.1584	0.1521	0.1492	0.0996
N	9648	9648	9648	8721

Notes: Five sector-dummies are included; p-values in parentheses.

technologies, external cooperations are above average in 8 of these fields. The significance of this result is reported in columns two and three in table 4.5.

4.6   SUMMARY AND CONCLUSIONS

Providing an analysis of cooperative behavior in research which takes into account findings from the innovation systems literature and acknowledges firms' difficulties in finding appropriate partners for such endeavors, we were able to construct hypotheses on research cooperations on the level of the technology region. Our empirical results imply, with respect to our hypotheses, that: (i) tech-regions which are intermediately specialized show the highest number of research cooperations, (ii) the higher a tech-region's technological specialization the higher its share of internal cooperation compared to cooperation with partners outside that region.

Moreover, tech-regions with a strong university, large firms embedded in a region with a low degree of technological diversification, a low concentration of local innovators, and a sufficient level of know-how are most conducive to cooperation. Regarding the distinction between density and the openness of a local network, we find that tech-regions with a high degree of specialization, embedded in a large region with large firms seem to be most conducive to dense local networking. A higher share of external linkages is found in regions with high diversity and a higher degree of concentration of local innovators.

To put the empirical analysis into perspective, we have to admit that our definition of the region is rather ad hoc, as the local system might easily consist of more than one region according to our definition. Often firms settle close to a city, but this location might belong to a different administrative region. The patenting practice of large patentees (to name the headquarters' address, rather than the actual research location) leads to the problem, that large, diversified regions probably account for more patents than they should. However, since we cannot identify these patents to check for systematic differences regarding characteristics in terms of cooperations or technology, we cannot assess the influence of this problem on our results.

We believe that our approach to measure and explain the degree of interaction serves as a good complement to the literature conducting case studies on local innovation systems. Further research in this direction will have to take account of the structure of the networks we investigate but also strengthen the role of geography when it comes to explaining the interaction between actors of distinct regions.

For Jena we find a highly interactive structure, documented by a large amount of cooperation, internal as well as external to the system. While the risk of spatial lock-in is decreased by the high numbers of external relations, it still becomes apparent that the local technological trajectories are subject to a dominating influence of internal actors as indicated by the higher share of internal linkages.

5. High-tech Firms in Jena

5.1 INTRODUCTION

The results of the previous chapter suggest a highly interactive structure in Jena. We find a large amount of cooperation, internal as well as external to the system. As these observations are merely based on patent data, the purpose of the present chapter is to validate these results by the means of other data and to identify the main actors in Jena as well as their modes of interaction.

In the summer of 2002, we conducted a survey of high-tech firms in Jena under the heading 'Innovationssystem und Gründungsgeschehen' (Innovation system and firm foundings). The research was performed in cooperation with the Max-Planck Institute for research into economic systems in Jena. The research methodology as well as the questionnaire are documented in the Appendix (see figure A.1). This chapter covers the results of this survey in the topics that are relevant to describe the economic landscape in Jena, its systemic nature, and the research environment of local high-tech firms.

In particular, we are interested in the different modes of interaction between local firms, as well as their connections to the university and public research. In the classical, Marshallian district, we would expect to see a large number of small, locally owned firms in a dominating industry, which maintain strong trade relations amongst each other and seldom cooperate external to the district. In addition, it should be characterized by a flexible local labor market with high personnel turnover within the district, which is able to attract workers from outside (Markusen, 1996). If Jena were to be characterized as a cluster in Maskell's (2001) sense, we would expect to see competition between horizontally related firms and cooperation and local trade between suppliers and customers. An ideal type local innovation system (or a regional networked innovation system, according to the typology by Asheim and Isaksen (2002)) should at first be able to produce new and valuable knowledge. For the system to accomplish this goal, we expect a high share of qualified labor, knowledge transfer within and between the system poles (scientific, technical, and market), and the actors to be embedded in the technological systems as well as the national system. Knowledge transfer channels are: inter-relationships between suppliers and customers; formal and informal collaborative and other links between innovating organizations; interfirm mobility of workers in localized markets for high skill; and the spin-off of new firms from existing firms, universities and public sector research laboratories (Cooke, 1998; Keeble and Wilkinson, 1999; Asheim and Isaksen, 2002).

The chapter is organized as follows: section 5.2 describes the sample firms with respect to size and industry. The market environment the firms are embedded in is presented in section 5.3. Responses regarding innovation activities, and firms' interaction with other actors via the labor market and through cooperation in research and development are summarized in section 5.4. Patterns of firm foundation in Jena are covered in section 5.5, with a special focus on variables that influence firms' location decisions and performance. The main findings are summarized in the final section.

5.2   CHARACTERIZATION OF THE LOCAL FIRMS

Our sample of firms characterizes Jena as a city, rooted in the tradition of the great entrepreneurs and researchers at the end of the 19th century, Otto Schott, Carl Zeiss and Ernst Abbe, who accomplished great progress in the fabrication of glass and its usage in optical applications.[1] Looking at the number of firms, the dominating industry is optics[2] with 28 firms, followed by services and data processing with 22 and 15 firms respectively. Other relevant industries present are chemicals, metal products, metals and machinery.[3] Figure 5.1 shows the share of industries in number of firms (light colored) and their employment shares (dark colored). Optics and data processing dominate also in employment with a share over 50%. Firms within services are significantly smaller (13.2 employees per firm) than in chemicals (112 employees per firm) and therefore these industries switch ranks (see table 5.1).

Besides the fields of activity, the size distribution of firms is also of interest for the following discussion. We measure size in terms of employment, since physical capital or turnover are measures too insecure given the large number of very young firms. We capture firms with an overall number of employees of 3277. The average firm employs a labor force of 35.2, with half of the firms employing less than ten employees. The labor force ranges between one and 534. In table 5.2 the size distribution of firms is given.

---

[1] For a detailed discussion of the historical tradition in Jena, see Walter (2000) and Länger (2003).

[2] The official description and the short terms we use here are given in table A.3 in the Appendix.

[3] The industry classification of firms is in general according to the IHK. To ascertain this assignment, we asked the firms for their major field of activity according to the list in table A.3 and a verbal description of what they do. In (the few) cases where this approach leads to ambiguity, we assigned the appropriate industry after gathering more information.

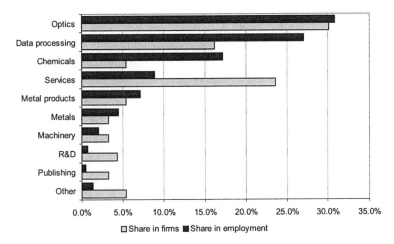

Figure 5.1: Industry distribution

Table 5.1: Industry distribution and firm size

Industry	Number of firms	Share in all firms	Number of employees	Share in all employees	Employees per firm
Optics	28	30.1%	1010	30.8%	36.1
Services	22	23.7%	291	8.9%	13.2
Data processing	15	16.1%	887	27.1%	59.1
Metal products	5	5.4%	233	7.1%	46.6
Chemicals	5	5.4%	563	17.2%	112.6
R&D	4	4.3%	24	0.7%	6.0
Publishing	3	3.2%	15	0.5%	5.0
Machinery	3	3.2%	65	2.0%	21.7
Metals	3	3.2%	147	4.5%	49.0
Other	5	5.4%	42	1.3%	8.4
Total	93	—	3277	—	35.2

The smallest firms with up to five employees represent 35.5% of the firms, but only 3.4% of the labor force in the sample. The seven largest firms employ more than half of the workers.

5.3 MARKET ENVIRONMENT

The type and intensity of innovation activities as well as the success of firms is strongly related to the market structure and the market environment. The benefits of clustering, which are discussed in chapter 3, are said to depend

Table 5.2: Size distribution of firms

Size range (employees)	Frequency	Cumulative	Sum of employees	Sum of employees (cumulated shares)
0–5	33	35.5%	113	3.4%
6–10	17	53.8%	130	7.4%
11–15	5	59.1%	64	9.4%
16–20	6	65.6%	108	12.7%
21–25	7	73.1%	165	17.7%
26–50	12	86.0%	455	31.6%
51–100	6	92.5%	432	44.8%
more than 100	7	100.0%	1810	100.0%

upon the market relations between co-located firms, i.e. whether they are horizontally or vertically related. On the other hand, there are urbanization economies or advantages from a diversified but related knowledge-base, which arise when firms that are neither competing nor positioned along the value chain but share a complementary knowledge-base, are interacting and therefore able to generate novelty from combining different types of knowledge.

In order to shed light on the horizontal relations, we summarize the responses towards the competitive environment in the following subsection, and vertical trade relations are analyzed in the second part of this section.

5.3.1 Competitive environment

To characterize firms according to their competitive position, it is useful to measure the number of direct competitors. In figure 5.2 we can observe that the firms in Jena are quite heterogeneous in that respect. While six firms view themselves as monopolists, the majority competes on small markets with less than five competitors and only 31 firms have more than ten competitors.

With respect to the geographical distribution we find no evidence for a strong competitive cluster. The number of firms reporting no direct competitors in Jena is 66.3% (55 out of 83) and 60.9% (53 out of 87) do not even have competitors in Thuringia.

On average, local firms have 1.75 competitors in Jena, 5.75 in Thuringia, 3.82 in Germany, 3.57 in Europe, and 3.48 in the rest of the world.[4] Only 9.5% of local competitors seem relatively small, but many firms compete locally when Thuringia is included (40.8%). Refining the picture, it shows that firms that are specialized producers (ten or less competitors) compete on a

---

[4]The regions are exclusive, i.e. the 5.75 competitors in Thuringia do not include the 1.75 located in Jena.

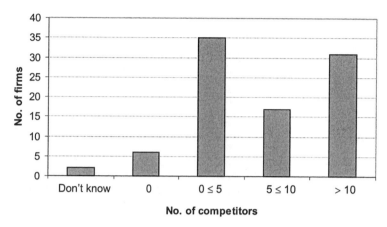

Figure 5.2: Number of competitors

supraregional market with 76% of their competitors being outside Thuringia (Germany 32%; Europe 18%, world 27%). Firms that face strong competition, on the other hand (more than ten competitors), rather work on a regional market, with 57% competitors from Jena and Thuringia (see figure 5.3).

As noted above, the literature is not clear as to what extent competition and collaboration respectively add to the success of a cluster. To get an impression what the firms themselves think about local competitors, we asked them to agree or disagree with four statements about local competition. The results are illustrated in figure 5.4. In principle, the respondents agree on the importance of a good relationship with competitors. Nonetheless, there is more objection towards the other statements: while only 15 firms do not believe in the positive effects of competition on the performance of their own firm, almost twice as many (27) disagree with the proposition that the local business environment is strengthened by a large number of competing firms. Regarding the second statement, the majority of firms view local competitors as a threat to their technological knowledge and feel that secrecy gains importance with an increasing number of local competitors.

5.3.2 Local trade

Our second interest regarding the market environment is in the trade relations between local firms. We asked for the share of sales to customers in the region and for the share of inputs they purchase from local suppliers. Answers should be given according to five classes (0–20%, 20–40%, 40–60%, 60–80%, 80–100%).

The answers of 84 firms are depicted in figure 5.5. Thirty-five firms are

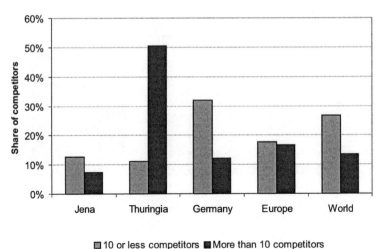

☑ 10 or less competitors ■ More than 10 competitors

Figure 5.3: Localization of strong competitors

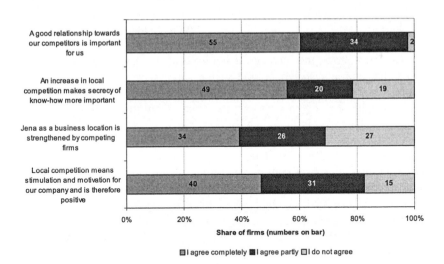

☑ I agree completely ■ I agree partly ☐ I do not agree

Figure 5.4: Attitude towards (local) competition

only loosely linked to local firms, buying and selling less than 20% locally. Only four firms can be considered strongly local in the sense that they sell more than 40% to local customers and also buy more than 40% of their inputs from local suppliers. One of these four firms is in the optics industry and the others provide internet or other services. Fifty-three (63%) firms sell less than

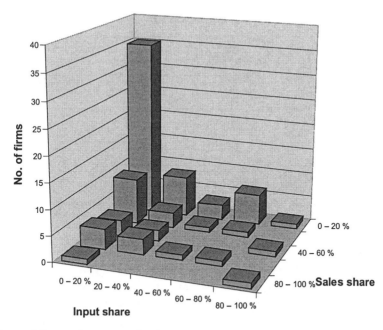

Figure 5.5: Local inputs and sales

20% to local customers and 52 (62%) firms purchase less than 20% of their inputs locally. These results indicate that the innovation system in Jena is not characterized by strong trade relations or by a value chain of production like typical clusters.

5.4   INNOVATION ACTIVITIES

We know from the map in figure 7.7 that Jena is very successful in terms of patents. As will be shown in chapters 6 and 7, public research is very active in that field. To get an impression of how business firms engage in that process, we asked them about their internal innovation related activities and how they interact with other actors in the local system and also on a wider geographical scale. We account for interaction via the labor market and direct relations in cooperative R&D projects.

5.4.1   R&D intensity and innovativeness

Firms were asked to provide information about the input side of the innovation process as well as the output side. Production factors in innovation are R&D

Table 5.3: R&D activities – descriptive statistics

| | Input oriented | | | Output oriented | | |
	R&D personnel	R&D personnel/ employees	R&D/ sales	Sales share $\leq$ 1 year	Sales share $\leq$ 3 years	Innova- tiveness
Mean	9.25	0.32	0.21	0.41	0.76	–
Median	2.00	0.22	0.10	0.28	0.95	2
Standard dev.	27.43	0.34	0.26	0.37	0.31	–
Minimum	0	0	0	0	0	1
Maximum	200	1	1	1	1	4
N	86	86	79	70	69	84

Notes: Innovativeness is a self-assessment relative to competitors; answer categories were: 1 = 'leading', 2 = 'above-average', 3 = 'average', 4 = 'below-average' and 5 = 'not innovative'.

personnel and R&D expenditures; output is measured in sales share of new products and a self-assessment of innovativeness.

The descriptive statistics for these variables are summarized in table 5.3. The average firm in Jena employs 9.25 workers engaged mainly in R&D, hence making up almost a third of the total workforce. Sales invested in R&D amount to 21%, 41% of sales are accomplished with products that are marketed for less than one year and 76.4% with products younger than three years. More than half of the firms view themselves as being leading innovators or at least above average in comparison to their competitors.

The distribution of R&D intensity with respect to personnel and expenditures is given in figure 5.6. Most of the firms lie in the range between 0 and 10% and the number of firms declines steadily with rising R&D intensity. The rise in the number of firms with a share of R&D personnel between 90 and 100% is worth noticing. These ten firms are either still in the phase of developing their first product or provide external research.

The average share of new products for the whole sample is presented in table 5.3. An analysis of the distribution of firms into different classes allows us to provide some information about the structure of the firms in Jena (see table 5.4). Half of the firms make less than 25% of their sales with products younger than one year. Firms making more than 50% of their sales with such products amount to 35.7%. Only three firms do not sell any product younger than three years and in 60% of the firms, the sales share of products younger than three years is more than 75%.

As noted above, we asked firms to self-assess their innovativeness. To validate their subjective responses we group the firms according to this assessment and calculate the average R&D intensity for each group (figure 5.7). 18 out of 84 firms view themselves as being technologically leading in their field. On

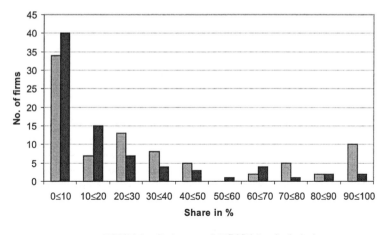

Figure 5.6: Distribution of R&D intensity

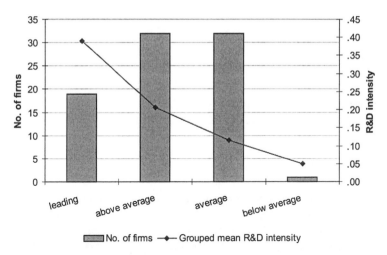

Figure 5.7: Subjective innovativeness and R&D intensity

average, these firms invest 40% of their sales in R&D. The R&D intensity of the 32 firms that responded to be above-average innovative is 20% and the 32 firms that consider themselves as average innovative have a R&D intensity of 12%. Only one firm is below average innovative (R&D intensity of 5%), while no firm responded to be not innovative at all.

Table 5.4: Firm distribution with respect to sales share of new products

Sales share	New products	
	≤ 1 year	≤ 3 years
0%	14	3
0–25%	21	4
25–50%	10	7
50–75%	5	13
75–100%	20	42
N	70	69

Notes: Table reads as follows: 14 firms sell no products that are less than a year on the market, 21 firms make between 0–25% of their sales with products that are less than a year on the market, and so forth.

Table 5.5: Employed academics and their origin

	Number	Share in...		
(1) Employees	3277			
(2) Academics	1675	...all employees	51.1%	(2)/(1)
(3) Academics from Jena	823	...all academics	49.2%	(3)/(2)
(4) Academics from Jena – professional contact	317		38.4%	
(5) Academics from Jena – personal contact	252	...all academics from Jena	30.6%	[4,...,7]/(3)
(6) Academics from Jena – moved from competitor	51		6.2%	
(7) Academics from Jena – moved from research	67		8.1%	

5.4.2 Employees

After the discussion of activities that are related to internal aspects of knowledge generation and utilization, we now turn to a topic which combines internal and external elements of the innovation process: the structure and background of the academic labor force. As stakeholders, the employees are engaged in firm specific processes of research and development, which are internal to the firm, while firms access external knowledge in hiring workers and scientists with useful capabilities and knowledge from other organizations.

In this context, we asked for the number of employed academics and the share that resided in Jena before this employment. Further, we wanted to know if the firms had contact (either personal or professional) with these academics before employment and whether they were recruited from local competitors or research institutes. A summary of the results is presented in table 5.5. We report the sum across all responses and the respective shares.

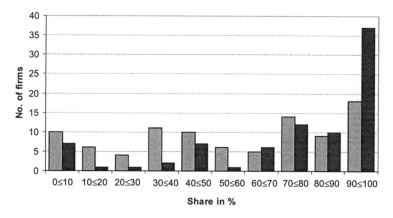

Figure 5.8: Share of academics and local recruiting

The firms in our sample have a very high share of academics on total employment. More than half of the workforce has a university degree and almost half of these resided in Jena before employment.

A more detailed picture of the distribution of these two variables (share of academics and share of academics from Jena on all academics) is given in figure 5.8. The histogram shows that all types of firms – from a very low to a very high share of academics – are present, with the highest number of firms employing more than 90% academics. With respect to the share of academics from Jena, we find a large number of firms (37), which recruit more than 90% of their academics locally.

5.4.3 Cooperations in R&D

Formal R&D cooperations are considered to be another important aspect of innovative networks and a possibility for firms to access external knowledge. Empirical studies have shown that cooperating firms perform better than others with respect to innovation (Palmberg et al., 1999; Czarnitzki and Fier, 2003). Research cooperations are considered an important mode of interaction in innovation networks where the partnering firms can learn from each other and accumulate a common knowledge-stock (Pyka, 2002). Besides, firms can access larger spillover pools where knowledge is shared on a voluntary basis (e.g. Nelson, 1987).

The firms were asked about their ongoing research projects and collaborations within those projects. Seventy-one firms answered this part of the survey, with 51 (68%) pursuing at least one research project. Forty-four of these re-

Table 5.6: R&D cooperation – type of partner

	Type of cooperation partner					
	Public institute	Direct competitor	Supplier	Customer	Same industry	Other
Number of firms that have at least one cooperation partner of this type	33	3	17	22	12	15
Share	79%	7%	40%	52%	29%	36%
Total number of cooperation partners of this type	118	14	60	43	28	35
Share in all cooperation partners	40%	5%	20%	14%	9%	12%

Notes: N = 42, firms that conduct research or development in cooperation and gave valid answers; non-ambiguous assignment of cooperation partners.

sponded to carry out at least one of those projects with an external partner. Summing up all responses results in 173 research projects, 126 of which are cooperative, which is equivalent to 72.8%. Taking the mean across firms' cooperation share, we find the average firm to cooperate in 75.9% of its research projects.

We gathered additional information regarding the partners in these research cooperations. The firms were asked to provide information about the number of partners, their type, i.e. supplier, customer, public research institute, etc. (table 5.6), and their location (table 5.7). In the first row of table 5.6 we report the number of firms that have at least one cooperation partner in the respective category indicated as column heading. Out of 42 firms that gave valid answers, 79% (second row) cooperate with a public research institute. Cooperations along the value chain are also often named (customers (52%), suppliers (40%)). Cooperative research with direct competitors is performed in 7% of the firms.

The third row in table 5.6 is the sum of all cooperation partners of a certain kind (e.g. public research institute in the first column) that were named by the participants. For example, the entry 14 in the third row, second column means that three firms which cooperate with competitors perform these cooperations with an overall of 14 partners, which are competitors. Most of the cooperation partners are public research institutes (40% as indicated in the fourth row), followed by suppliers (20%), and customers (14%). Direct competitors and firms within the same industry add up to 14%, too. This result emphasizes the important role of universities and public research institutes in the process of innovation as discussed in 2.1.2. Besides, the relevance of user – producer relationships, which make up one third of the partnerships, is also supported.

The regional distribution of cooperation partners is summarized in table 5.7.

Table 5.7: R&D cooperation – regional distribution of partners

	Location of cooperation partners				
	Jena	Thuringia	Germany	Europe (EU)	World
Number of firms that have at least one cooperation partner located in this region	31	25	30	13	8
Share	72%	58%	70%	30%	19%
Total number of cooperation partners located in this region	71	49	131	39	29
Share in all cooperation partners	22%	15%	41%	12%	9%

Notes: N = 43, firms that conduct research or development in cooperation and gave valid answers; non-ambiguous assignment of cooperation partners.

The number of firms cooperating with partners located in Jena is 72%, 58% perform research in collaboration with Thuringian organizations, and 70% have at least one partner in the rest of Germany. The number of non-local partners from Germany (131) is almost twice as high as the number of local partners (71). This result fits into the picture of a local innovation system, which uses internal (to the region) knowledge where it is appropriate, but also maintains external linkages to keep up with the progress made in the respective field. The picture of Jena developed in section 5.3 is supported by the 21% international research partners (Europe and the world) and the 37% of the firms which stated to have at least one international partner.

5.5 ENTREPRENEURSHIP AND LOCALIZATION

Rates of firm foundation differ substantially between regions (Longhi, 1999; Fritsch and Niese, 1999; Bade and Nerlinger, 2000). It has been shown that in many cases high rates of firm foundation are associated with a better economic performance on the regional level (Audretsch and Thurik, 2000; Audretsch and Fritsch, 2002; Acs and Storey, 2004). The ability to spur on the establishment of new firms is therefore regarded as an important function in innovation systems (Edquist, 2004).

In order to evaluate entrepreneurial activities in Jena, we present the development of start-up activities over time, ask for the geographic heritage of founders, and try to get an insight into which factors are decisive for the location decision of firms. Finally, we focus explicitly on spin-offs from incumbent firms and public research to infer to interactive aspects of entrepreneurship and new businesses.

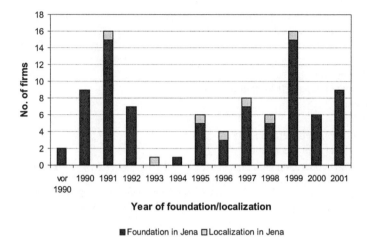

Year of foundation/localization

■ Foundation in Jena ☐ Localization in Jena

Figure 5.9: Firm foundation in Jena

5.5.1   Two waves of firm foundation

Except for two firms, all respondents answered the question regarding the date of the founding of the firm. We distinguish local foundations and firms that moved to Jena (movers) according to the concurrence of firm founding and the date of localization in Jena. Localization can mean that the firm actually moved or that it established a subsidiary. A rather high number of firms, namely 84 (92%) of the responding firms, are to be considered as local firms in this sense. Figure 5.9 depicts the number of foundations for the years 1990 until 2001, with the number of local firms colored in gray and the movers in black. The moving firms enter with the date of their establishment in Jena.

Figure 5.9 shows two waves of entry, which can be divided into the periods before and after 1993 with no local foundations in 1993. The first wave, directly after the German reunification, can be explained by the change of the economic system and its side effects, as the break-up of the Carl-Zeiss combine led to a number of spin-offs. The second wave, with its peak in 1999, can be explained by the new economy hype, but it is also triggered by Jena's success in the BioRegio contest, indicated by the high number of firms in optics and data processing.[5] In both peak years (1991 and 1999) we observe 15 local foundations and one moving firm. Between 1995 and 1999 one firm per year enters from outside, but none in 2000 and 2001. Overall, Jena is dominated by local firms with a share of 92% in firm numbers (there are 84 local firms and 7 movers).

---

[5] 19 out of 28 firms in optics and 10 out of 15 data processing firms were established after 1993.

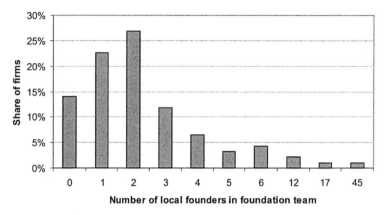

Figure 5.10: Relative frequency of local founders

5.5.2 Local founders

Firm foundations are said to be highly local, i.e. the founders of firms avoid the costs and risks associated with moving to a different place (Cooper and Folta, 2000; Fornahl and Graf, 2003). To analyze the background of local firms, we asked how many founders resided in Jena the year before firm foundation (local founder). Seventy-four firms were established by at least one local founder, in 12 cases none of the founders was local. The average number of local founders is 2.91, with a modal and median of 2. This result can also be seen in figure 5.10. Firms with no local founder amount to 15%, whereas more than 50% have one or two local founders.

Figure 5.11 depicts the composition of foundation teams. Fifty-five firms were established by teams with a majority of local founders. Thirty-nine firms were completely founded by locals.

To come up with a more detailed picture of the local founders, we asked for the types of connections to the region. In the following representation (figure 5.12) we only consider the answers given by actual members of the founding team, a requirement met by 76 of the respondents. It turns out that only 18 founders are born in Jena, a large number of founders had either vocational training or were employed in Jena. Within the group of 'other', the majority answered to have had their residence in Jena (six counts).

5.5.3 Location factors

As indicated above, many firm founders had a relationship to Jena before firm establishment. Residence and choice of firm location have been shown to be

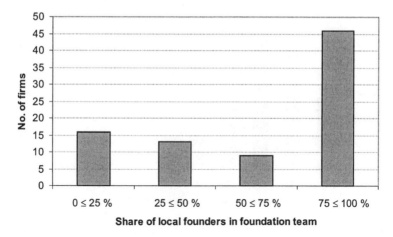

Figure 5.11: Composition of foundation teams

strongly dependent on each other (Cooper and Folta, 2000; Sorenson, 2003). Before asking the respondents to evaluate specific location factors, we attempt to find out to what degree firms actively pursue a search for an 'optimal' location for their endeavor. Within 87 valid answers, 26 (31%) firms evaluated more than one location. On average 2.3 locations were considered within this group. The distribution of considered alternatives is given in figure 5.13. The maximum number of locations that came into question is five. Overall, we find that only a rather small number of firms made an active location decision and even if such a decision was made, the number of alternatives was low.

Even though firm founders do not seem to consider alternative locations, the local conditions influence the founding decision itself (Fornahl and Graf, 2003). Of course, location factors also influence the performance of local firms. Participating firms were asked to evaluate several location factors according to their relevance in the location decision, to grade them at the time of firm founding and to indicate in what direction the conditions have changed up to the present moment. The most relevant factors for the location decision are the 'qualified labor force', the existence of 'other firms' (other than direct competitors), the 'personal social network', 'universities', and the 'image of Jena'. 'Research institutes', 'quality of life', 'transport infrastructure', 'public funding', and 'IT infrastructure' are of moderate importance. Least relevant are the 'site availability', the existence of 'competing firms', 'low wages', the existence of 'technology parks', and the availability of 'venture capital' (see table 5.8). The low relevance of venture capital might be explained, first, by the types of firms that were surveyed, with a high share of low capital intensive industries such as services. Second, venture capital cannot be considered to be

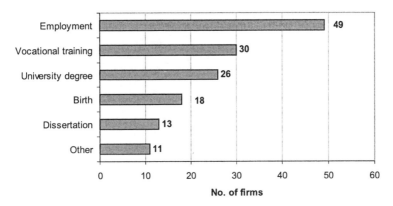

Figure 5.12: Type of founders connection to Jena

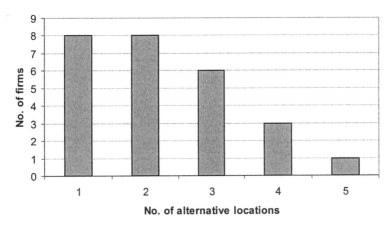

Figure 5.13: Distribution of the number of considered alternative locations

bound to a specific location and is therefore irrelevant for the location decision. The overall picture shows a clear tendency towards knowledge and innovation related factors, with soft factors like quality of life and the image of Jena being considerably more relevant for the location decision than site availability or low wages.

A more disaggregated analysis of the relevance of universities and research institutes reveals that they are appreciated as a partner for cooperation (universities 68.7% / research institutes 55.6%). Their relevance with respect to the shared use of facilities (46.3%/35.9%) and the training and education of workers (33.3%/15.6%) is far less valued.

In the literature on regional clusters, it is the combination of cooperative

Table 5.8: Relevance of location factors

Rank	Location factor	Relevance (in %)		Valid answers (%)
		Yes	No	
1	Qualified labor	83.1	16.8	89.2
2	Other firms	77.4	22.6	90.3
	cooperation	63.9	36.1	89.2
	customer	55.4	44.6	89.2
	supplier	48.1	51.9	87.1
	use facilities	21.0	79.0	87.1
	training	10.0	90.0	86.0
3	Personal social network	75.3	24.7	87.1
4	Universities	73.5	26.5	89.2
	cooperation	68.7	31.3	89.2
	use facilities	46.3	53.8	86.0
	training	33.3	66.7	87.1
5	Image of Jena	64.6	35.4	88.2
6	Research institutes	55.6	44.4	87.1
	cooperation	55.6	44.4	87.1
	use facilities	35.9	64.1	83.9
	training	15.6	84.4	82.8
7	Quality of life	54.4	45.6	84.9
8	Transport infrastructure	51.9	48.2	87.1
9	Public funding	49.4	50.6	89.2
10	IT infrastructure	41.6	58.4	82.8
11	Site availability	38.8	61.3	86.0
12	Competing firms	32.5	67.5	89.2
	cooperation	24.7	75.3	87.1
	follow joint interests	23.1	76.9	83.9
	training	3.8	96.2	83.9
13	Low wages	28.1	71.9	88.2
14	Technology parks	29.5	70.5	83.9
15	Venture capital	16.1	84.0	87.1

and competitive elements in the relationships between located firms that drive the success of the cluster (Porter, 1990). To investigate the relationship towards competitors, the respondents were asked how they might be influenced by co-located competitors. We find that these firms do not seem to influence many firms' location decisions. Firms which thought them to be relevant as possible cooperation partners amounted to 24.7%, 23.1% thought them helpful in combining efforts to follow joint interests, and only 3.8% appreciate them for educating workers. 'Other firms' are seen relevant as they are a possible cooperation partner (63.9%), customer (55.4%), or supplier (48.1%); joint usage of facilities (21%) and training of workers (10%) are of minor importance.

Besides the sheer relevance of different factors in the decision making process, we asked the firms to evaluate these factors during their own foundation

Table 5.9: Evaluation of location factors at the time of firm foundation

Rank	Location factor	Mean	Standard dev.
1	Qualified labor	1.7	0.84
2	Personal social network	1.8	0.81
3	Image of Jena	2.0	0.80
4	Research institutes (cooperation)	2.0	1.00
5	Universities (facilities)	2.1	0.84
6	Universities (training)	2.1	0.80
7	Research institutes (facilities)	2.1	1.16
8	Universities (cooperation)	2.2	1.04
9	Quality of life	2.2	0.95
10	Other firms (cooperation)	2.3	1.09
11	Other firms (suppliers)	2.3	0.87
12	Site availability	2.4	1.24
13	Low wages	2.4	1.10
14	Research institutes (training)	2.4	1.10
15	Technology parks	2.5	1.35
16	Public funding	2.5	1.21
17	Other firms (customers)	2.5	1.07
18	IT infrastructure	2.7	1.20
19	Competing firms (common interests)	2.7	1.39
20	Venture capital	2.8	1.48
21	Other firms (facilities)	2.9	1.18
22	Competing firms (cooperation)	3.0	1.30
23	Transport infrastructure	3.1	1.22
24	Other firms (training)	3.1	1.18
25	Competing firms (training)	3.3	1.29

process. Answers had to be given on a scale from 1 (very good) to 5 (poor). In table 5.9 the mean is reported and location factors are ranked accordingly. We observe a strong overlap between the most relevant factors for locating in Jena and the best valued ones. 'Qualified workers', the 'personal social network', and the 'image of Jena' are to be highlighted here. 'Universities' and and 'other firms' (subdivided according to their functions) are also top ranked. The respondents were least satisfied with 'transport infrastructure', 'competitors as educators', 'competitors as cooperation partners', as well as 'other firms for usage of facilities' and 'other firms as educators'. It has to be noted that the incumbent organizations (e.g. 'other firms') have to be differentiated according to their functions.

The changing perception of location factors between the time of foundation and the time of this survey is analyzed in table 5.10. It shows that the 'IT infrastructure', 'quality of life', 'technology parks', 'other firms (suppliers)', and the 'image of Jena' have improved most. Overall, only five out of 25 factors are perceived to have worsened by a majority of firms: 'site availability', 'venture capital', 'public funding', 'qualified labor', and 'low

Networks in the Innovation Process

Table 5.10: Changing perception of location factors

Rank	Location factor	Mean	Standard dev.
1	IT infrastructure	0.56	0.50
2	Quality of life	0.39	0.56
3	Technology parks	0.37	0.58
4	Other firms (suppliers)	0.36	0.53
5	Image of Jena	0.32	0.57
6	Research institutes (facilities)	0.29	0.56
7	Other firms (cooperation)	0.28	0.52
8	Universities (training)	0.26	0.55
9	Research institutes (cooperation)	0.25	0.56
10	Research institutes (training)	0.25	0.44
11	Universities (cooperation)	0.22	0.58
12	Universities (facilities)	0.22	0.60
13	Other firms (training)	0.22	0.42
14	Other firms (customers)	0.21	0.64
15	Other firms (facilities)	0.19	0.40
16	Competing firms (common interests)	0.14	0.58
17	Competing firms (training)	0.12	1.29
18	Personal social network	0.09	0.43
19	Competing firms (cooperation)	0.09	0.61
20	Transport infrastructure	0.03	0.66
21	Site availability	-0.15	0.76
22	Venture capital	-0.27	0.77
23	Public funding	-0.32	0.70
24	Qualified labor	-0.39	0.62
25	Low wages	-0.40	0.57

Note: A mean value of 0 means that an equal number of firms perceive the respective factor to have changed for the better and for the worse, positive values correspond to a majority that perceives improvements, and negative values correspond to a change for the worse.

wages'. Qualified labor is probably the most valuable asset of Jena, as the scores on relevance and its evaluation show. The decline is supposedly due to an abundance of skilled workers after the breakdown of the combines, which cannot be achieved again. A comparison of responses of the older firms (founded before 1993) and the younger ones (founded after 1993) supports this hypothesis. The younger firms found local supply of skilled labor less relevant at the time of foundation, which might be due to increasing mobility. As the image of Jena and the quality of life are perceived as good, it might have become easier to attract people from outside. The young firms also evaluated supply of skilled labor worse and perceived a smaller decrease than older firms. Unfortunately, we are not able to distinguish between a singular event and a persistent trend. However, it will be important to educate, to train, and to attract capable people for future performance.

5.5.4   Local spin-offs

Spin-off firms are considered a main driver of the dynamics in successful local clusters (e.g. Klepper, 2001a; Klepper and Sleeper, 2002). Besides their function in creating variety by pursuing innovations, which might otherwise not have been followed, they provide a strong basis for interaction with incumbent firms, as the founders are close to former colleagues in terms of cognitive and social proximity. We define spin-offs as start-up firms which are founded by individuals who 'market technological know-how, which was acquired and accumulated during their previous employment.' In our sample 34.8% of the firms confirm to be public or private spin-offs. Compared to a study by Bhidé (2000), who observed 71% spin-offs in a sample of Inc. 500 companies in 1989, this value is rather low. In a recent study by the German ministry for education and research (BMBF) the authors calculate 22% as the share of spin-offs (including academic start-ups with relevant technology transfer) on all foundations in research and knowledge intensive industries during the second half of the 1990s in Germany (BMBF, 2002b).

Fifteen firms stated to have acted as an incubator for an overall of 25 spin-off firms. From a networking perspective (viewing linkages between spin-offs and incubators) we can summarize that 50 firms are neither incubator nor spin-off, i.e. isolated in that respect, seven are spin-offs which have produced spin-offs themselves, 25 are spin-offs without 'offspring', and eight firms have only acted as incubators.

Thirty out of the 32 spin-offs answered the question regarding their incubator organization. Figure 5.14 shows the share of spin-offs and their incubators. Seven spin-offs are rooted in the public sector and 23 stem from private firms. The incubators with the highest numbers of spin-offs are also the central actors of the networks in chapter 6. Carl-Zeiss, Jenoptik, and Schott are the largest private incubators, Friedrich Schiller University was mentioned by five out of seven public spin-offs.[6]

In order to understand the forms of interaction between spin-offs and their incubators, we asked for the modes of assistance. In table 5.11 we report the shares of firms which have benefited from or have provided the various types of assistance.[7] The most common aid according to the spin-offs is 'knowledge exchange with incubators' employees' and 'usage of facilities' of the incubator. The incubators also named 'knowledge exchange with incubators' employees' but only roughly half of them provided facilities for their spin-offs. Incubators rather provided 'consulting during foundation process' (86.7%), which only

---

[6]Some firms mentioned more than one incubator, in which case these incubators were accounted for an equal share of the respective spin-off.

[7]It has to be noted that the answers by spin-offs and incubators are not referring to the same relations, as neither all incubators of the surveyed spin-offs are included in the sample, nor all spin-offs from the surveyed incubators are included.

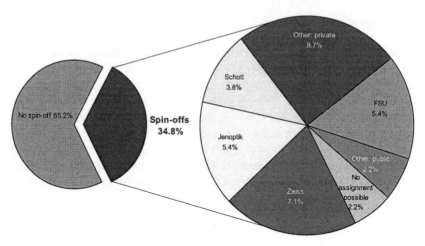

Figure 5.14: Spin-offs and their incubators

Table 5.11: Assistance during foundation process

	Spin-offs	Incubators
Knowledge exchange with incubators' employees	75.0%	86.7%
Usage of facilities (equipment, laboratory, etc.)	75.0%	53.3%
Usage of business contacts	65.6%	80.0%
Consulting during foundation process	59.4%	86.7%
Financial assistance (loans, shareholding, etc.)	56.3%	60.0%
N	32	15

59.4% of the spin-offs received. Being able to use the business contacts of the former employer is also of strategic relevance for the spin-offs. Notably, the only two spin-offs that received no assistance by the former employer were established in 1990 and 1991 by employees from former combines and none of the incubators answered to have given no assistance.

To assess the future development of this mode of knowledge transfer and innovation, we asked the firms about planned spin-offs. It shows that four experienced incubators, three spin-offs, and six firms without active or passive spin-off experience plan to spin-off new firms in the near future.

5.6   SUMMARIZED FINDINGS

This chapter is an attempt to characterize the market pole of the local innovation system of Jena and its interactions with external actors and the actors of the technical and scientific poles in Jena.

We find the majority of firms which are located in Jena to be local foundations, in the sense that they were founded in Jena as opposed to having moved. A majority of firms was established – at least partly – by local actors. The endogenous potential of the region is therefore highly responsible for the development of start-up firms. The local firms were established in two waves with peaks in 1991 and 1999. The first wave is explained by the transformation process in Jena, where the dominant Carl-Zeiss combine was broken up and the former employees started their own businesses. In the second wave we find an increasing share of firms in optics and data processing, which is interpreted as a combined effect of the new economy hype and Jena's success in the BioRegio contest.

Regarding the local conditions for the decision to found and locate in Jena, we find some factors being especially relevant: the qualified labor force, the incumbent firms, the personal social network of founders, the universities and the image of Jena are highlighted here. These factors not only influence the location decision but also the decision to start an own business in the first place. This is indicated by the fact that only one third of the firms considered alternative locations for their establishment. Again, this indicates the relevance of the endogenous potential for firm founding, which is not only incorporated in the people but also in the business and research environment. This point is also strengthened by the following findings: 1) 85% of the firms were founded by teams with at least one local actor; 2) 35% of the firms are regarded as spin-offs from either incumbent firms or public research institutes (which include the university); 3) more than 50% of the labor force have a university degree; 4) approximately half of these academics were educated in Jena and often had professional or personal contacts with their employers before employment.

The literature tells us that regional clusters or industrial districts are characterized by strong user–producer relationships within the value chain. We find only four companies to be strongly engaged in local trade as they buy and sell more than 40% locally. The innovation system of Jena is rather characterized as a region with a stronger focus on external relations with respect to these material and product flows. Analyzing the competitive situation also shows that most firms are specialized producers competing on international markets.

However, we observe strong local interaction in the process of knowledge generation. In addition to the relevance of spin-offs and local networks, we find 73% of the research projects to be conducted in cooperation, with the preferred partners being public research institutes, suppliers, and customers. The regional distribution of cooperation partners hints at a broad common knowledge-base of local actors, as 72% of cooperating firms have at least one research partner located in Jena. This makes up 22% of all research partners. This finding suggests that firms try to absorb local knowledge where it is appropriate, but seek out for partners elsewhere for external (to the region) knowledge.

The internal relations in the processes of learning and innovation turn out to be of major importance for the success of the local innovation system. In the subsequent chapter, we concentrate on the innovator network and its evolution.

6. Networks of Innovators[*]

6.1 INTRODUCTION

The previous chapters suggest that Jena is a learning region, where actors, who are involved in the processes concerned with the generation of knowledge and novelty, are highly interactive. The larger fraction of these interactions are internal to the system, i.e. they take place between actors who are located in Jena. By applying the methodology of social network analysis, we are able to generate graphical representations of these interactions and to perform statistical analyses on these networks.

The purpose of this chapter is threefold: first, we provide a detailed description of the networks which result from interaction based on a common technological knowledge-base, on the job mobility of scientists, and on co-operations between innovators. Second, we analyze actors' positions in these networks. Based on measures for the centrality of actors in a network, we retrieve information on the central innovators in Jena and how their positions have changed over time. The third focus of our work is on the determinants of the cooperative linkages. We analyze the network resulting from R&D co-operation and explain – by means of network regression techniques – which relations between the actors can best explain the resulting structure.

The chapter proceeds as follows. In the next section we give a short introduction to the methodology and the data used for the empirical analysis. In section 6.3 we apply social network analysis methods and visualizations to describe the evolution of the innovator networks of Jena in the period from 1995 to 2001. Besides the overall structure of the networks, we also investigate the change in relative positions of the core network members. Section 6.4 concentrates on the explanation of cooperative linkages between the actors. Finally, section 6.5 concludes the chapter by summarizing the main findings.

---

[*] A version of this chapter is published as Cantner and Graf (2006).

6.2   RESEARCH METHODOLOGY AND DATA

6.2.1   Social network analysis

Social network analysis is an interdisciplinary methodology developed mainly by sociologists and researchers in social psychology, further developed in collaboration with mathematics, statistics, and computing that led to a rapid development of formal analyzing techniques which made it an attractive tool for other disciplines like economics, marketing or industrial engineering.

> [...] [S]ocial network analysis is based on an assumption of the importance of relationships among interacting units.[...] relations defined by linkages among units are a fundamental component of network theories.
> (Wassermann and Faust, 1994, p. 4)

There is a wide range of topics in economics, that employ methods of social network analysis. Some recent examples include the work of Cowan and Jonard, who evaluate the impact of the network structure on its performance by means of simulation (Cowan and Jonard, 2003). Owen-Smith et al. (2002) compare the organization and structure of scientific research in the United States and Europe by building networks of R&D cooperation. Breschi and Lissoni (2003) as well as Singh (2003) expand the study of Jaffe et al. (1993) and find that social proximity has a stronger relevance for the degree of knowledge spillovers than geographical proximity. Balconi et al. (2004) analyse Italian networks of inventors resulting from common team membership in patenting. They focus on the specific role of academic inventors in different technological classes. Another example is the work of Potts (2000), who places the existence and generation of linkages between actors at the center of his evolutionary microeconomic theory.

The data requirements constitute a problem for empirical application of this approach in the field of economics. The usual procedure of taking samples of firms is not appropriate in analysing networks. Even if relational data were available one might miss firms that link unconnected parts of the network or the most central players of the network. The observed network structure would then not at all correspond to the actual relations. Samples can only be taken on the level of relations, i.e. not all possible relations between firms have to be analyzed, but only the ones that are in the focus of the study. As a consequence, many empirical applications which study networks of innovators or inventors make use of patent data either by building citation or co-authorship networks. Patent data are widely available and databases are complete in the sense above (Balconi et al., 2004; Fleming et al., 2004); as an indicator for innovative activity, patents are widely used and widely criticized (Lanjouw and Schankerman, 2004). The use of patents is problematic since not all novelties are or can be patented and information about the quality of patents is difficult to retrieve.[1] Since we are interested in the connections between actors in the process of innovation, the output in terms of patent quality is not of critical importance.

The insights that are and might be obtained by means of this methodology in accounting for specific linkages and the resulting structure outweigh its drawbacks if one is aware of the difficulties with the underlying database. We can obtain interesting and relevant information by asking not just 'how many cooperative research projects do you perform?' but rather 'with whom do you cooperate on research projects?'.

6.2.2 Data

The following example should provide the reader with a short introduction to the methodology and our data setup. For more details, please refer to the widely cited book by Wassermann and Faust (1994). Since we use patent data it is natural to use a small number of patents as the raw data for our example given in table 6.1. On each patent you find information about the applicant(s), let us call them innovator, which is usually a firm or public research laboratory, but might also be an individual. You also find the actual inventor(s), i.e. the people who generated the knowledge that has been patented as well as the technological classification of the patent.

Table 6.1: Example raw data

Patent	Innovator	Inventor	Class
P1	A_1	I_1, I_4	1
P2	A_2	I_2	2
P3	A_3	I_3, I_4	2
P4	A_4	I_1, I_4	1
P5	A_4	I_2, I_3	2
P6	A_4	I_5	2

If one wishes to build a network of innovators where a linkage between the innovators A_1 and A_2 result from people having worked for both of them, one has to generate the 2-mode sociomatrix X, where the rows are the innovators and the columns represent the inventors. Inventors are then the

---

[1]For a more detailed discussion on the usage of patent statistics in economics see Griliches (1990) or Pavitt (1988).

common 'events' of the innovators.

$$X = \begin{pmatrix} 1 & 0 & 0 & 1 & 0 \\ 0 & 1 & 0 & 0 & 0 \\ 0 & 0 & 1 & 1 & 0 \\ 1 & 1 & 1 & 1 & 1 \end{pmatrix}$$

The square matrix that indicates the number of linkages a_{ij} between A_i and A_j, is called the adjacency matrix A, which is computed as the product of X and its transposed X'.

$$A = XX' = \begin{pmatrix} -- & 0 & 1 & 2 \\ 0 & -- & 0 & 1 \\ 1 & 0 & -- & 2 \\ 2 & 1 & 2 & -- \end{pmatrix}$$

Since I_4 has worked both for $A_1 (i_{14} = 1)$ and $A_3 (x_{34} = 1)$, there is a linkage between A_1 and A_3, indicated by $a_{13} = 1$. The graphical or network representation of A is then given in figure 6.1.

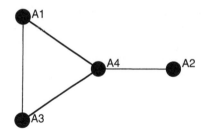

Figure 6.1: Example network

We use data on patents that were applied for at the German patent office and were disclosed between 1995 and 2001. To include all patents that are relevant for Jena as an innovation system we filtered out all patents where at least one of the inventors named on the patent had their residence in Jena at the time of application (inventor-based approach). Altogether we could identify 368 distinct innovators on 1181 patents in 29 out of the 30 technologies,[2]

---

[2]For the technological aggregation, patents have been classified according to a technology-oriented classification that distinguishes five industries and 30 technologies based on the International Patent classification (IPC). This classification has been elaborated jointly by the Fraunhofer-Institut für Systemtechnik und Innovationsforschung (FhG-ISI), the Observatoire des Sciences et des Techniques (OST), and the Science and Technology Research Policy Unit of the University of Sussex (SPRU).

employing 1888 inventors (1113 of which resided in Jena). To investigate the dynamics of the networks, we split the sample into two periods of equal length, i.e. the first period includes all patents disclosed between 1995 and 1997 while the second period covers the years 1999 through 2001. By dropping the year 1998 from the sample we lose 42 innovators. The rest can be divided into 173 innovating entrants, 117 innovators that exit, and 36 permanent innovators, which make up the core of the system that is analyzed in more detail in section 6.4.

6.3   INNOVATOR NETWORKS

According to the outline of this chapter given in the introductory section, we now proceed to map the actors that build up the innovation system of Jena. We pursue two different approaches in building innovator networks with our data. The first approach to build such a network is to link the innovators by the kind of technological knowledge they have created. The more fields of research the innovators have in common, the closer they are related (technological overlap). The second possibility is related to the notion of knowledge transfer through workers mobility (e.g. Saxenian, 1994; Almeida and Kogut, 1999). The main idea is that organizations, i.e. firms or research institutes, are closely related if scientists move from one organization to the other or know each other through working on joint projects.

Based on our data we analyse three different types of networks, all of which are built for the two consecutive periods (1995–1997 and 1999–2001):

i)   **Technological overlap:** Linkages between innovators are formed whenever they patent in the same technological class. This network can be interpreted as the potential for cooperation.

ii) **Personal relations** divided into:

   a)   **Cooperation:** If there is more than one innovator on a patent, there are as many linkages between all co-applying innovators as there are inventors.

   b)   **Scientist mobility:** If a specific inventor is mentioned on patents applied for by distinct, not cooperating innovators, a link between those innovators exists since we assume the inventor to have worked for both.

6.3.1   The innovator network based on technological overlap

Innovators can be specialized in a certain field of knowledge or instead be diversified. Building a network where innovators are connected by the overlap in technological interest we would expect diversified actors forming the center of the network, whereas the specialized innovators are positioned in the periphery. This exercise serves three purposes. First, it gives us a picture of the structure of the innovation system in different time periods. Are the innovators all focussing on the same technologies or do we see several specialized groups of firms that form clusters in the periphery of the network? Second, we can identify the innovators in the center and the periphery, thereby investigating the roles of particular actors. Third, this type of network can be viewed as the potential for innovators to cooperate since the connected firms share a common knowledge-base, a topic that will be addressed in section 6.4.

Figure 6.2 visualizes the Jena network of innovators, where nodes are innovators and edges result from an overlap in at least two technologies.[3] It comes as no surprise, that the larger innovators form the center of these networks. Jenapharm is the only exception, being a specialized firm in pharmaceuticals. Carl Zeiss Jena and Jenoptik are the successors of the former VEB Carl Zeiss which dominated the economic structure of Jena during the socialist era in the GDR. This VEB was a highly differentiated combine, i.e. integrated firm and already by visual inspection we see that they move towards the periphery of the network as they follow a strategy of higher specialization. The university (FSU) on the other hand moves towards the center of the network and covers the broadest range of research fields in the second period (see also table 6.7).

We do not observe any clear cut cluster formation within Jena for either period, and it rather seems that the core has become denser while small innovators position themselves in the same types of technologies as the core. Even though we applied equal time-spans for the division of the data, the size of the network almost doubles from 25 innovators,[4] that have at least two technologies in common, to 48 innovators in the second period.

Table 6.2 summarizes the descriptives of these two networks. If g is the size of the network and $d(n_i)$ is the degree, the number of connections, of actor i, then the density D of the network is defined as the number of all linkages divided by the number of possible linkages within the network $D = \sum_{i=1}^{g} d(n_i)/(g^2 - g)$. The observation from the visual inspection that the network has become more tightly connected is confirmed by the measures (0.15 to 0.17).

The degree centrality of an actor i is the number of its ties divided by the

---

[3]This restriction is only used for visualization of the network. The size of a node is determined by the number of patents granted, the width of an edge is related to the number of overlapping technologies. Isolated innovators (isolates) are not displayed for reasons of lucidity. The network visualization for this and the following figures was performed using NetDraw as implemented in UCINET 6 software (Borgatti et al., 2002) and multidimensional scaling with node repulsion and equal edge length bias as layout. Network regressions and structural variables were calculated using the sna-package by Carter T. Butts for R statistical software and UCINET 6.

[4]Innovators that have patented in at least two technologies, that are also covered by other network members.

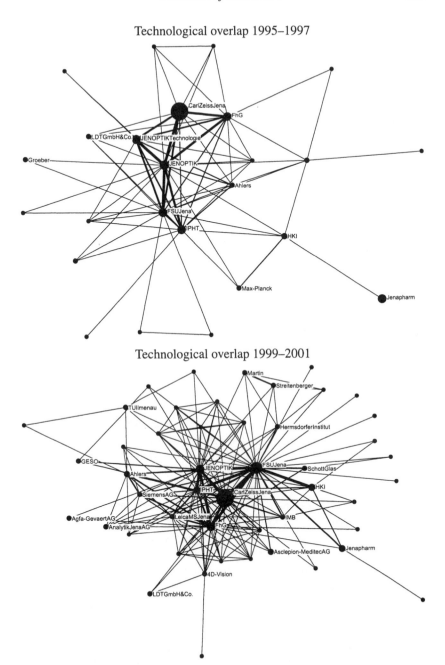

Figure 6.2: Potential for cooperation in Jena

Table 6.2: Descriptive statistics of the networks of technological overlap

	tech$^{95\text{-}97}$	tech$^{99\text{-}01}$
No. of actors	153	209
Density	0.151	0.165
Network centralization[a]	0.598	0.700
Overall graph clustering coefficient	1.238	1.178
No. of components	5	2
Components with 2 or more members	2	1
Size of largest component	148	208

Note: [a] Networks have been dichotomized.

number of possible ties $C_D(n_i) = d(n_i)/(g-1)$. The *network centralization* is then given by $C_D = \sum_{i=1}^{g} (\max(C_D(n_i)) - C_D(n_i))/(g-2)$. We find an increase in centralization of the network from 0.6 to 0.7, which means that the periphery of the network has more connections to the core but less connections within itself. Since there are only 30 technological classes, the *number of components* (disconnected parts of the network) is very small. But the fact that the number of components decreased from five to two, so that in the second period all innovators – except one – are connected, hints towards a stronger concentration on core competencies of the network.

Another structural measure for a network is the *overall clustering coefficient*. It is calculated by averaging the clustering coefficients of all actors within the network. The node level clustering coefficients are calculated as the density of the neighborhood (i.e. the network of actors directly linked to the respective actor) of this actor. The decrease of the overall graph clustering coefficient from 1.238 in the first period to 1.178 in the second period provides another result in favor of the above argument.

As was already noted before, we can characterize the innovators according to their innovator status (entry, exit, permanent). If network positions really matter for the performance of single actors, one would suspect that innovators that exit the system have to do this because of a weak position therein. For the entering firms we should observe a close relation to the core of the existing network. Why would this be so? The literature on entrepreneurship tells us that people often found their firms where they are already located (e.g. Fornahl and Graf, 2003; Cooper and Folta, 2000). Being educated within a particular system or having worked there would lead to a higher probability of being engaged in the same activities as before. Even if there are firms that are relocating, we could expect them to be quite aware of the characteristics of this site, and technological competencies of the region would – at least for innovative firms it should – be a relevant criterion.

Table 6.3: Technological overlap: block-densities/average value within and between blocks

		Exiting innovators	Permanent innovators	Entering innovators
P1	Exit	0.0903 (0.2877)	0.2056 (0.4466)	
	Permanent	0.2056 (0.4466)	0.4317 (0.8550)	
P2	Permanent		0.5413 (1.0067)	0.2336 (0.4692)
	Entry		0.2336 (0.4692)	0.1206 (0.3310)
	N	117	36	173

Note: Standard deviations in parentheses.

Analyzing these differences we calculate block densities for the network of both periods, where the blocks are the different groups mentioned. The resulting values and standard deviations within and between the groups are given in table 6.3. First, we notice an increase in the density of the network of permanent innovators between the two periods from 0.43 to 0.54 (second and third row, second column). The technological overlap of the core members of the innovation system has increased. Second, regarding the different roles of exiting innovators and entrants we observe a stronger connectivity within the entering group itself (0.12 compared to 0.09 for the exiting group), but also with respect to the linkages with the permanent group (0.23 compared to 0.21 for exit). This can be interpreted as a result of a self-organizing process where actors in technologies with a number of co-located innovators below the critical mass either leave the system and search for a better location or just stop innovating at all, and new entrants on the other hand are attracted by the strengths or core capabilities within the network.

6.3.2 The innovator network weaved by interpersonal relations

In the previous section we focussed on the technological competencies of the innovators in Jena. Performing within the same technological field, however, does not imply an actual relationship to one another. What really matters when we talk about local innovation systems, innovator networks, clusters or whatever, are the interpersonal relationships in such systems.

Arrow (1962b) already recognized labor mobility as a distinct source of knowledge spillovers. Saxenian (1994) and Almeida and Kogut (1999) show that the mobility of individuals is one possible mechanism of knowledge diffusion to existing firms, whereas Klepper (2001a) as well as Gompers et al. (2003) focus on start-ups as a means of commercializing knowledge. Cooper

(2001) shows theoretically that a higher rate of job mobility corresponds to greater overall technological progress because parts of the knowledge generated by the worker can be utilized by both firms involved.

Due to the data that we use, we have the possibility of analyzing a network of innovators that can be viewed as the lower barrier of actual relationships. On each patent we find information about all the scientists and engineers that were involved in the creation of the knowledge that led to this innovation (inventors). By creating a 2-mode sociomatrix where the innovators are the nodes (rows) of the network and the inventors on the patent are the characteristics (columns) of these innovators we can identify those inventors that have worked on research projects for more than one innovator, thereby creating linkages between these innovators. We assume that the more scientists have worked for two distinct innovators, the closer the latter are related.

We can distinguish two different possibilities how this relationship is established. The first way is by direct cooperation. Whenever we find a patent with more than one innovator (co-application), we assume it to be a cooperation. Of course, all the inventors on such a patent are then a 'common event' of all the innovators. We call the resulting network *cooperation*. The other possibility is less direct. If an inventor is mentioned on patents applied for by different, not co-applying innovators within one of the two periods of observation (1995–1997 and 1999–2001) we end up with a link between those innovators that is referred to as *scientist mobility*.

Besides the obvious increase in size of the visualized networks (figure 6.3) both types of networks are characterized by a different evolution of the network structure.[5] In table 6.4 we report the same statistics as in the last section for the networks of cooperation (co^t), scientist mobility (sm^t), and the network of personal relationships (pr^t) which does not distinguish between the two former types of relations.

The density of the cooperation network decreases (0.026 to 0.022) while it increases slightly for the scientist mobility network (0.004 to 0.005). The overall effect is dominated by the effects of cooperation, which leads to a network of personal relationships that is less connected in the second period (0.036 to 0.031). The overall network becomes more centralized (0.113 to 0.171), which is also due to the development in formal cooperation (0.046 to 0.124) whereas centralization decreases in the scientist mobility network (0.048 to 0.040). This network also shows a tendency towards stronger clustering (0.638 to 0.885), which is opposite to the development for cooperation

---

[5]In the network visualization, nodes are innovators irrespective of organizational form, edges between A and B result from an inventor named on patents held by both A and B. In the first period the two largest components are displayed, in the second period only the largest one. Linkages through cooperation are light grey, linkages through scientist mobility are black. If both types of linkages apply, we use a dark grey. For large firms such as Siemens, which are not located in Jena, we only include patents with at least one inventor living in Jena.

Cooperation and scientist mobility 1995–1997

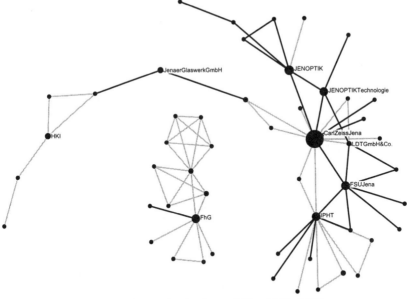

Cooperation and scientist mobility 1999–2001

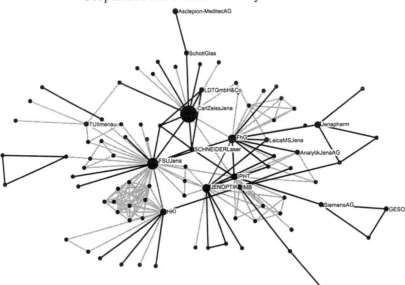

Figure 6.3: The network through interpersonal relations in Jena

Table 6.4: Descriptive statistics of the interpersonal networks

	$pm^{95\text{-}97}$	$pm^{99\text{-}01}$	$co^{95\text{-}97}$	$co^{99\text{-}01}$	$sm^{95\text{-}97}$	$sm^{99\text{-}01}$
N	153	209	153	209	153	209
Density	0.036	0.031	0.026	0.022	0.004	0.005
Network centralization[a]	0.113	0.171	0.046	0.124	0.048	0.040
Overall graph clustering coefficient	2.758	2.044	3.835	2.808	0.638	0.885
No. of components	67	80	100	135	126	150
Components with 2 or more members	17	19	20	14	7	14
Size of largest component	63	101	14	61	20	39

Note: [a] Networks have been dichotomized.

(3.835 to 2.808). Again the combination of both networks is dominated by co-operation (2.758 to 2.044). Only the analysis of components shows a similar trend towards less fragmentation. The share of innovators that are part of the largest component of the cooperation network increased from 0.09 to 0.29 and the share of innovators connected by scientist mobility in the largest component increases from 0.13 to 0.19. If we abstract from the type of interaction connecting the innovators, almost 50% of all innovators are part of the largest component of the network.

It seems that the large core actors within the network focus more on formal cooperation while the smaller surrounding or peripheral actors have more contacts through informal personal relations.

As in the analysis of the network of technological overlap we are interested in the relative positions of different groups of the network. Tables 6.5 and 6.6 report the results for block-densities, calculated for exiters, permanent innovators, and entrants in the two periods.

The first observation regards the change in structure of the networks of permanent innovators. Its density almost doubled for cooperative linkages (0.057 to 0.102) and more than tripled for scientist mobility (0.016 to 0.051). We also notice a higher density within the exiting group (0.0237) compared to the entrants (0.0119) in the cooperation network. On the other hand, the entrants are better connected with the permanent innovators (0.0390) than are the exiters (0.0254).

Regarding the scientist mobility network, we observe higher density for the entrants within the group (0.0012) compared to the exiters (0.0010), and also more connections between entrants and permanent innovators (0.0103) than between the exiters and the core network (0.0078).

Overall, entrants in Jena seem to be better integrated into the network as actors who, for whatever reasons, stopped innovating. This finding is consistent with the results of Powell et al. (1999) that the network position has an important influence on firm performance.

Table 6.5: Cooperation: block-densities/average value within and between blocks

		Exiting innovators	Permanent innovators	Entering innovators
P1	Exit	0.0237 (0.3173)	0.0254 (0.3405)	
	Permanent	0.0254 (0.3405)	0.0571 (0.5827)	
P2	Permanent		0.1016 (0.8428)	0.0390 (0.4292)
	Entry		0.0390 (0.4292)	0.0119 (0.2189)
	N	117	36	173

Note: Standard deviations in parentheses.

Table 6.6: Scientist mobility: block-densities/average value within and between blocks

		Exiting innovators	Permanent innovators	Entering innovators
P1	Exit	0.0010 (0.0364)	0.0078 (0.2279)	
	Permanent	0.0078 (0.2279)	0.0159 (0.1586)	
P2	Permanent		0.0508 (0.3952)	0.0103 (0.1407)
	Entry		0.0103 (0.1407)	0.0012 (0.0418)
	N	117	36	173

Note: Standard deviations in parentheses.

Since we only analyze two periods, its difficult to view this finding as a general result. Surely, it needs to be qualified through further research. Let us nevertheless assume this conjecture holds: would this not lead to ever increasing density of the network? We think not. Since the ties that constitute the networks cannot assumed to be persistent over very long periods of time, it might well be that formerly well connected actors become more isolated over time, therefore becoming candidates for subsequent exit.

6.3.3 The core network members

The last two sections provided a description of the network as a whole. Now we will focus on the role of the core network members. To measure the importance of single actors, social network theory employs several measures for centrality. We use degree centrality, explained above, and the betweenness of an actor, i. It is defined as $C_B(n_i) = \sum_{j<k} \frac{g_{jk}(n_i)}{g_{jk}}, \forall i \neq j, k$, where g_{jk} is the number

of geodesics (shortest paths) linking j and k and $g_{jk}(n_i)$ is the number of geodesics from j to k that pass through i. Conceptually, high-betweenness vertices lie on a large number of non-redundant shortest paths between other vertices; they can thus be thought of as 'bridges' or 'boundary spanners'.

In table 6.7 we report the ranking of the innovators according to these centrality measures for the 15 innovators that were most active in both periods. For reasons of clarity we only present the rank scores on degree and betweenness centrality within the three different types of networks (cooperation, scientist mobility, and technological overlap), separate for each period.

The first observation is that the local innovation system is clearly dominated by public research institutions (marked with an asterisk) and the large successors of the VEB Carl Zeiss (Jenoptik and Carl Zeiss Jena). Second, we notice the centrality of the three actors within the top 15 that are not located in Jena (Hermsdorfer Institut, Siemens AG and LDT GmbH & Co.) to be decreasing over time. Finally, the University of Jena (FSU) can strengthen its position and is top ranked in all types of networks of the second period. The betweenness measures indicate in particular that the university plays the central role in mediating between the local actors. The FSU is central within the technology-based network, meaning that it covers the knowledge fields most important for the region. It is the central partner for research cooperations and for the transfer of knowledge to the private sector via scientists.

6.4   EXPLAINING THE COOPERATION NETWORK

6.4.1   Research cooperation

In this section we want to investigate whether certain linkages between the actors in one period will lead to stronger interaction in the following period. More specifically: how can we explain the linkages between innovators in Jena that arise through co-applications during one period by various linkages between these actors in a preceding period? Before we attempt to give an answer, we first have to briefly discuss the incentives for firms to cooperate and, second, to identify possible explanatory variables.

An innovative firm planning to either improve its products or to place a completely new product on the market, always faces a number of strategic questions before starting the new project. Usually a large amount of research and development is necessary to succeed, but when creating something new it is also the already existing knowledge of scientists and engineers working on those projects that is relevant. Forming an alliance with competitors, upstream and downstream firms or public research institutes might be advantageous for the project.

Harabi (2002, p. 94) summarizes the arguments as follows: (i) overcoming

Table 6.7: Centrality ranks of the core network members

	Degree						Betweenness					
	1995–1997			1998–2001			1995–1997			1998–2001		
	co	sm	tech	co	sm	tech	co	sm	tech	co	sm	tech
FSU Jena*	10	2	2	1	1	1	6	1	1	1	1	1
Carl Zeiss Jena	2	3	3	5	3	2	1	2	4	5	4	3
FhG*	3	7	5	3	2	4	3	6	3	3	2	5
JENOPTIK	7	1	1	6	5	3	6	3	2	2	8	2
IPHT*	1	3	4	4	11	5	2	4	5	4	6	6
HKI*	5	8	7	2	3	9	4	6	6	6	3	8
Jenapharm	10	8	10	10	6	11	6	6	8	8	7	7
Ahlers	10	8	6	10	15	6	6	6	9	8	12	4
IMB*	10	8	14	7	9	10	6	6	13	7	5	11
Schott Glas	4	6	9	10	13	14	6	6	10	8	10	13
Hermsdorfer Institut*	6	8	12	9	9	13	5	6	12	8	11	10
LDT GmbH&Co.	8	3	8	10	8	15	6	5	11	8	12	15
Siemens AG	10	8	13	10	11	8	6	6	13	8	9	9
Leica MS Jena	10	8	15	8	6	7	6	6	13	8	12	12
GESO	9	8	11	10	13	12	6	6	7	8	12	14

Notes: Innovators are sorted according to the average rank across all columns; * public research institutes.

the R&D financial constraints in individual firms (i.e. expensive research projects can be realized as a result of cost-sharing); (ii) exploitation of economies of scale and scope in R&D; (iii) reduction of wasteful duplication in R&D; (iv) internalization of technological spillovers and other forms of externality; (v) better use of synergies because each firm can contribute distinct capabilities to a common research project; and, finally, (vi) reduction of investment risks due to demand uncertainties.

Since we examine cooperations that exist or have existed and since we have no information about firms having thought about it and decided against it, we turn our focus to the question of how the cooperating actors find each other.

In the last decades a strong policy towards technology transfer from universities to industry has emerged. Universities all over the world institutionalize this mode of knowledge transfer. Also when searching the internet there are numerous networking platforms where firms and non-profit research organizations present themselves to be found as a networking or cooperation partner. We view this development as a strong indication that the matching of cooperation partners is not a marginal problem. Besides these transaction cost reducing institutions there are definitely other ways by which appropriate partners come together. Powell et al. (1996, p. 117) mentions, '[...]each partner's size and position in the "value chain," the level of sophistication, resource constraints, and prior experiences with alliances' as factors influencing the partnering decision. In the following sections we will examine the role of existing relations between actors as an explanation of future cooperations.

6.4.2 The data sample

We attempt to identify these relations by building networks of innovators according to the three types of commonalities that we discussed above: the first commonality, which can be viewed as a necessary condition for a research cooperation, has to be a common knowledge-base. Even though research partners want to create something new, they need to have an overlapping knowledge-base to facilitate know-how exchange and development, i.e. for cooperation to be mutually beneficial, the partners both need the absorptive capacity to learn from each other (Cohen and Levinthal, 1990). In their empirical study on interfirm cooperation, Mowery et al. (1998) find strong evidence in favor of their hypothesis that joint venture partners display a higher degree of technological overlap compared with non-collaborators. We define technological overlap as the number of technological classes in which two actors both hold patents.

When this condition is fulfilled the firm might approach someone with whom they have successfully cooperated before. This is an idea of know-who on the institutional level since researchers of the earlier cooperation do

Table 6.8: Network correlations

	$co^{99\text{-}01}$	$co^{95\text{-}97}$	$sm^{95\text{-}97}$	$tech^{95\text{-}97}$	$sm^{99\text{-}01}$
$co^{99\text{-}01}$	–	-0.012	0.095	0.294	0.456
$co^{95\text{-}97}$	-0.012	–	-0.010	0.145	0.056
$sm^{95\text{-}97}$	0.095	-0.010	–	0.277	0.038
$tech^{95\text{-}97}$	0.294	0.145	0.277	–	0.245
$sm^{99\text{-}01}$	0.456	0.056	0.038	0.245	–

not need to be involved directly. The third commonality involves scientists who have worked for both companies or organizations. Usually the contacts between colleagues are not terminated (straightaway) when they change the job. Actually sometimes firms hire skilled people especially for their contacts, hoping to benefit from their networks.

We use the networks of permanent innovators for the regressions, i.e. those innovators that patented in both periods of observation. This constraint decreases our sample dramatically from 326 innovators, patenting in either of the two periods, to 36 permanent innovators in Jena. The correlations between the networks, as shown in table 6.8, suggest that cooperation partners have overlapping technologies in the period before. This result is not very surprising but table 6.8 also suggests that it is not the cooperations between firms in the former period that determines who will cooperate in the second period, but rather the linkages between the firms that result from the job mobility of the scientists. Further we notice an increase of the correlation between technological overlap and cooperation comparing the two periods. This is probably due to the fact that overall cooperation activity has increased. Another result is that firms do not seem to have both types of personal linkages in the same period. We observe almost no correlation between $sm^{95\text{-}97}$ and $co^{95\text{-}97}$.

6.4.3 Network regression

To investigate these differences with more sophisticated methods, we employ multiple regression analysis with dyadic data (e.g. Krackhardt, 1988; Butts and Carley, 2001). This literature provides us with tools to investigate the structural equivalence of different networks. Think of the network as a $n \times n$ adjacency matrix, Y, where $y_{i,j}$ equals zero if the actors i and j have no relation and $y_{i,j}$ is equal to any positive integer representing the strength of the relation between both. The structural representation of our network variable is then given by:

$$
\mathbf{Y} = \begin{pmatrix}
0 & y_{1,2} & \cdots & y_{1,n} \\
y_{2,1} & 0 & \cdots & y_{2,n} \\
\vdots & \vdots & \ddots & \vdots \\
y_{n,1} & y_{n,2} & \cdots & 0
\end{pmatrix}
$$

For using regression techniques the original adjacency matrix, without the diagonal elements, is transformed into vector form as follows:

$$
\mathbf{y} = \begin{pmatrix}
y_{1,2} \\
y_{1,3} \\
\vdots \\
y_{n,n-1}
\end{pmatrix}
$$

Performing this transformation with all network variables leads us to the generalized formulation of the regression equation

$$
y_{ij} = \alpha + \boldsymbol{\beta}' \mathbf{x}_{ij} + \varepsilon_{ij} \quad \forall i \neq j, \text{ where}
$$

y_{ij} is the value of the interpersonal link between i and j that is to be explained. The matrix $\mathbf{x}_{ij}$ contains the explanatory variables relating i and j. This model is estimated using a standard OLS procedure with the usual interpretation of the coefficients. As opposed to regular regression data, a problem of structural autocorrelation might appear either in rows or in columns of the network matrix (Krackhardt, 1987). Therefore the significance levels of the regression coefficients as provided by the t-statistic or the p-value have to be handled with care.

Krackhardt (1987) suggests a different method to evaluate the significance of the coefficients.[6] QAP-tests (Quadratic assignment procedure) (Hubert, 1987) are applied to make more correct inferences about the significance of the coefficients. In these tests the null-hypothesis is that the test-statistic of association equals the expected value of the test-statistic under a permutation distribution. A major advantage of that technique is that the test makes no assumptions about the distribution of the parameters. QAP constructs a reference distribution of random parameters that could have been derived from a dataset with the same structure but different node assignments as the dataset under evaluation. A permutation distribution is constructed that is similar to the underlying distribution for which inference is drawn by randomly permuting the rows and columns of the dependent variable. When related to the independent variables these permutations of the dependent network

---

[6]For a more detailed explanation than the following see the illustrative example in Krackhardt (1987) on pages 175–178.

provide random estimates of the relation between the variables. Since there are too many (n!) possible permutations, random samples of these permutations are used to generate a reference distribution (Hubert, 1987). If the observed coefficient is greater than 95% of the coefficients based on random permutations, for instance, then, according to this randomization test, it is said to be significant at the 5% level, because an index that large or larger was found just five times out of 100 total permutations.[7]

Performing the above transformation with all network variables leads us to the econometric model:

$$y_{ij}^{99\text{-}01} = \alpha + \beta' \mathbf{x}_{ij}^{95\text{-}97} + \varepsilon_{ij} \quad \forall i < j, \, [8] \text{ where}$$

$y_{ij}^{99\text{-}01}$ is the number of interpersonal linkages between innovators i and j which result from a formal cooperation of both in the second period. The matrix $\mathbf{x}_{ij}^{95\text{-}97}$ contains the explanatory variables from the first period, such as cooperation linkages, linkages through scientists mobility, and technological overlap between i and j. We also include dummy variables for linkages between public funded research institutes (uni) and private organizations (priv).

The difference between the two models reported in table 6.9 is the inclusion of 'scientist mobility[99-01]' in the second regression. In the first model we only include the explanatory variables from the first period thereby assuming long term relations being relevant for cooperative linkages. In the second regression we also control for scientists changing their jobs in the same period where the cooperations that are to be explained take place. Our results can at least give some hints on the mechanisms relying the matching process of cooperation partners. Regarding the R^2's we observe a tremendous increase in explanatory power when controlling for short term relationships. The variance in the data explained by our model increases from about 0.1 to 0.25. This is still rather small but not surprising given the data that we use. One factor that we have left aside is the role of the above mentioned technology transfer institutions. As has already been said, their purpose is to bring actors together that did not know each other before. Also, we admit that there are definitely more linkages between innovators than are documented in patents.

After these drawbacks let us focus on the relationships between the different types of linkages. Without the information documented in table 6.8 we would have expected a positive influence of the earlier cooperation network on the later one. Seemingly though, the theoretical argument of the persistence of linkages does not apply to this case. This result is confirmed by both network regressions of table 6.9. The estimated coefficient for cooperations in the first period (co[95-97]) is negative and significantly different from what we should

---

[7]Referring to table 6.9 this means that in 17 out of 1000 permutations of the co[99-01]-network the observed coefficient of the scientist mobility network was larger than 0.061.

[8]Since our data is undirected, only the upper triangle of the relevant matrices are used.

expect under the random assignment hypothesis.[9]

The importance of personal linkages in weaving a network of organizations is quite obvious. Even though the coefficients of scientist mobility (sm^{95-97}) are not significant by standard measures in both regressions they are close enough to be analyzed. Here we can also see the largest difference between the standard p-value, which would suggest absolutely no influence of scientist mobility on cooperations, and the significance provided by testing the QAP hypothesis. We observe a positive influence of this type of network which is even getting stronger when we control for the mobility of scientists in the same period as the observed cooperations (sm^{99-01}). This is actually the variable that adds most information to our model. The coefficient is by far the largest, is highly significant and, as already said, more than doubles the R^2. This result speaks strongly in favor of the prominent role of interpersonal linkages in building networks of innovators or local innovation systems.

Our results concerning technological overlap of the first period ($tech^{95-97}$) come as no surprise and affirm our predictions that actors have to share a common knowledge-base. There are only two (out of 12) linkages by cooperation where there is no technological overlap in the first period. Finally, chances of a collaborative agreement between two public organizations are higher than between two private ones.

6.5 CONCLUDING REMARKS

The usage of patent data for social network analysis proved fruitful in its application on the local innovation system of Jena. The analysis of the network of technological overlap leads us to conclude that the dynamics of the system are directed towards an increasing focus on core competencies of the local innovation system; i.e. innovators on the periphery of the network exit and new entrants position themselves closer to the core of the network. Thus, new innovators and exiting innovators in Jena have shown to be different regarding their network positions. From this we presume that a critical mass of innovators is necessary for a specific technology to 'survive' within an LIS. A success-breeds-success mechanism on the level of the technology will then lead to an increasing specialization of the LIS in these technologies. The same dynamics regarding the network positions of entering and exiting innovators are observed when analyzing the cooperation and scientist mobility networks. Other studies of this type will have to find evidence in favor of the hypothesis that network positions are a crucial factor in the explanation of innovative performance.

---

[9]Significance is the minimum of $Pr(\geq b)$ (which is documented) and $Pr(< b)$. If the observed coefficient is larger than all coefficients resulting from the permutation of $\mathbf{Y}$ the influence is significantly higher than we would expect from random assignment. If, on the other hand, our observed coefficient is exceptionally low, this is also a significant, since not random, result.

Table 6.9: Network regression

Dependent variable: $co^{99\text{-}01}$	β		$Pr(>|t|)$	$Pr(\geq\beta)^a$	β		$Pr(>|t|)$	$Pr(\geq\beta)^a$
(Intercept)	−0.007	**	0.893	0.984	0.014	**	0.782	0.956
$co^{95\text{-}97}$	−0.100	***	0.073	1.000	−0.104	***	0.041	1.000
$sm^{95\text{-}97}$	0.068		0.745	0.120	0.127		0.508	0.110
$tech^{95\text{-}97}$	0.273	***	0.000	0.001	0.177	***	0.000	0.007
$sm^{99\text{-}01}$					0.858	***	0.000	0.000
Public linkages	0.406	**	0.002	0.024	0.238	*	0.048	0.081
Private linkages	−0.065		0.337	0.741	−0.088		0.155	0.815
Res.st.err.:	0.800				0.730			
Mult. R^2 (Adj.):	0.108		(0.101)		0.258		(0.251)	
F-statistic (p-value):	15.160		(0.000)		36.040		(0.000)	
Obs. (Nodes):	630		(36)		630		(36)	

Notes: ^{a} Null hypothesis is QAP; i.e. the probability to observe a coefficient of this magnitude or larger under the assumption of random assignment of actors to nodes; significance levels according to QAP: *** ≤ 0.01, ** ≤ 0.05, * ≤ 0.1; significance is the minimum of $Pr(\geq b)$ (which is documented) and $Pr(<b)$; no. of permutations: 10000.

It shows that the local innovation system is clearly dominated by the local university and public research institutes. Our inventor-based definition of the system, leads to the inclusion of non-local organizations. Some of them even hold prominent positions within the network, but we observe decreasing centrality for these actors. As a consequence of economic transformation in Jena, the dominating firm(s), the successors of the Carl-Zeiss combine, are losing their central position to the local university.

It has been suggested that the partnering in R&D cooperation is a problem for firms and has even led to political intervention. We showed that personal relationships that arise through the job mobility of scientists are an important variable in explaining the formation of cooperation networks.

7. Local Innovation Systems in Comparison: Jena, Dresden, Heidelberg and Ulm

7.1 INTRODUCTION

This chapter aims at questioning the favorable statements about Jena by evaluating the technological and economic performance of the local innovation system. The approach we take is comparative, in contrasting the figures for Jena with the ones of Ulm, Dresden, and Heidelberg. The theoretical concepts behind the approach that is taken, is in line with the systemic approach to innovation (as discussed in chapters 2 and 3), where successful innovation is characterized as a result of interactive processes of learning, research, and innovation.

In this light, we view the four regions as innovation systems, and try to evaluate them according to the strengths of the respective poles, the functions, that are served in the innovation process, and the economic success of the innovation systems. The order in this chapter is as follows: in the next section the selection of regions is justified by characterizing the regions and the elements of the respective systems. We compare the innovation systems with respect to the technological development in section 7.3 and with respect to economic characteristics in section 7.4. A short summary will close the chapter.

7.2 REGIONAL CHARACTERISTICS

7.2.1 Selection of regions

If one seeks to detect specificities in the technological or economic development of a region, there are by and large two ways to approach this topic. One method is to compare the region in question to larger geographical entities, such as a state or nation. The problem with this approach is that the larger entity is rather heterogenous with respect to the constituting elements. Metropolitan areas, smaller cities and rural areas are mixed up and their systematic differences in the organization of economic and innovative processes are blurred. A second method aims at comparing entities at the same level of geographical aggregation. Differences between the regions then depend with a higher probability on local characteristics. Throughout this chapter, we largely stick to the second approach but, whenever it is appropriate, we compare the four regions with Germany as a whole.

We chose the regions according to the following criteria:

i) The regions for comparison should be cities of similar size.
ii) The scientific pole should be present, i.e. a university which covers many scientific fields and/or public research institutes.
iii) Cities should have a reputation in local innovation.
iv) Two regions should be located in the eastern and western parts of Germany, respectively.

Jena is included, as it is at the center of this study. With a population of roughly 100,000, it is the smallest of the four cities (see table 7.1). The Friedrich Schiller University Jena covers all natural and social sciences, the Fachhochschule (polytechnical university) offers courses of study in technical and engineering fields. In addition, there are three institutes of the Max-Planck society, the Fraunhofer-Institute for Applied Optics and Precision Engineering, the Institute of Molecular Biotechnology (IMB), and the Hans-Knöll Institute für Naturstoff-Forschung (HKI),[1] and the Institute for Physical High Technology Jena (IPHT).

As noted above, Jena is often named as a positive example for regions in eastern Germany. In Zukunftsatlas 2004 (Prognos, 2004), a recent ranking of German regions by the Prognos AG in cooperation with the German daily paper *Handelsblatt*, which evaluated chances for future performance, Jena is ranked 24th out of 439 regions and top ranked among east-German regions.

Despite its size, which is roughly four times that of Jena, Dresden is included, as it is also often mentioned as a successful region in eastern Germany. Dresden is ranked 110th by Prognos (2004), but the second best region in the east. The Technical University Dresden and the Fachhochschule cover all scientific disciplines. Public research is further strengthened by the location of ten institutes of the Fraunhofer society, four research institutes belonging to the Science Association Gottfried Wilhelm Leibniz, and three Max-Planck-Institutes.

Heidelberg is a traditional university city, which – like Jena – was successful in the BioRegio contest instigated by the German ministry of education and research (BMBF). Besides the German Cancer Research Center (DKFZ) and

[1] IMB and HKI belong to the Science Association Gottfried Wilhelm Leibniz.

the European Molecular Biology Laboratory, four Max-Planck Institutes are located in Heidelberg. Prognos (2004) ranks Heidelberg in 6th position with excellent chances for future development.

Ulm, with its 'Wissenschaftsstadt', can be considered as an initiated innovation system (Boucke et al., 1994). This science and innovation park was founded in 1986, initiated by the former prime minister of Baden Württemberg, Lothar Späth.[2] In contrast to the other three regions, there are no large, national funded research institutes, but some smaller research institutes are located in Ulm. The university is close to the Wissenschaftsstadt, where a science park and a large Daimler Chrysler research center is located.

In setting the boundaries of the four locations and in classifying them as economic area or innovation system, one has to deal with certain methodological problems. Economic areas as well as (regional or local) innovation systems are not constituted by clear-cut physical boundaries (Koschatzky and Zenker, 1999). They might include cities belonging to different administrative regions or might even cross national boundaries, like the euro-region 'Pro Europa Viadrina' around Frankfurt/Oder. A glance at the web-site 'Kompetenznetze.de', sponsored by the BMBF, shows Jena presenting itself together with Erfurt, Dresden with Chemnitz, Ulm as part of the region 'Bodensee-Oberschwaben-Ulm,' and Heidelberg as part of the 'Rhein-Neckar-Dreieck'. This makes it also difficult to find accurate boundaries of the respective innovation systems, as Jena might as well be part of a system called Jena-Ilmenau-Erfurt or Jena-Halle-Leipzig.

Being aware of the problem of adequately defining a region, we define the regions according to their administrative boundaries, i.e. the level of the 'Kreis'. Thereby we can diminish problems of data availability and compatibility, as most information, except for data on unemployment, is given at that level. For the comparative study, we use data on patents and public research funding to capture the technological structure, the innovative performance, and the main actors in the innovation systems. Regional statistics are used for information on population, industrial structure, education, and economic performance. The remainder of this section is concerned with a description of the local innovation systems with respect to population, industrial structure, and education.

7.2.2 Population

Population and its development over time is an important measure to describe the four regions. On the one hand it just indicates the size of a region, on the other hand it can serve as an indicator for the economic development.

---

[2]Later, he was engaged in Jena, first, in the splitting-up of the VEB Carl-Zeiss and later, as CEO of the Jenoptik AG.

Networks in the Innovation Process

Table 7.1: Development of regional population

	1995	1996	1997	1998	1999	2000	2001
Dresden	472697	465968	464255	456478	477590	476683	478631
Heidelberg	138873	138825	139405	139613	139479	139966	141509
Jena	101724	100774	99958	99052	99419	99763	101157
Ulm	115422	115871	115825	115665	115902	116668	118347

Sources: Statistische Ämter des Bundes und der Länder (2002), Statistische Landesämter Sachsen, Thüringen and Baden-Württemberg (for 2001).

The most important factors influencing the change in population are migration and natural change (birth vs. mortality rate). Being capable of attracting people from other regions indicates the economic strength of the respective region, whereas regions with poor economic performance often shrink, as the youth seeks chances elsewhere in prospering regions. The development of the regional population for the years 1995–2001 is given in table 7.1. We observe a decline in Jena and Dresden until 1997 and 1998 respectively, a trend which is observed for the whole of eastern Germany (Kempe, 1998).[3] Heidelberg and Ulm show a moderate growth in population.

7.2.3   Industrial structure

Besides the size of a region, the industrial structure is also an informative way of describeing and characterizing a region. In figure 7.1, differences in the importance of sectors according to their employment shares within the regions are shown. Services are divided into 'public and private services' and 'services (other),' which include amongst others, commerce, hotel and restaurants, and financial services.

Overall, the four regions do not differ substantially in their sectoral structure. In Jena and Heidelberg, the dominating sector is public and private services, accounting for 41% of employment respectively, followed by other services (dominant in Dresden and Ulm). This is due to the prominence of universities and public research laboratories in these two cities. Manufacturing employs less than 25% in all four regions, with the strongest relevance in Ulm. Agriculture and forestry is – expectedly – of no importance. An alternative analysis based on shares in regional GDP leads to similar results, with a stronger role of industry, especially in Ulm with a share of 35%.

---

[3]The reason for the sharp increase in Dresden between 1998 and 1999 is due to the incorporation of surrounding communities with an area of 90 km^2 (corresponding to 38%).

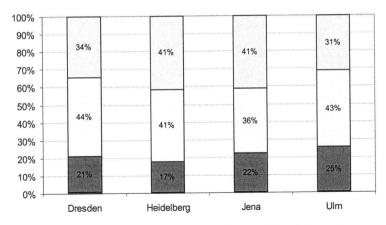

□ Agriculture and forestry ■ Industry □ Services (other) □ Public and private services

Source: Own calculations based on Statistische Ämter des Bundes und der Länder (2002).

Figure 7.1: Regional sectoral structure – employment shares in 2000

7.2.4   Human capital and education

The results from the previous section indicate the dominating role of services in the economic landscape of the four regions. A large part of this sector is knowledge intensive and therefore relies on a high level of education within the workforce. Further, human capital is the decisive factor in the production of knowledge and is critical in the process of innovation. Even though managers of business firms call for mobility of employees, it is actually the case that firms often recruit their employees locally, which makes the availability of skilled workers an important location factor (see chapter 5). A similar argument is put forward by Cooper and Folta (2000) and Fornahl and Graf (2003), who question the mobility of entrepreneurs during the foundation process. Using the data discussed in chapter 5, Fornahl and Graf (2003) find that only a minority of founders even considered alternative location for their ventures, but rather establish their firms where they are located at the time of foundation. Education is therefore not only a requirement for the supply of skilled workers but also serves as a local pool for future generations of entrepreneurs in high-tech industries.

We compare the structure of school leavers according to the type of degree and the relative importance of universities in table 7.2. Jena and Heidelberg, with a respective 16% and 19% share of university students in population, can be characterized as 'university cities'. These two cities also show the highest

Table 7.2: Structure of education

	Dresden	Heidelberg	Jena	Ulm
School leavers 1998				
without degree (%)	8.8	6.3	8.2	7.8
with CSE (after 9th grade) (%)	10.2	20.4	14.0	28.0
with degree (after 10th grade) (%)	48.1	27.2	30.5	35.5
with higher education entrance qualification (Abitur) (%)	32.8	45.4	47.4	28.7
University students 1998 in % of population	6.4	19.2	16.2	5.6
Foreign students 1998 (%)	5.2	13.4	3.8	7.9

Source: Bundesamt für Bauwesen und Raumordnung (2000).

share of school leavers with a higher education entrance qualification. It seems as if the presence of a strong university makes it more attractive to study there. Another reason for this difference might be the relationship between the social background and school performance. If the career is strongly influenced by parents' social status (Mare, 1980; Kodde and Ritzen, 1988; Dearden et al., 1997), then a higher share of academics might translate to a higher education degree of their children. This hypothesis might explain why Jena shows the highest share of school leavers with 'Abitur' and Ulm the lowest, since the share of employees with a university degree is highest in Jena (21.7%) and lowest in Ulm (12.5%), but it does not explain why the youth in Heidelberg (academics share of 16.9%) is higher educated than in Dresden (18.7%).[4]

After this short presentation of the four regions, we proceed with a discussion of specific technological structures and developments in the following section.

7.3 INNOVATIVENESS AND TECHNOLOGICAL DEVELOPMENT

As has been pointed out in the introduction to this chapter, we discuss regional innovativeness and technological development following the concept of innovation systems. Such a system includes a number of actors which interact during the processes of invention, innovation, and diffusion of new knowledge. On this basis we present some measures to compare the regions according to the extent of public funding of research, innovativeness, forms of cooperative research between business firms and between firms and public research (universities and institutes), technological specialization, and the local knowledge-base. Of course these are only part of the dimensions making up an

[4]Data for 2000 (Statistische Ämter des Bundes und der Länder, 2002).

Table 7.3: Research funding – annual sum (million €)

	1990	1991	1992	1993	1994	1995	1996	1997	1998	1999	2000	2001	2002
Dresden	1.3	28.1	29.7	34.4	38.8	43.0	40.7	38.9	51.5	53.4	55.5	64.7	44.8
Heidelberg	22.3	18.9	21.1	19.5	16.9	17.3	17.8	19.8	19.1	22.9	28.9	40.8	37.6
Jena	0.1	17.1	20.6	19.9	25.1	28.3	27.8	29.3	23.7	23.8	23.8	32.9	27.1
Ulm	9.4	8.7	11.7	12.7	15.6	18.0	22.0	20.6	20.3	21.0	18.5	18.1	19.3

Source: Own calculations, based on BMBF (2002a).
Note: Project sum is equally distributed across run time.

innovation system. Others might include internal mechanisms regarding the phase of invention or a more detailed analysis and classification of the actors (e.g. as small, medium-sized firms, position in the value chain, etc.). Also, we do not go into sociological factors like mentality and culture, ability to learn or resolve conflicts, which clearly influence the performance of an innovation system.

7.3.1 Public funding of research activities

Innovation systems normally include a political dimension, which provides the institutional setting but also takes direct influence on the innovation process by providing funding to the actors of the system. In this subsection, we compare the four regions, according to the public funding of their research activities. Of course, research funding is a policy instrument not only for research policy, but for regional policy as well. But still, to receive funding, the actors must be capable of recognizing and starting interesting and promising research projects and to have the potential to successfully carry them out.

We use data on research funding provided by the German federal ministry of education and research (BMBF) and the German federal ministry of economic affairs (BMWi). The data is available on the internet as 'Förderkatalog des Bundesministeriums für Bildung und Forschung' (BMBF, 2002a). The analysis serves two purposes. First, it documents the capability of local actors to acquire funding and, second, it allows identification of the main actors of the respective system.

Table 7.3 gives the sum of research funding, received by organizations of the respective region for the years 1990–2001. Since the projects usually run longer than one year, we spread the funding for each project equally across the run time of the project. Comparing regional funding, we observe a strong effect of regional policy on the funding structure in the mid 1990s. Starting from almost zero in 1990, Jena and Dresden received more funding than Heidelberg or Ulm by 1993. Jena was second behind Dresden until 1999, but from 2000 onwards, we observe a ranking, in line with the size of the regions according to population.

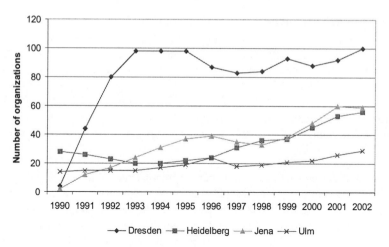

Figure 7.2: Number of organizations receiving research grants

The number of organizations that receive research grants, is depicted in figure 7.2 for each year to illustrate the development of variety in the local research landscape. Even though Dresden is almost five times as large as Jena, only twice as many organizations received public funding in 2002, while the average organization in Dresden receives less compared to Jena (figure 7.3). Despite its small size, the number of funded organizations in Jena exceeds those in Ulm and in Heidelberg in almost every year after 1993. In contrast to Dresden, this lively research landscape in Jena has been growing throughout most years, while the development has stagnated there since 1993. We also observe a continuous growth in Heidelberg after 1994 and a slight increase in Ulm over the period.

Another indication of the different structure of the local research landscape is provided by the funding per organization. Figure 7.3 shows clearly that in 1991 and 1992, a large amount of money went to only few organizations in Jena, but this concentration sharply declined in the following years. By 2002, Jena and Dresden show a similar level, about €200,000 lower than in Ulm or Heidelberg.

The organizations can be distinguished into universities, business firms, and research institutes.[5] By comparing the regions according to the shares of funding that the different types of actors receive, we can analyze the relevance of the different system poles in the respective innovation system. Figure 7.4 shows that the market pole is, by far, most prominent in Ulm, where 67% of the

---

[5]This category also includes individuals or organizations that do not fall into the other two categories.

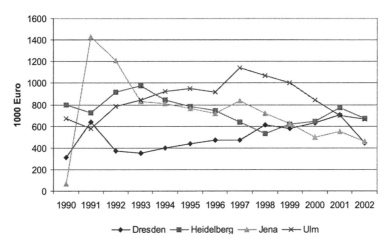

Figure 7.3: Average funding per organization

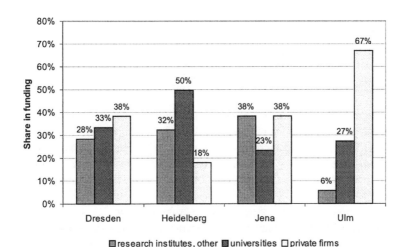

Figure 7.4: Research funding according to type of receiver (1990–2002)

research grants go to business firms. In Heidelberg the university is the largest actor, receiving almost 50% of funding, while business firms only account for 18%. In Jena, business firms and research institutes receive equal shares of 38% leaving 23% to the universities.

The analysis of research funding provides us with two insights. Since public grants are an input to the innovation process, it is only possible to infer to innovativeness by assuming that part of the scientific or inventive work must be accomplished before applying for funding. Besides, it seems as if other political goals (adjustment of regional disparities) influence the funding decisions. It is possible though, to distinguish the local innovation systems with respect to the structure, concentration, and relevance of actors. It shows that, in Ulm, the business firms are not only most prominent in terms of employment, but also in performing research. Heidelberg is clearly a more science and research driven system and Dresden and Jena lie somewhere in between.

7.3.2 Innovative performance

We use patent data to compare the regions with respect to technological competitiveness and innovative performance. Of course, the number of patents is not a perfect measure for innovativeness since not all novelties are or can be patented and no information about the quality of the patents is provided. On the other hand, patents have the great advantage of a consistent and comparable database for longer time periods.[6] For our purposes we use patents that were granted by the German patent office as provided in DPMA (Deutsches Patent-und Markenamt). We use patents which name at least one inventor residing in Germany at the time of application and which were disclosed between 1995 and 2001. In assigning the patents to a region, we use the residence of inventors.[7] In cases of more than one inventor, the patent is counted for each inventor's residence region.

To get a first impression of regional patenting and its development, figure 7.5 shows the absolute number of patents for the period covered in the four regions. We observe an increase in patenting for all regions, with the ranking of regions corresponding to differences in size, and notably Jena is stronger in the number of patents as Ulm despite being smaller. Here, information about the relative importance in Germany, in relation to general trends in patenting, or in relation to size of the regions are not accounted for.

In figure 7.6, the regional share of patents in Germany is depicted, thereby revealing information about the relative importance of the region and account-ing for macro-trends in patenting. All regions gain importance as their patent-ing shares rise over the period. Except for small fluctuations the larger patent-ing regions Heidelberg and Dresden and the smaller ones Jena and Ulm per-form in quite a similar way.

Finally, to account for differences in size we calculate the patent intensity (Greif, 1998), i.e. patents per 100,000 inhabitants in accordance with the numbers given in table 7.1. Figure 7.7 shows a map of Germany, where the

---

[6]For a more detailed discussion on the usage of patent statistics in economics see Griliches (1990) or Pavitt (1988).

[7]For advantages of the inventor-based method compared to an applicant-based approach see Greif (1998, S. 13).

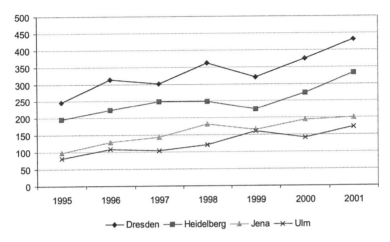

Figure 7.5: Development in patenting (absolute numbers)

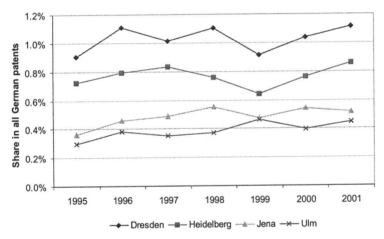

Figure 7.6: Development of patenting shares

'Kreise' (NUTS 3 level) are colored on the basis of the patent intensity and the four regions are highlighted. Besides the spatial distribution of patenting activities in Germany, this map also indicates the different environment of our regions. The characterization of Jena as a 'lighthouse' seems adequate since the surrounding regions are all patenting below national average, whereas Jena lies between 2 and 3 standard deviations above the mean. Jena and Dresden are somewhat outstanding in the eastern part of Germany while Ulm does not stand out in Baden-Württemberg. Heidelberg falls in the same category as Jena. We also observe that Heidelberg is embedded in a larger region mentioned above, namely the 'Rhein-Neckar-Dreieck,' including Mannheim, Ludwigshafen, and the surrounding regions, with an outstanding patenting performance. A list of all NUTS 3 regions in Germany with their respective numbers on patents and patent intensities is given in table A.4 in the Appendix, where we report the measures resulting from the inventor-based and the applicant-based method of counting the patents on the regional level.

Measuring the innovativeness of regions in patent intensities leads to a different ranking than before (see figure 7.8 in contrast to figures 7.5 and 7.6). Dresden – the largest region – drops to fourth place, Heidelberg is first, followed by Jena and Ulm. With the exception of 1998 and 1999, where Jena lies above Heidelberg, this ranking remains stable throughout the whole period but analyzing the respective average growth rates shows that especially Ulm (average annual growth rate of 12.23%) and Jena (11.81%) are more dynamic than Heidelberg (8.39%) and Dresden (9.10%).

7.3.3   Interaction and innovation

It has been argued above, that interaction between actors within the innovation process is essential to functioning innovation systems. Cooperations in research and development (not only as formal agreements) are one type of interaction. One possible way of measuring the degree of interaction is to measure cooperative patents. In chapter 4, cooperative patents were defined as patents which are co-applied, i.e. more than one applicant named on the patent. Here we use an inventor-based definition, i.e. a cooperative patent is invented by a team of inventors. Patents can be invented by individuals or by teams, and these teams might be from the same or different localities. Observing a large number of cooperative patents achieved by local teams, indicates dense local networking. If the teams are often formed by members from different localities (external cooperations), the actors might rather be integrated in a technological system or a larger regional system.

We want to answer the following questions: (i) are the regions different in terms of cooperative behavior?; (ii) are the cooperating teams rather local, i.e. residing within the region, or external (research teams from different localities)?; (iii) do the regions differ with respect to patenting by public research (research institutes and universities), which might influence the cooperative behavior?

Table 7.4 already provides some eye-catching differences between the regions in the shares of internal and external cooperations and the shares of patents by public research. In particular, it seems to make a difference if the patent is developed in the eastern or western part of Germany. While the share of internal cooperations is 18% in Dresden and 21% in Jena, Heidelberg and

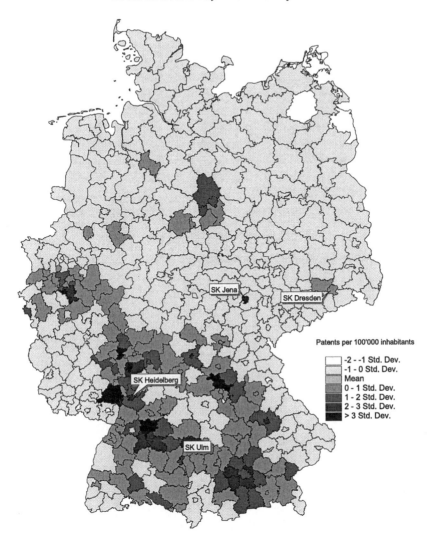

Note: Patent counts based on inventor residence.

Figure 7.7: Patents per 100,000 inhabitants in Germany

Ulm show a share of internal cooperations strikingly lower (each around 3.7% and 3.4% respectively). Public research also seems to contribute considerably more to regional innovation in the east (27% and 29%) than in Heidelberg with 9.4% or Ulm with 3%.

130Networks in the Innovation Process

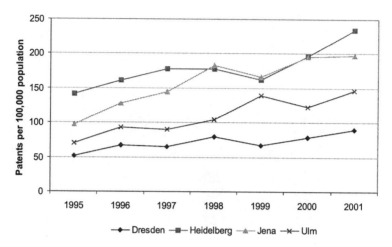

Figure 7.8: Development of the patent intensity

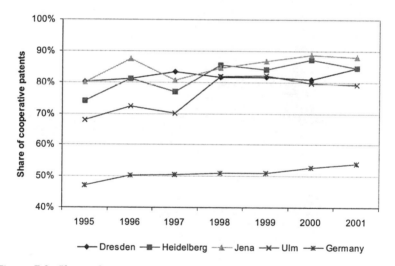

Figure 7.9: Share of cooperative patents

On this basis, we can proceed and answer the above questions.

i) First, we examine cooperations without making the distinction between internal and external linkages. In Germany 51% of the patents are invented by teams. The share of cooperative patents in our regions is 82%. In total, Jena shows the highest share of cooperations and Ulm the lowest. Regarding the development of this variable over time, we observe

*Table 7.4: Patenting behavior in regions**

	Dresden	Heidelberg	Jena	Ulm
Patents	2345	1750	1114	892
Cooperative patents	1925	1442	954	689
internal	419	65	229	30
external	1506	1377	725	659
Patents by individuals	420	308	160	203
Patents by public research	636	165	320	27
Share of cooperative patents	82.1%	82.4%	85.6%	77.2%
internal	21.8%	4.5%	24.0%	4.4%
external	78.2%	95.5%	76.0%	95.6%
Share of patents by public research	27.1%	9.4%	28.7%	3.0%

Note: *Patents with at least one inventor residing in that region at time of application (disclosure between 1995 and 2001).

an increase in all four regions with a notable increase in Ulm between the first and the second half of the period (see figure 7.9).

ii) Looking at the share of internal cooperations in figure 7.10, we see that the two eastern regions have a much higher share than the western ones. While this share remains almost constant in Ulm and Heidelberg over time, we observe a sharp decrease in Dresden and Jena. One part of this difference might be due to our setting of regions' boundaries. If workers in the west rather live in communities surrounding the cities as compared to the east than we observe external cooperations that are actually none. But, if we follow the reasoning of Markusen (1996) or Bathelt et al. (2004), we can understand that actors in Jena and Dresden just did not have enough time to build up the capabilities and capacities to establish these external relations.

iii) Finally, we consider the relevance of public research in the local innovation systems. Figure 7.11 depicts the share of patents which name at least one public research institute or university as applicant. As noted above, this share is highest for Jena and Dresden, ranging between 19% and 36%, whereas in Ulm it oscillates between 0% and 6%, and in Heidelberg it increases from 4% to 14% in 2000. Taking a closer look at the development, no significant time trend is perceivable except for Heidelberg, where, on average, the share of public research patents increases by 1% each year.[8]

Since there are quite some similarities between figures 7.10 and 7.11, a

[8] A simple OLS regression of the share of public research on a time variable shows significant results only for Heidelberg, with an R^2 of 0.57 and a coefficient for the time variable of 0.0115 with a p-value of 0.0493.

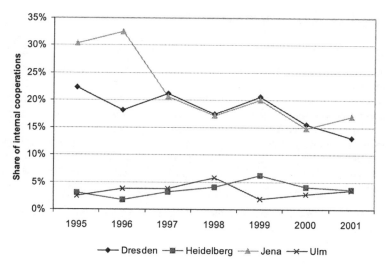

Figure 7.10: Share of internal cooperations in all cooperations

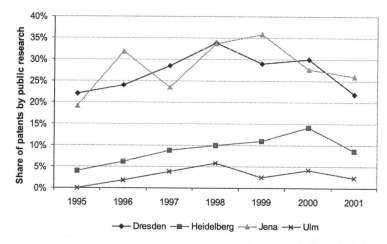

Figure 7.11: Patenting shares of universities and public research institutes

relationship between patents by public research and internal cooperations could be suspected. Table 7.5 shows that in public research, a higher share of patents is developed by teams of researchers (91.8%) than in all patents in the sample (82.0%). Within these cooperative patents, the internal ones make up 27.1% compared to only 14.9% in total patenting. Public research therefore is more focussed on team work and especially local in its contacts.

Table 7.5: Cooperation and public research

	Public research	Total
Patents	1130	6071
Cooperations	1037	4980
Internal cooperations	281	743
Share of cooperations	91.8%	82.0%
Share of internal cooperations in cooperations	27.1%	14.9%
Share of internal cooperations in all patents	24.9%	12.2%

Note: The sum of patents here is not equal to the resulting numbers from adding up the first row in table 7.4, since 30 patents are external cooperations between the regions covered.

Table 7.6: Technological specialization

Dresden	Heidelberg	Jena	Ulm
1 Surface technology, coating (4.22)	Organic fine chemistry (7.40)	Optics (8.64)	Materials, metallurgy (2.50)
2 Nuclear engineering (3.65)	Biotechnology (6.75)	Biotechnology (5.30)	Semiconductors (2.45)
3 Semiconductors (2.91)	Macromolecular chemistry, polymers (2.84)	Analysis, measurement, control technology (2.91)	Telecommunications (2.30)
4 Materials, metallurgy (2.20)	Pharmaceuticals, cosmetics (2.59)	Pharmaceuticals, cosmetics (2.89)	Surface technology, coating (1.81)
5 Thermal processes and apparatus (2.00)	Handling, printing (2.18)	Medical technology (2.86)	Chemical engineering (1.58)

Note: TRCA in parentheses.

7.3.4 Technological knowledge-base

A further aspect in examining innovativeness and technological development in the four locations deals with their specific technological strengths and the local technological knowledge-base. It can be questioned whether the usage of patents for mapping the knowledge-base is an adequate approach. As discussed in chapter 2, it is clearly wrong to assume that all knowledge is patented, but still, in many industries, a large part of knowledge that is believed to provide a competitive advantage is patented (Levin et al., 1987; Cohen et al., 2000).

One measure, that reveals technological strengths, is the specialization index, $TRCA$, used in chapter 4. Table 7.6 gives those five technologies for the four regions, with the highest scores in the $TRCA$.[9]

---

[9]For classifying the patents in technological classes we use the concordance between patent classes and technologies according to table A.2 in the Appendix.

Table 7.7: Share of innovating firms (in %)

	1994	1995	1996	1997	1998	1999	2000
Manufacture of medical, precision and optical instruments	49	76	83	86	76	84	80
Mechanical engineering	61	72	76	85	81	81	75
Electrical engineering	52	53	65	82	88	80	74
EDP/Telecommunication	84	81	78	77	65	62	73
Chemical industry	67	53	75	77	80	80	70
Motor manufacturing industry	46	70	68	72	72	74	64
Rubber and plastics	68	42	49	65	69	71	63
Wood production and publishing	42	45	52	42	40	56	59
Metal industry	52	59	57	50	69	62	57
Furniture, jewellery, toys, musical instruments, and sports goods	45	60	63	66	71	64	56
Textile and leather	40	54	57	53	65	66	55
Glass/Ceramic	31	74	68	57	58	52	55
Food, beverages, and tobacco	50	39	43	71	67	64	54

Source: ZEW – Mannheimer Innovationspanels.

Dresden and Ulm are quite similar in their technological specialization, as three technologies (Surface technology, Semiconductors, Materials) show up in both their top five. Jena and Heidelberg have two overlaps in this list, Pharmaceuticals and Biotechnology. The second position of nuclear engineering in Dresden exemplifies that this index measures the relative importance of a region within a technological field and not typically the major fields of activity. Nuclear engineering is a very small field of patenting in Germany, ranked last in the number of patents of all 30 technologies with a share of 0.35%. So, even though this technology would only be ranked 25th by numbers of patents in Dresden, it is specialized, as its share (1.28%) is higher than the national average.

Comparing these findings with results from the 'Mannheimer Innovationspanel' about innovativeness in industries, allows us to evaluate the fields of specialization in our regions as more or less innovative. In table 7.7, we report 13 selected industries with their respective shares of innovating firms. This list serves us as an indicator, as to whether a certain industry is characterized by importance of novelties in products and processes. Unfortunately, there is no direct match of industry classifications between tables 7.7 and 7.6, but the industry with the highest share of innovators in the years 1999 and 2000 is 'medical technology, optics'. This industry encloses three of the top five technologies in Jena (Optics; Analysis, measurement, control technology; Medical technology), which indicates good prospects for the competencies in Jena.

The literature on agglomeration economics suggests that the growth of

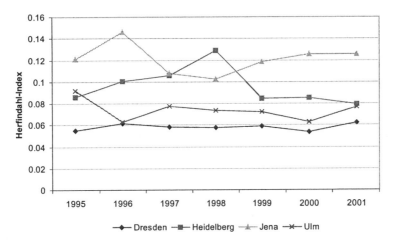

Figure 7.12: Concentration of technologies

cities is dependent on the degree of productive and/or technological special-ization and diversification (Glaeser et al., 1992). For a detailed description of the development of these aspects, we calculate the concentration of technolo-gies for each year. A high value of the Herfindahl-Index[10] indicates greater specialization, whereas low values indicate a diversified innovation system. A benchmark value is $1/n$ if the same number of patents is applied for in each out of n technological classes.

Figure 7.12 shows the development of the concentration of technologies between 1995 and 2001. Jena is the most specialized of the four regions, followed by Heidelberg, Ulm and Dresden. While Heidelberg and Ulm are becoming more diversified, Jena and Dresden seem to be more stable in their degree of concentration. These trends, which are obtained by visual inspection, are, however, not statistically significant.

The Herfindahl-index alone is not appropriate if one wants to detect shifts beyond this global measure. To investigate changes in the ranking of technologies within the innovation systems, we calculate rank correlations between consecutive years, where the ranking is based on the TRCA for each year. A value of one indicates stability between two observations (years). The other extreme of complete inversion of this measure would lead to a value of -1. As documented in figure 7.13, Ulm shows the least stability over all years, whereas Heidelberg and Dresden show a more stable pattern. In Jena, the years 1996 to 1998 show significantly more turbulence than the three consecutive years.

---

[10]$C_i = \sum_j p_{ij}^2$, where p_{ij} is the patent share of technology j in region i.

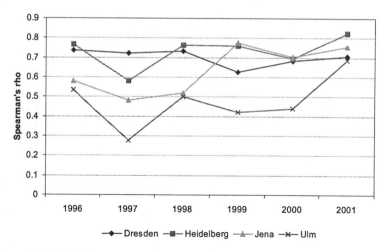

Figure 7.13: Stability of technological fields

This analysis has to be interpreted in light of the cumulative character of innovation and learning. A high stability in technologies indicates that a region pursues technological progress within its fields of competence. Deepening the local knowledge-base would seem to be more promising for innovative success, than experimenting in different fields. As long as the technological strengths provide a promising future, a certain stability should be beneficial for the local innovation system. Turbulent patterns indicate disruptive tendencies in the local knowledge-base. While this cannot be considered a positive feature as a general rule, it might well occur if technologies on the periphery of the knowledge-base provide more opportunities than formerly dominating fields. This might lead to a stronger focus of incumbents in these technologies, but might also attract entrants in these fields, as indicated by our results in chapter 6 for Jena. Of course, such a shift can also be triggered by policy, if it is the political will to attract a promising industry and establish a local cluster. Dresden, for example was able to attract some major players in the semiconductor industry. In any case, such a shift in technological opportunities and consequent turbulence should only be a temporary phenomenon.

7.3.5 Mapping the technological knowledge-base

So far, in this section, we have learned about the technological strengths of the four regions, their degree of focus on certain technologies and the development within this structure. In the following, we try to dig deeper into what is called the technological knowledge-base of a local innovation system. Systems are not only described by their composition and changes therein.

To provide a proper picture of the knowledge-base, we need to account for the linkages that exist between parts of such a system. By describing the strengths of e.g. Dresden, we do not know whether nuclear engineering is, while small, still an important part of a system as its knowledge components link certain other technologies and competencies, and therefore provide the basis for cross-fertilization effects. Neither do we know if this technology is completely different from other technological fields within that system and cannot contribute to other fields as the cognitive distance is too large, or it is just useless to be combined with other parts of knowledge.

Inspired by the work of Saviotti and co-authors (Saviotti et al., 2003), we apply social network analysis to map the knowledge-base of local innovation systems. Saviotti et al. (2003) performed this kind of analysis to investigate the knowledge-base of firms in the pharmaceutical sector (pre- and post-merger) to draw a dynamic picture and analyze whether stated goals of the management were achieved. There is no one to one correspondence to our approach, since local innovation systems are not organized in a way that makes it easy to test the achievement of managerial goals. But still, the following description of the evolution of the knowledge-bases has to be seen in the context of changed common goals in the respective period. Jena and Heidelberg, for example, were supposedly influenced by their success in the BioRegio contest. Dresden might have experienced a push towards semiconductors by the location of Infineon or AMD.

The knowledge-base (KB) of a firm is defined as the collective knowledge that a firm can use for its productive purposes (Saviotti, 1996). Thus:

> [It] evolves in the course of time, since any set of interactions modifies the KB but the interactions themselves are determined by the KB. However, the KB achieves a certain stability since the firm has a set of routines and decision rules that are modified very infrequently. The KB of a firm can thus be expected to be very specific and to have a considerable degree of path dependence.
> (Saviotti, 2004, p. 132)

Within this statement, the word 'firm' can easily be replaced by 'local innovation system' without being afraid of major criticism.

To apply this methodology, we divided our data on patents into two overlapping periods. The first period covers the years 1995 to 1998 and the second period covers 1998 to 2001. Besides the main patent class, each patent names up to six (at least in our data base) secondary classes. These secondary classes are either provided by the applicant or by patent examiners during the process of review and further specify the relevant technological fields. As patents, which share common technological classes, are assumed to be more closely related than other patents, the frequency of co-occurrence is assumed to be proportional to the intensity of the linkage (Saviotti, 2004). We use this information to link the technologies in our network in the following way: if a patent names main class i and secondary class j, there is one link between nodes i and j. The more linkages between two technologies are observed, the stronger these two are assumed to be related. We do not discriminate between giving and receiving classes; i.e. we symmetrize the resulting adjacency matrix.

We build networks for two different aggregations of patent classes. The lower level aggregates patents according to the first four digits of the International Patent classification (IPC-network). For the higher level, we assign every patent to one of the 30 technological classes according to table A.2 in the Appendix (TECH-network).

In addition to the networks statistics introduced in chapter 6, the following two statistics are calculated to describe the structure of each network in tables 7.8 and 7.9:

i) **Average distance:** The average number of edges that have to be passed between any two nodes. In disconnected networks, only reachable pairs are included.

ii) **Diameter:** Within a connected graph, the diameter is the longest distance between any two nodes. A cohesive knowledge-base is characterized by a small diameter, since the maximum cognitive distance between technologies is lower.

For the IPC-network (table 7.8), we find Jena to have the most cohesive knowledge-base. It is the network with the smallest average distance, the highest density, and the smallest diameter for both periods. Compared to Dresden and Ulm, Jena and Heidelberg are far more dense and centralized around the core of the network. Regarding the evolution of the knowledge-base, the structure of Jena does not change much. With the number of IPC-classes increasing (nodes), cohesion slightly decreases. Heidelberg and Dresden develop into different directions. Cohesion in Heidelberg increases, as density and centralization increase, with average distance and diameter decreasing, whereas for Dresden the opposite is true. Ulm becomes more focussed on core competencies between the two periods.

The TECH-networks, which are more aggregated, are described in table 7.9 and the corresponding visualizations of the knowledge-base are provided in the Appendix (figures A.2 to A.9).[11] Here, linkages between IPC-classes that belong to the same technology are absorbed into the nodes themselves. This aggregation might therefore lead to different results than in the IPC-networks.

---

[11] The network visualizations are performed with the software tool NetDraw, included in UCINET. The size of nodes is proportional to the number of patents with the main IPC classification in the respective technology. The thickness of edges is proportional to the intensity of the linkages, i.e. the number of patents that are relevant for the two or more technologies that are connected by main and secondary class. The layout options used here are multidimensional scaling with node repulsion and equal edge length bias.

Table 7.8: Local knowledge-base – IPC-network – statistics

Region	Dresden		Heidelberg		Jena		Ulm	
Network	IPC-p1	IPC-p2	IPC-p1	IPC-p2	IPC-p1	IPC-p2	IPC-p1	IPC-p2
Ave. dist.	3.954	4.004	4.375	4.152	3.443	3.537	5.165	4.752
Density	0.027	0.024	0.042	0.046	0.051	0.050	0.022	0.024
Centralization (degree)	0.321	0.298	0.659	0.709	0.684	0.682	0.169	0.184
Components	8.000	11.000	24.000	23.000	9.000	12.000	18.000	18.000
Diameter	9.000	11.000	12.000	9.000	8.000	8.000	12.000	13.000
Nodes	336	347	258	248	177	186	229	234

Table 7.9: Local knowledge-base – TECH-network – statistics

Region	Dresden		Heidelberg		Jena		Ulm	
Network	tech-p1	tech-p2	tech-p1	tech-p2	tech-p1	tech-p2	tech-p1	tech-p2
Ave. dist.	1.566	1.547	1.717	1.830	1.702	1.813	2.103	1.857
Density	2.485	2.294	2.241	2.368	1.379	1.466	0.777	1.054
Centralization (degree)	5.613	4.783	11.564	12.833	5.577	5.944	1.865	2.780
Components	1.000	1.000	1.000	2.000	3.000	1.000	1.000	1.000
Diameter	3.000	3.000	3.000	4.000	3.000	3.000	4.000	3.000
Nodes	30	30	30	30	29	29	30	29

For Dresden, this is not the case. Density and centralization develop in the same direction as above, indicating a knowledge-base of decreasing cohesion, even though the average distance slightly decreases. Heidelberg has, by far, the most centralized knowledge-base, and its increase as well as the increased density speak in favor of greater cohesion in the second period. This picture is not consistent though, as the average distance, the number of components, and the diameter increase. In Jena a similar development is observed. Increasing density and centralization is accompanied by a larger average distance in the second period. For Ulm the direction of development is clear from both types of networks. As in the IPC-network, we see increasing cohesion based on all types of measures in the technology network.

The centrality of network nodes is summarized in figure 7.14. The technologies are ranked in decreasing order of centrality scores in the first period. For the second period the positions on the x-axis are kept, so that changes in network positions correspond to upward and downward deviations from the line for the first period. A monotonous, downward sloping line for the second period would then correspond to no changes in network positions.

For Dresden, we observe a decreasing centrality of the five most central technologies of the first period, and a notable increase for semiconductors (5) and handling, printing (24), accompanied by a movement to the center by information technology (4) and telecommunications (3). These shifts suggest that the decreasing cohesiveness of the knowledge-base is due to a paradigmatic change in the local system towards an IT cluster. Comparing the most central technologies with the respective specialization index, we find only a weak correspondence for Dresden. Out of the five technologies mentioned in table 7.6, only surface technology, coating (17) is ranked in the top five according to centrality in both periods, and semiconductors (5) only in the second period. To evaluate the technological strength of a region, one has to take account of both types of measures. All-purpose technologies such as analysis, measurement, control technology (7) are probably central in many regions, because of their volume and breadth in applications, but they do not have to be a specific strength of the respective region. A comparative advantage in peripheral technology is not necessarily a core competence of a region.

In Heidelberg, the success in the BioRegio contest becomes evident in the changing position of biotechnology (12) and related fields. Organic fine chemistry (9), which is strongly related to biotechnology (as can be seen in figures A.-7 and A.-6) becomes even more central as well as analysis, measurement, control technology (7), which is an important field in linking different technologies (see the position of this technology in the other four regions). Technologies associated with the large local company Heidelberger Druck, like materials processing, textiles, paper (18) or handling, printing (24) are not that central and even lose positions despite their large patent numbers.

Here, the correspondence between specialization and centrality is higher. Organic fine chemistry (9), biotechnology (12), and macromolecular chemistry, polymers (10) are top-ranked according to both measures and therefore can be considered the core competence fields in Heidelberg.

In Jena, this correspondence is even higher. Except for biotechnology (12), all technologies, in which Jena is specialized, are also central parts of the knowledge-base (Optics (6); Analysis, measurement, control technology (7); Pharmaceuticals, cosmetics (11); Medical technology (8)). The curves in figure 7.14, also suggest a rather solidified structure of technologies in Jena. In contrast to Heidelberg, the gained importance of biotechnology (12) is not as pronounced, but also accompanied by a more central position of organic fine chemistry (9). This difference comes as no surprise, as the concept of Jena in the BioRegio contest focussed on bioinstruments as a specific part of the biotechnology, where the historical competencies (optics, instruments) are of strategic importance.

Finally, in Ulm, we observe the most dramatic changes in the local knowledge-base (consistent with figure 7.13). Major positive shifts in centrality arise in analysis, measurement, control technology (7), transport (26), chemical engineering (16), and especially materials, metallurgy (13). The negative development of telecommunications (3), electrical machinery and apparatus, electrical energy (1), macromolecular chemistry, polymers (10), and medical technology (8) is comparatively small. Telecommunications (3) scores high in the TRCA as well as centrality, materials, metallurgy (13) and chemical engineering (16) become central only in the second period. Altogether, these changes lead to the observed increase in cohesion of the knowledge-base.

Summarizing the analysis of the local knowledge-base, we find Heidelberg and Jena to be deepening their competencies, following their traditional strengths. Dresden and Ulm, on the other hand, seem to open up new trajectories for their future development and show therefore more turbulence with respect to the central technological strengths.

Some qualitative evidence for a relationship between system structure and performance is gained by comparing the regions pairwise. Average annual growth rates between 1992 and 2000 are higher in the innovation systems that show greater cohesion of the knowledge-base, more interaction, and stronger innovativeness. Jena grows by 8.0% on average, while Dresden grows slower by 6.9% per year. Within the second pair in the same macro environment, Heidelberg (2.3%) outperforms Ulm (0.9%).

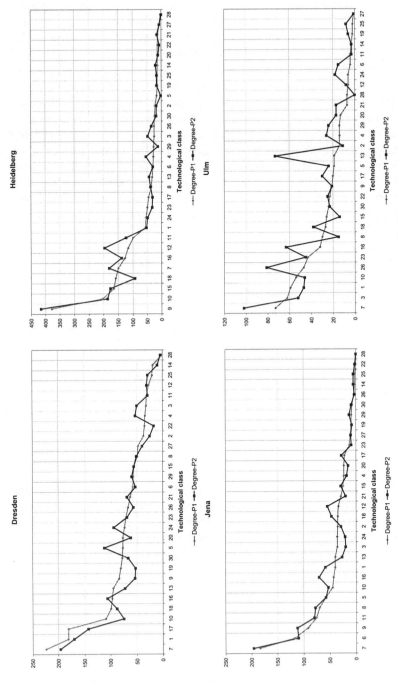

Figure 7.14: Centrality (degree) scores of technological classes within the knowledge-base of regions

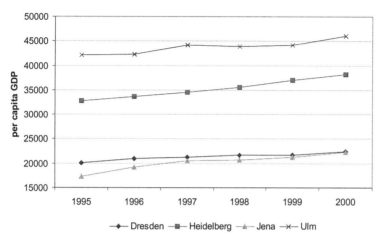

Figure 7.15: Development of regional per capita GDP (1995 prices)

7.4 ECONOMIC DEVELOPMENT

7.4.1 Regional GDP

From a welfare point of view, creativity and innovation are not ends in themselves. Rather, they are an intermediate step towards economic growth and wealth. If the economic consequences of technological change were not clear, the demands for technological progress would not be eligible. Even though, this chapter is mainly concerned with the analysis of innovation activities as well as technological structures and their development, this last section tries to give an answer to the question of whether the positive picture that is drawn for Jena translates to economic success.

We use data on regional GDP to characterize economic development between 1995 and 2000. Economic wealth is indicated by per capita GDP. To account for difference in the dynamics of the systems, we use growth rates of regional GDP.

In the given framework it is difficult to assess direct connections between technological characteristics and economic wealth. The period that is covered by this study is definitely too short, as there are many time lags and uncertainties involved – from the creative act to the application of a patent and further to a successful product. Taking a glance at figure 7.15, it becomes clear that the macroeconomic environment between the eastern and the western regions is dominating the differences. The figures might serve as a basis for speculation, though. The example of Ulm shows that a strong market pole, where innovations are commercialized, is necessary for a good economic performance. In

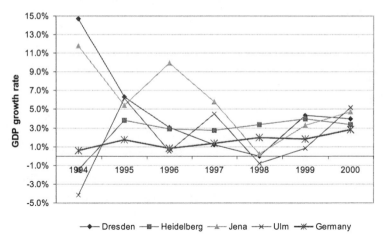

Figure 7.16: Regional GDP growth rates

2000 per capita GDP is 17% higher than in Heidelberg. Jena and Dresden, with a similar sectoral structure, also show a similar per capita GDP in 2000. Jena is growing faster than Dresden and is able to reduce the gap from 13.8% in 1995 to 1.1% in 2000.

To go further into the dynamics, regional growth rates are compared with the German average in figure 7.16. After the high growth rates that followed the transformation process in the New Länder in the beginning of the 1990s, the process of catching-up, where growth rates were far higher than the national average, seems to have stopped in Jena and Dresden in 1998 and 1997 respectively. In 1999 and 2000 growth is above the national average and on a similar level as Heidelberg, which constantly grows faster than Germany as a whole, whereas development in Ulm is subject to greater fluctuations.

7.4.2 Employment

High unemployment is a dramatic problem for every society and full employment is a central goal for government from a socio-political and from a fiscal point of view. How is unemployment to be judged from the perspective of innovation systems? On the one hand, innovation is related to creativity and risk taking but, on the other hand, successful innovation is also related to the acceptance of novelties in society, be it consumers, employees, or potential entrepreneurs. High unemployment leads to frustration, which might give rise to a hostile attitude towards people from outside the system. External contacts and external knowledge are essential to the functioning of innovation systems, though.

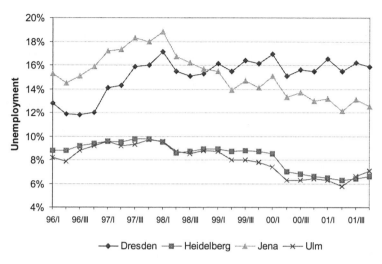

Figure 7.17: Unemployment

The large gap between unemployment rates in the eastern and the western parts of Germany is also present in this comparative study. Jena and Dresden have to deal with unemployment of 12.5% and 15.9% by the end of 2001, while unemployment in Heidelberg (6.6%) and Ulm (7.1%) is significantly lower. In all four regions, unemployment rises until 1998 and falls again, except in Dresden, where it remains high and fluctuates around 16%. One possible explanation for the continuous decline can be found in the analysis of chapter 5, where the years 1997 until 2001 are characterized by high numbers of new establishments. These newly founded firms might well be responsible for the generation of new job positions.

7.5 OVERALL PICTURE

Summarizing the findings of this chapter, we end up with, at least, two characteristics of the regions which let them fall into different categories. There are clear differences between Jena and Dresden on the one hand, and Ulm and Heidelberg on the other, which are due to history. Differences in unemployment, regional GDP, and the patenting behavior of the universities are to be named here. A consequence of the last point might also explain the lower usage of external knowledge in the innovation systems located in the eastern part of Germany, but even within the rather short time-span covered, these differences are already diminishing.

If the categories are set more internal to the systems of innovation, we find more similarities within the pairs Jena/Heidelberg and Dresden/Ulm. Jena and Heidelberg have dominating universities, a high degree of interaction and a clear technological focus. In this sense, they come closer to what is understood as a well functioning innovation system than the other two. Dresden and Ulm experience shifts in the local knowledge-base, whereby they lose some of the locally accumulated knowledge. This structural change leads to comparatively lower performance in welfare, but at least in Ulm, not in patenting.

8. Conclusions

The central research objectives of this study were to apply the innovation system approach to the East-German city of Jena and to employ novel methodology by applying social network analysis to the local system of innovating actors and the technological knowledge-base. We were interested in the local innovation system of Jena, since it is often named as an outstanding example for prospering economic development in the eastern part of Germany. The press has given labels like 'Silicon Valley des Ostens' or 'Boomtown des Ostens' and only recently, Jena was included as one of nine 'Stille Stars' (silent stars) in a series by the German newspaper *Handelsblatt*.

The fact that social network analysis, as well as the SI approach, is based on the assumption that relationships among interacting units are of critical importance, makes it almost inevitable that this methodology should be integrated with empirical research on innovation systems, but as yet only few applications exist. As the concluding sections of each chapter already summarize the findings of the respective parts of this research project, the purpose of this concluding chapter is to recapitulate on the structure of the study, to place the research results in a general perspective, and to identify prospects for subsequent research.

8.1 STRUCTURE

Within the theoretical, literature-based part, we sketched the roots of innovation as a systemic process and introduced the levels on which innovation systems are analyzed. Further, we provided explanations for economic differences at the regional level in terms of agglomeration economies which are thought to shape the geographical landscape of economic activity. Knowledge spillovers were identified as one factor which is especially important for the geography of innovative activity. The focus of analysis then shifted to regional and local innovation systems, an approach which is capable of explaining how interaction in the process of knowledge generation can influence the innovative success of regions. This approach is more interested in how these local spillovers are generated and mediated than merely providing evidence for their existence. Furthermore, it was suggested that local systems have to be considered as parts of the relevant technological and national systems to explain why – and to where – interactions, external to the local system, are directed.

The empirical part of this study was organized around the analysis of the local innovation system of Jena from different perspectives. In the first perspective, we made observations about the embeddedness of Jena within the national and technological systems. In search for specificities, we conducted a survey of high-tech firms in Jena. Thereby we could identify the actors, different modes of interaction, and the specific strengths of Jena. While the survey provided useful results at one point in time, we used information on filed patents to describe the evolution of the network over a longer time period. Thereby we could visualize explicit ties between local firms and research institutions via their overlap in technological competencies and contacts of the people who work for or own these organizations. Following this in-depth description of the local network, we again widened the view in comparing the local structures and innovative performance of Jena with three other successful cities in Germany.

We acknowledge that patent data, even though it is frequently used in studies on innovation, is subject to criticism and assuredly has some drawbacks. Despite the problems with the usage of patent data, we found similar results for local characteristics in other studies and in using survey data. Especially for comparative studies on innovation systems, patents provide an important data input.

8.2   RESEARCH RESULTS

Our main research results can be divided into findings that are specific to Jena and findings that are generally applicable. In particular, the results with a general claim guide the direction of further research as they state relationships which have to be tested in other settings. Other research questions open up as the developed tools are applied to other innovation systems and further improved.

The general picture that we could draw for Jena provides evidence for a successful innovation system which clearly stands out within the rest of eastern Germany. Jena is capable of competing not only with the average region in western Germany but with the most successful ones when it comes to the generation of technological knowledge.

Our approach towards interaction in the process of innovation at the regional level allowed us to compare Jena with the 'average' German region. In the econometric model, we included variables on the level of the technology-region, the region and the technology in our analysis to account for geographical as well as industrial or technological characteristics. Jena turned out to be a highly interactive region, where the relationships are largely internal to the innovation system.

Whether the internal cooperation in patenting is accompanied by internal relationships in other fields of economic interaction was questioned in a survey of high-technology firms in Jena. The resulting picture was in line with the previous finding, but additionally provided information about differences between trade-related and knowledge-related interaction: while local interaction is strong in the process of knowledge generation and entrepreneurship, it is comparatively weak in terms of product flows along the value chain.

The local university arises as a central player in the local innovation system. The results of our survey showed that its central functions are the education of the labor force, being a partner for cooperative research, and to spawn academic start-ups. Network analysis showed that the university became the most central actor in the networks of technological overlap and personal contacts (via cooperation and scientist mobility).

Jena has its technological strengths in the technological classes of optics, biotechnology, and analysis, measurement, control technology. We found that the local innovation system is characterized by a deepening of these core competencie, which can be explained by an evolutionary process where innovating entrants work on similar problems as the core members of the network and exiting innovators have rather worked in fields less related to the network core.

Results that are more generally applicable were obtained with respect to cooperation in R&D. In line with previous studies, we found that partners in cooperation need similar levels of competence in a related knowledge-base. On the level of the technology-region, the problem of finding adequate cooperation partners leads to the observation that moderately specialized technology-regions are the ones that cooperate most, since they are open to a larger pool of potential partners. It also showed that a higher degree of specialization goes along with a higher share of internal interaction, which is in line with the hypothesis that local interaction is stronger in clusters of related activities. With respect to the mechanisms that lead to the partnering decision, we found the scientists' mobility of major importance; i.e. uncertainty is reduced and trust is already existent if the partners know each other as former colleagues.

8.3 PROSPECTS

Possibilities for further research open up as the tools and the methodology developed in this study can be applied to other local innovation systems or other types of innovation systems. In future studies of innovation systems, the usage of social network analysis might be refined as we explicitly account for different types of ties or as techniques for network regressions are improved.

Also the existing gap between theoretical work on network dynamics and empirical work has to be closed. The predictions of theoretical work on the relationships between network structure and performance can be tested in panel or cross-section studies of innovation systems. In analyzing network data over longer periods, the premise that network dynamics generally lead to more efficient structures could also be tested. Regarding the efficiency of innovation systems the role of specific types of actors would be of special interest. Some organizations such as universities have to be in the focus as they are strongly engaged in education as well as generation of technological knowledge. An innovation system should only be able to benefit from such an institution if it is embedded in the system.

A mid- or long-term threat to every innovation system is the risk of technological lock-in. It has been argued that especially larger players can afford the resources to establish and maintain external relations as they cooperate, but also as they attract skilled workers and scientists from abroad. To test these arguments we will need to analyze specific actors within the network in how they are capable of serving this important function. Research on related aspects will have to relate the integration of local systems within the technological and national systems to long-term success in innovation.

Also, some results, such as the factors that influence cooperative R&D, could be tested for other regions to find out if our results can be generalized or if they are specific to Jena.

Finally, more research is necessary to understand how, when, and under which circumstances technological success leads to economic success. If the specific configuration of a local innovation system shows that the scientific pole has a strong position and the economic pole a weak one, too much focusing on the generation of knowledge might leave the economic benefits to other regions.

Appendix

Table A.1: Bivariate correlation between variables in the sample: N=9648

	(1)	(2)	(3)	(4)	(5)	(6)	(7)
(1) Specialization index (RSCA)	1.000	0.031	-0.056	0.077	-0.170	-0.225	-0.132
(2) University patents (UNI)	0.031	1.000	0.225	0.043	-0.051	0.011	0.053
(3) Population (POP)	-0.056	0.225	1.000	0.343	-0.254	0.053	0.059
(4) Technological diversity (DI)	0.077	0.043	0.343	1.000	-0.231	0.044	-0.174
(5) Concentration of innovators in tech-region (HERF)	-0.170	-0.051	-0.254	-0.231	1.000	0.219	0.003
(6) Geographical concentration of technology (HERFTEC)	-0.225	0.011	0.053	0.044	0.219	1.000	0.027
(7) Average firm size in region (FIRMSIZE)	-0.132	0.053	0.059	-0.174	0.003	0.027	1.000

Table A.2: Concordance between IPC and technology codes

Industry Technology	IPC-Code
I. ELECTRICAL ENGINEERING	
1. Electrical machinery and apparatus, electrical energy	F21; G05F; H01B, C, F, G, H, J, K, M, R, T; H02; H05B, C, F, K
2. Audiovisual technology	G09F, G; G11B; H03F, G, J; H04N-003, -005, -009, -013, -015, -017, R, S
3. Telecommunications	G08C; H01P, Q; H03B, C, D, H, K, L, M; H04B, H, J, K, L, M, N-001, -007, -011, Q
4. Information technology	G06; G11C; G10L
5. Semiconductors	H01L, B81
II. INSTRUMENTS	
6. Optics	G02; G03B, C, D, F, G, H; H01S
7. Analysis, measurement, control technology	G01B, C, D, F, G, H, J, K, L, M, N, P, R, S, V, W; G04; G05B, D; G07; G08B, G; G09B, C, D; G12
8. Medical technology	A61B, C, D, F, G, H, J, L, M, N
9. Nuclear engineering	G01T; G21; H05G, H
III. CHEMISTRY, PHARMACEUTICALS	
10. Organic fine chemistry	C07C, D, F, H, J, K
11. Pharmaceuticals, cosmetics	A61K, P
12. Biotechnology	C07G; C12M, N, P, Q, R, S
13. Agriculture, food chemistry	A01H; A21D; A23B, C, D, F, G, J, K, L; C12C, F, G, H, J; C13D, F, J, K
14. Materials, metallurgy	C01; C03C; C04; C21; C22; B22; B82
15. Surface technology, coating	B05C, D; B32; C23; C25; C30
16. Macromolecular chemistry, polymers	C08B, F, G, H, K, L; C09D, J
17. Chemical industry and petrol industry, basic materials chemistry	A01N; C05; C07B; C08C; C09B, C, F, G, H, K; C10B, C, F, G, H, J, K, L, M; C11B, C, D
IV. PROCESS ENGINEERING, SPECIAL EQUIPMENT	
18. Chemical engineering	B01B, D (without -046 to -053), F, J, L; B02C; B03; B04; B05B; B06; B07; B08; F25J; F26
19. Materials processing, textiles, paper	A41H; A43D; A46D; B28; B29; B31; C03B; C08J; C14; D01; D02; D03; D04B, C, G, H; D05; D06B, C, G, H, J, L, M, P, Q; D21
20. Handling, printing	B25J; B41; B65B, C, D, F, G, H; B66; B67
21. Agricultural and food machinery and apparatus	A01B, C, D, F, G, J, K, L, M; A21B, C; A22; A23N, P; B02B; C12L; C13C, G, H
22. Environmental technology	A62D; B01D-046 to -053; B09; C02; F01N; F23G, J
V. MECHANICAL ENGINEERING, MACHINERY	
23. Machine tools	B21; B23; B24; B26D, F; B27; B30
24. Engines, pumps, turbines	F01B, C, D, K, L, M, P; F02; F03; F04; F23R
25. Thermal processes and apparatus	F22; F23B, C, D, H, K, L, M, N, Q; F24; F25B, C; F27; F28
26. Mechanical elements	F15; F16; F17; G05G
27. Transport	B60; B61; B62; B63B, C, H, J; B64B, C, D, F
28. Space technology, weapons	B63G; B64G; C06; F41; F42
29. Consumer goods and equipment	A24; A41B, C, D, F, G; A42; A43B, C; A44; A45; A46B; A47; A62B, C; A63; B25B, C, D, F, G, H; B26B; B42; B43; B44; B68; D04D; D06F,N ; D07; F25D; G10B, C, D, F, G, H, K
30. Civil engineering, building, mining	E01; E02; E03; E04; E05; E06; E21

CONDUCT OF THE SURVEY

Between May and July 2002, we asked 173 firms to take part in our survey. Starting with two lists[1] of local firms provided by the local chamber of commerce (IHK Ostthüringen), we selected firms in high-tech industries according to the listing in table A.3. The resulting list included 293 companies located in the city of Jena. The firms were then arranged in random order and the first 100 firms were approached to be interviewed. If there was a negative response, the next firms on the list were contacted. The interviews, based on the questionnaire in figure A.1, were conducted by pairs of economics and business students of the Friedrich Schiller University, Jena, who were instructed by Dirk Fornahl and the author. At the end of the survey, 173 companies had been addressed, 93 of which responded (return rate: 53.8%). The questionnaire was designed by Dirk Fornahl and the author, under the supervision of Uwe Cantner and Ulrich Witt. Thomas Brenner, Silke Scheer, Veronika von Lintel, and Jens Krüger provided helpful comments.

Table A.3: Selected industries

NACE	Industry	Short*
22	Publishing, printing and reproduction of recorded media	publishing
24	Manufacture of chemicals and chemical products	chemicals
25	Manufacture of rubber and plastic products	none
26	Manufacture of other non-metallic products (glass, ceramics)	other
27	Manufacture of basic metals	metals
28	Manufacture of fabricated metal products, except machinery and equipment	metal products
29	Manufacture of machinery and equipment	machinery
30	Manufacture of office machinery and computers	other
31	Manufacture of electrical machinery and apparatus	other
32	Manufacture of radio, television, and communication equipment and apparatus	other
33	Manufacture of medical, precision and optical instruments, watches and clocks	optics
34	Manufacture of motor vehicles, trailers and semi-trailers	none
37	Recycling	none
40	Electricity, gas, steam and hot water supply	other
41	Collection, purification, and distribution of water	none
72	Computer and related activities	data processing
73	Research and development	R&D
74	Other business activities	services
including only:		
742	Architectural and engineering activities and related technical consultancy	
743	Technical testing and analysis	

Notes: * Short labels of the respective industry are used in text and figures, 'none' if no firms in that industry are present in the sample, 'other' meaning an aggregate of industries with a small number of firms in the sample.

[1] One list provided directly by the IHK and the second obtained from the internet site of the IHK, http://unternehmen.gera.ihk.de, queried May 2002.

MAX-PLANCK-GESELLSCHAFT
Max-Planck-Institut
zur Erforschung von Wirtschaftssystemen
Max Planck Institute for Research into Economic Systems
Abteilung Evolutionsökonomik

seit 1558
Friedrich-Schiller-Universität Jena

Wirtschaftswissenschaftliche Fakultät
Lehrstuhl für Volkswirtschaftslehre/Mikroökonomik

Questionnaire concerning the founding of a company and of innovative systems in Jena

For us to get a better idea of companies within Jena and to compare your answers with other sources of information (Patent data base), we would be grateful if you could mention the name of your company. **Any given details will be kept strictly confidential.** This means, your information will not be passed on to any third party. Any analysis gained as a result of this questionnaire, will only be publicised in such a way that no links can be made with any company.

Name of firm: _____

<u>Questions regarding your person</u>

Position respectively.
Your area of responsibility: _____

Were you part of the original founding team?   Yes ❑ No ❑

If „No", since when have you been working for this company? (Year)   _____

Thank you for your assistance!

Name of the Interviewer: _____

Figure A.1: Questionnaire

1. General Information to Company

1.1. When was your company founded? (month and year)   _____

1.2. Since when is your company based in Jena? (month and year)   _____

1.3. How many people founded the company?   _____

1.4. How many employees does your company have?   _____

1.5. In what branch are you primarily active? (Please choose a branch number from the list attached.)   _____

1.6. Please describe briefly your company's field of work (For example, Bioinformatics, Web-Design, Laser or e-commerce).

1.7. Is your company part of a corporate group?   Yes ❑   No ❑

1.8. If yes, please name the parent company.   _____

1.9. If your company is not based in Jena, please select the relevant region.

Thuringia	Germany	Europe (EU)	World
❑	❑	❑	❑

2. General information to the founders

2.1. How many of the founders had before they founded this company already set up other companies? (number)   _____

2.2. How many of the founders before setting up the company had lived and worked in Jena? (number)   _____

2.3. What connection did you have with Jena before the company was founded? (Multiple answers are possible)

Connection	Yes?	Connection	Yes?
Birth	❑	Studies	❑
Job. Training	❑	Promotion	❑
Dependant employment	❑	Other:	❑

If "Other", please specify: _____

2.4. How many of the founders before setting up the company had no connection to Jena? (number)   _____

Figure A.1: Questionnaire (continued)

---

3. Business Idea

Questions will be asked in this section that relate to the founding process. If you did not belong to the founding team, we would like to ask you to let this section be filled out by one of the founders. This section of questions is split up into three chronological areas: 1) The time spent actively looking for a business idea, 2) The time after finding a business idea and the search after product ideas as well as 3) The founding decision time.

3.1. How many of the founders searched actively for a fundamental business idea, that is for example invested time and financial means in the search, because they intended to set up a company? (number) _____

3.2. How many of these actively searching persons had economic training / degree? (number) _____

3.3. Which of the following factors was relevant for the people actively searching in the Decision to search? (More than one answer is possible)

Friends and acquaintances also searched for founding possibilities	❑	(Imminent) Unemployment ❑
Friends and acquaintances have also set up a company	❑	The strive after money ❑
National founding mood	❑	The strive after self-fulfilment ❑
Regional founding mood	❑	The strive to be self-employed ❑
Other:	❑	

If "Other", please specify: _____

3.4. Which factors respectively which technological areas influenced the active search for setting up a company in this business sector?

_____

_____

3.5. When did the fundamental business idea come into being? (month and year) _____

3.6. When did the first product idea come into being? (month and year) _____

3.7. Were product ideas actively searched for?   Yes ❑   No ❑   Do not know ❑

3.8. How strongly were these products modified during the time elapsed?

Strongly ❑   Weakly ❑   Not at all ❑   Do not know ❑

3.9. When did the product idea come to being, which the company introduced to the market respectively. will introduce? (month and year) _____

3.10. How important were the following factors to the point in time as the product idea came into being and were they relevant?

	Occurrence			Relevant	
	Often	Sometimes	Rarely	Yes	No
Other companies were founded with similar ideas	❑	❑	❑	❑	❑
Research results opened up new possibilities	❑	❑	❑	❑	❑
Increasing demand for products in the focused sector	❑	❑	❑	❑	❑
Many other companies were founded	❑	❑	❑	❑	❑
Other:_____	❑	❑	❑	❑	❑

3.11. When was it decided to set up the company? (month and year) _____

Figure A.1: Questionnaire (continued)

3.12. Were the following factors present at the point in time as the company was founded and were they relevant for the founding of the company?

	Factors?			Relevant	
	Yes	Partly	No	Yes	No
A patent was pending	❑	❑	❑	❑	❑
A product idea respectively, business plan had been drafted	❑	❑	❑	❑	❑
The prototype was finished respectively, the idea was ready for the market	❑	❑	❑	❑	❑
Good market opportunities	❑	❑	❑	❑	❑
Venture Capital obtained	❑	❑	❑	❑	❑
(Imminent) Unemployment	❑	❑	❑	❑	❑
Good founding mood	❑	❑	❑	❑	❑
Friends and acquaintances have also founded companies	❑	❑	❑	❑	❑
Good opportunity to earn money	❑	❑	❑	❑	❑
Good opportunity for self-fulfilment	❑	❑	❑	❑	❑
Other:_____	❑	❑	❑	❑	❑

3.13. Have the founders prepared especially for the founding?   Yes ❑   No ❑

3.14. At which preparation possibilities did the founders take part in? If they took part, please tell us which of these possibilities were useful for the setting up activities?

		If taken part, please note usefulness			
	Took part	Very helpful	A little helpful	Not helpful	Do not know
GET-UP Seminar	❑	❑	❑	❑	❑
Adult Education Centre	❑	❑	❑	❑	❑
Exchange with other founders	❑	❑	❑	❑	❑
Chamber of commerce and industry-Offers	❑	❑	❑	❑	❑
Other founding seminars	❑	❑	❑	❑	❑
Other	❑	❑	❑	❑	❑

If "Other", please specify: _____

3.15. How would you evaluate the commercial competence of the founders to the time of the company founding?

Do not know Continue with 3.17	Very Good 1	2	3	4	Inadequate 5
❑	❑	❑	❑	❑	❑

3.16. Retrospectively would you say, that the evaluation of the founders regarding their commercial competence back then...

Was overrated?	Was adequately evaluated?	Was underestimated?	Do not know (yet)
❑	❑	❑	❑

Figure A.1: Questionnaire (continued)

3.17. How would you evaluate the technological competence of the founders to the time of the company founding?

Do not know Continue with 3.19	Very Good 1	2	3	4	Inadequate 5
❑	❑	❑	❑	❑	❑

3.18. Retrospectively would you say, that the evaluation of the founders regarding their technological competence back then...

Was overrated?	Was adequately evaluated?	Was underestimated?	Do not know (yet)
❑	❑	❑	❑

3.19. Please check the relevant box, which of the following years would you consider to have been a bad year to found a company? (Multiple answers are possible)

Before 1993	1993	1994	1995	1996	1997	1998	1999	2000	2001	2002
❑	❑	❑	❑	❑	❑	❑	❑	❑	❑	❑

3.20. Please check the relevant box, which of the following years would you consider to have been a good year to found a company? (Multiple answers are possible)

Before 1993	1993	1994	1995	1996	1997	1998	1999	2000	2001	2002
❑	❑	❑	❑	❑	❑	❑	❑	❑	❑	❑

3.21. Please note down the following factor characteristics for the different years. Note the quantity / quality of the factors in the different years. Use a ,+' for a particularly good year, a ,o' for an average year and a ,-' for a bad year.

	before 93	93	94	95	96	97	98	99	00	01	02
Good regional founding mood											
Good national founding mood											
Venture Capital present											
By setting up a company a good opportunity to earn money											
Lots of friends and acquaintances have set up companies											
Market demand high											
Other employment opportunities were limited											
Transfer of information and advice through other founders											
Political support for setting up companies was strong											
Other:											

If "Other", please specify: _____

Figure A.1: Questionnaire (continued)

4. Market Conditions

Please note down, how you prepared yourself for the market conditions before setting up your company, and order the competitor situation using the mentioned categories into their main distribution sectors.

4.1. Did you carry out market studies before setting up your company?   Yes ❑   No ❑

4.2. How did you carry out these market studies and does the reality today deviate from the prognoses obtained? (positive = better Market growth than was forecast) (More than one answer is possible)

		Deviation				
	Usage	Very positive	Positive	Not at all	Negative	Very negative
Internet research	❑	❑	❑	❑	❑	❑
Questioning of potential customers	❑	❑	❑	❑	❑	❑
Your own experience or feeling for the market	❑	❑	❑	❑	❑	❑
A professional market research institute	❑	❑	❑	❑	❑	❑
Venture-Capital-Provider for example a bank	❑	❑	❑	❑	❑	❑
Discussions with other company founders	❑	❑	❑	❑	❑	❑
Other	❑	❑	❑	❑	❑	❑

If "Other", please specify: _____

If possible please note down an explanation for the deviations : _____

4.3. How many companies are you directly competing with?

Do not know	0	≤5	≤10	>10
❑	❑	❑	❑	❑

4.4. How many of your strongest competitors are based in the following areas?

	Jena	Thuringia	Germany	Europe (EU)	World
Number	___	___	___	___	___

4.5. Is there one or more regions where the most of your competitors are based, and if so which regions are they? (The term *Region* in this case covers a smaller area, for example, Silicon Valley, southern England or Munich, but not south east Asia or the USA)

_____

4.6. Please not down your stand point to the following statements.

	This statement I...		
	...agree with.	...partly agree with.	...do not agree with.
Local competitors for our company mean incentive and motivation and we evaluate it therefore positively	❑	❑	❑
The company's location in Jena is strengthened by competing companies	❑	❑	❑
Through the increase of competitors locally it is becoming more important to keep know-how secret.	❑	❑	❑
A good relationship to our competitors is important for us.	❑	❑	❑

Figure A.1: Questionnaire (continued)

5. Business partners

5.1. What proportion of your turnover do you achieve through sales to companies within the region Jena?

0 - 20 %	20 - 40 %	40 - 60 %	60 - 80 %	80 - 100 %
❑	❑	❑	❑	❑

5.2. How many customers are needed to reach this proportion?   _____

5.3. Which part of your input did you get out of the region Jena?

0 - 20 %	20 - 40 %	40 - 60 %	60 - 80 %	80 - 100 %
❑	❑	❑	❑	❑

5.4. From how many companies in Jena did you receive this input?   _____

6. Innovation Activity

6.1. How many of your employees are predominantly occupied with research and development? (Number)   _____

6.2. How much of your turnover do you use for research and development purposes? (In %)   _____

6.3. How high is the turnover proportion of products, that are...

...not older than a year?	...1 to 3 years old?	...3 to 5 years old?
_____	_____	_____

6.4. How innovative would you say your company is compared with your competitors?

leading	Above average	average	Below average	Not innovative
❑	❑	❑	❑	❑

7. Increasing capacity (Planning)

Are you planning on increasing capacity in one of the years mentioned below and if so I how large a quantity? If you have no plans in undertaking something in this sector, please skip this section and carry onto question 8.

7.1. Increasing production capacity

	Year(s)				
	2002		2003 - 2004		2005 - 2006
Increasing capacity	Yes ❑	No ❑	Yes ❑ No ❑	Yes ❑	No ❑
Amount (Thousand €)	_____		_____		_____

7.2. Increasing the amount of employees

	2002		2003 - 2004		2005 - 2006
Employing	Yes ❑	No ❑	Yes ❑ No ❑	Yes ❑	No ❑
Number	_____		_____		_____

7.3. Expansion in the sector research and development

	2002		2003 - 2004		2005 - 2006
Increasing capacity	Yes ❑	No ❑	Yes ❑ No ❑	Yes ❑	No ❑
Amount (Thousand €)	_____		_____		_____

Figure A.1: Questionnaire (continued)

8. Deciding Location (Influencing factors)

This section deals with your assessment to the point in time as the company was founded/established, if the decision was made after 1990, as well as an actual evaluation.

8.1. When making the decision to locate your company did you also consider other locations, if so how many? No ☐   Yes ☐   Number: ___

8.2. Have the following factors influenced your decision to choose the location Jena for your company (Relevance)? Please assess the situation in Jena at that time considering the given factors on a scale from 1 (very good) to 5 (inadequate). Please also note down, if the situation presently compared to back then, has improved or worsened.

	Relevant		Assessment made to the point in time as the company was founded					Change compared to the present day		
	Yes	No	Very Good ←			→ Inadequate		better	The same	worse
			1	2	3	4	5			
Venture Capital	☐	☐	☐	☐	☐	☐	☐	☐	☐	☐
Government Funds	☐	☐	☐	☐	☐	☐	☐	☐	☐	☐
Qualified Workers	☐	☐	☐	☐	☐	☐	☐	☐	☐	☐
Low wages	☐	☐	☐	☐	☐	☐	☐	☐	☐	☐
Founding centres	☐	☐	☐	☐	☐	☐	☐	☐	☐	☐
Industrial Real Estate	☐	☐	☐	☐	☐	☐	☐	☐	☐	☐
Personal social network	☐	☐	☐	☐	☐	☐	☐	☐	☐	☐
Transportation infrastructure	☐	☐	☐	☐	☐	☐	☐	☐	☐	☐
IT-Infrastructure	☐	☐	☐	☐	☐	☐	☐	☐	☐	☐
Quality of Life (Landscape, Culture)	☐	☐	☐	☐	☐	☐	☐	☐	☐	☐
The city Jena its image	☐	☐	☐	☐	☐	☐	☐	☐	☐	☐
Universities...										
As (possible) co-operation partners	☐	☐	☐	☐	☐	☐	☐	☐	☐	☐
For utilisation of facilities	☐	☐	☐	☐	☐	☐	☐	☐	☐	☐
As a training centre	☐	☐	☐	☐	☐	☐	☐	☐	☐	☐
Research institutes...										
As (possible) co-operation partners	☐	☐	☐	☐	☐	☐	☐	☐	☐	☐
For utilisation of facilities	☐	☐	☐	☐	☐	☐	☐	☐	☐	☐
As a training centre	☐	☐	☐	☐	☐	☐	☐	☐	☐	☐
Rival Businesses...										
As (possible) co-operation partners	☐	☐	☐	☐	☐	☐	☐	☐	☐	☐
As a training centre	☐	☐	☐	☐	☐	☐	☐	☐	☐	☐
The pursuit of similar interests	☐	☐	☐	☐	☐	☐	☐	☐	☐	☐

Figure A.1: Questionnaire (continued)

Other companies...										
As (possible) co-operation partners	❑	❑	❑	❑	❑	❑	❑	❑	❑	❑
As a training centre	❑	❑	❑	❑	❑	❑	❑	❑	❑	❑
For utilisation of facilities	❑	❑	❑	❑	❑	❑	❑	❑	❑	❑
As a supplier	❑	❑	❑	❑	❑	❑	❑	❑	❑	❑
As a customer	❑	❑	❑	❑	❑	❑	❑	❑	❑	❑

Other reasons _____

9. Regional and personal founding context

9.1. How was your decision to establish a company influenced through other founders out of your town / region?

Very positively	Positively	No influence	Negative	Very negative	Do not know
❑	❑	❑	❑	❑	❑

9.2. In what manner were the general conditions for establishing a company in your town / region influenced by the activities of other founders / or founded companies? How strong was their influence (Strong)? Have these factors affected your decision to establish a company (relevance)? If you happen to remember an example of such a founding, please name it in the last column.

Type and manner	Influence			Relevance		Example
	Strong	Light	Not at all	Yes	No	
A customer of our products und / or co-operations partner	❑	❑	❑	❑	❑	_____
They gave information and advice	❑	❑	❑	❑	❑	_____
They showed that it is possible to establish a successful company	❑	❑	❑	❑	❑	_____
Have made the town / region internationally well known	❑	❑	❑	❑	❑	_____
Have improved the political backing for founders	❑	❑	❑	❑	❑	_____
Have eased the access to capital (Venture Capital, stock exchange, etc.)	❑	❑	❑	❑	❑	_____

Other important influences from other founders:

_____

_____

Figure A.1: Questionnaire (continued)

9.3.   Which of the following persons is or was self-employed (before you established your company)? If one of the persons was self-employed, please note down how they influenced you by your own founding consideration.

	Self-employed?	manner of influence				
		Strongly positive	Positive	No influence	Negative	Strongly negative
Father / Mother	❑	❑	❑	❑	❑	❑
Grandparents	❑	❑	❑	❑	❑	❑
Rest of the family	❑	❑	❑	❑	❑	❑
partner	❑	❑	❑	❑	❑	❑
Close circle of friends	❑	❑	❑	❑	❑	❑
Work- / research groups	❑	❑	❑	❑	❑	❑
People out of University	❑	❑	❑	❑	❑	❑
People out of University	❑	❑	❑	❑	❑	❑

10. Employees

10.1. Qualification

    a) How many of your employees possess a university degree?   _____

    b) How many of your employees hold a doctorate?   _____

10.2. Background (Due to your central function in the innovations process the following questions refer only to employees who possess a university degree.)

    a) How many of your academic employees were previously also employed in Jena (includes. graduates that studied in Jena)?   _____

    b) How many of the a) mentioned employees did you or other employees already in your company nurture professional contacts with before they became employees? (Work experience, co-operations)   _____

    c) How many of the a) mentioned employees did you or other employees already in your company have personal contact with before they became employees?   _____

    d) How many of your academic employees worked previously for a business competitor in Jena?   _____

    e) How many of your academic employees worked previously for a public research institute situated in Jena?   _____

10.3. Fluctuation

    a) How many new workers do you employ per year?   _____

    b) How many of your employees leave your company per year?   _____

Figure A.1: Questionnaire (continued)

11. Membership

With which associations and institutes is your company a member? Please write down the official name of the organisation and the year you became a member. How often do you or a company representative take part at events from these organisations?

Associations / Institutes	Year of Entry	Take part at events		
		Often	Seldom	Never
_____	____	☐	☐	☐
_____	____	☐	☐	☐
_____	____	☐	☐	☐
_____	____	☐	☐	☐
_____	____	☐	☐	☐

12. Spin-offs

The term Spin-off we understand to be the new establishment of a business out of an existing organisation (for example. Businesses, Universities, other research institutes), which we will call in this instance "Incubator". The reason for these new or spin-off businesses is the sale of technological "Know-how", which is acquired from the original business "inkubator".

12.1. Was your company established as a Spin-off?	Yes ☐	No ☐
		Carry on with 12.4.
12.2. Who is the "Incubator" of your company?		_____
12.3. In what way are you supported from the "Incubator"?		
Usage of facilities (Equipment, Laboratories, etc.)	Yes ☐	No ☐
Financial (Credit, Interests, etc.)	Yes ☐	No ☐
Advice in establishing process	Yes ☐	No ☐
The use of the "Incubators'" business contacts	Yes ☐	No ☐
Knowledge exchanged with employees from the "Incubator"	Yes ☐	No ☐
12.4. Were Spin-offs founded out of your business?	Yes ☐	No ☐
		Carry on with 12.8.
12.5. How many businesses were established?	Number: ___	
12.6. Which businesses were established?		
_____		
_____		
12.7. In what way did you support the Spin-offs?		
Usage of facilities (Equipment, Laboratories, etc.)	Yes ☐	No ☐
Financial (Credit, Interests, etc.)	Yes ☐	No ☐
Advice in establishing process	Yes ☐	No ☐
The use of your business contacts	Yes ☐	No ☐
Knowledge exchanged with employees	Yes ☐	No ☐
12.8. Are Spin-offs planned by your company and if "yes" how many?	No ☐ Yes ☐	Number: ___

Figure A.1: Questionnaire (continued)

13. Research Projects and co-operations

By the term research projects we understand as a thematic well defined concrete research objective with associated research efforts, which must be completed in the given period and with a given budget. If you do not have any projects of this kind please skip this part of the questionnaire.

13.1. Current research projects

a) How many research projects are you currently carrying out?   Number _____

b) How many of these projects are you carrying out in co-operation with other organisations?   Number _____

c) With how many different organisations are you co-operating with?   Number _____

d) Please arrange your co-operation partners into the following categories.

	Public organisation	Competitor	Supplier	Consumer	Same sector	None of these categories
Number	_____	_____	_____	_____	_____	_____

e) Please arrange your co-operation partners into the following regions.

	Jena	Thuringia	Germany	Europe (EU)	World
Number	_____	_____	_____	_____	_____

f) How many of these co-operation partners are linked to your company via equity investments (corporate group)?   _____

13.2. Planned research

a) How many research projects are being planned?   Number _____

b) With how many of these projects are you planning to co-operate with other organisations?   Number _____

c) With how many different organisations do you plan to co-operate with?   Number _____

d) Please arrange your co-operation partners into the following categories.

	Public organisation	Competitor	Supplier	Consumer	Same sector	None of these categories
Number	_____	_____	_____	_____	_____	_____

e) Please arrange your co-operation partners into the following regions.

	Jena	Thuringia	Germany	Europe (EU	World
Number	_____	_____	_____	_____	_____

f) How many of these co-operation partners are linked to your company via equity investments (corporate group)?   _____

Thank you for your support!

Do you have any criticism or suggestion, or you would like to inform us concerning something else? Please use the following lines.

_____

_____

_____

Would you be so kind as to answer any further questions we might have?   Yes ❑   No ❑

Figure A.1: Questionnaire (continued)

Appendix

Table A.4: *Patenting in German regions*

NUTS 3 ('Kreis')	Population (2000)	Patents (1995–2001) – inventor-based number	per 100' pop.	rank	Patents (1995–2001) – applicant-based number	per 100' pop.	rank
Erlangen-Höchstadt (LK)	128,547	2946	2291.77	1	1334	1037.75	11
Frankenthal	47,930	1030	2148.97	2	200	417.28	36
Bad Dürkheim (LK)	133,671	2691	2013.15	3	128	95.76	273
Ludwigshafen (LK)	146,644	2816	1920.30	4	87	59.33	342
Erlangen	100,730	1875	1861.41	5	343	340.51	62
Ludwigsburg (LK)	496,604	7921	1595.03	6	1863	375.15	44
Neustadt a.d.Weinstrasse	53,937	826	1531.42	7	21	38.93	388
Main-Taunus-Kreis (LK)	219,223	3333	1520.37	8	401	182.92	146
Ludwigshafen	163,039	2462	1510.07	9	5136	3150.17	2
Leverkusen	160,904	2415	1500.89	10	4516	2806.64	5
Darmstadt	138,028	2068	1498.25	11	1860	1347.55	9
Böblingen (LK)	363,518	5071	1394.98	12	990	272.34	92
Speyer	49,779	694	1394.16	13	49	98.44	269
München (LK)	292,159	4030	1379.39	14	1261	431.61	33
Schweinfurt	54,439	737	1353.81	15	1534	2817.83	4
Starnberg (LK)	124,010	1676	1351.50	16	632	509.64	27
Heidenheim (LK)	136,933	1849	1350.30	17	1900	1387.54	7
Rheinisch-Bergischer Kreis (LK)	275,494	3482	1263.91	18	553	200.73	132
Heidelberg	139,966	1750	1250.30	19	1911	1365.33	8
Darmstadt-Dieburg (LK)	285,873	3353	1172.90	20	574	200.79	131
Regensburg	125,180	1461	1167.12	21	360	287.59	81
Fürstenfeldbruck (LK)	191,817	2203	1148.49	22	483	251.80	102
Stuttgart	583,159	6638	1138.28	23	18688	3204.61	1
Esslingen (LK)	499,246	5650	1131.71	24	2636	528.00	26
Jena	99,763	1114	1116.65	25	892	894.12	16
Bodenseekreis (LK)	198,603	2136	1075.51	26	2054	1034.22	12
Rems-Murr-Kreis (LK)	408,255	4380	1072.86	27	1224	299.81	74
Enzkreis (LK)	192,221	2055	1069.08	28	715	371.97	48
Mettmann (LK)	507,052	5310	1047.23	29	1890	372.74	47
Gifhorn (LK)	170,719	1784	1044.99	30	51	29.87	405
Aachen	244,031	2480	1016.26	31	1176	481.91	29
Schweinfurt (LK)	116,344	1182	1015.95	32	85	73.06	325
Ebersberg (LK)	117,475	1174	999.36	33	324	275.80	89
Altötting (LK)	108,024	1059	980.34	34	312	288.82	80
Hochtaunuskreis (LK)	224,760	2195	976.60	35	960	427.12	35
Braunschweig	246,070	2386	969.64	36	563	228.80	119
Wolfsburg	121,940	1182	969.33	37	3511	2879.28	3
Dachau (LK)	128,652	1191	925.75	38	278	216.09	127
München	1,201,871	10938	910.08	39	25804	2146.99	6
Aschaffenburg (LK)	173,849	1572	904.23	40	507	291.63	78
Nürnberger Land (LK)	167,702	1500	894.44	41	422	251.64	103
Freising (LK)	150,648	1329	882.19	42	470	311.99	69
Rhein-Neckar-Kreis (LK)	522,991	4607	880.89	43	1501	287.00	82
Regensburg (LK)	174,924	1519	868.38	44	353	201.80	130
Landsberg a.Lech (LK)	104,997	901	858.12	45	293	279.06	88
Bad Tölz-Wolfratshausen (LK)	115,357	967	838.27	46	401	347.62	60
Göppingen (LK)	256,464	2078	810.25	47	1049	409.02	38
Remscheid	119,714	964	805.25	48	1197	999.88	14
Bergstrasse (LK)	262,987	2043	776.84	49	462	175.67	157
Aschaffenburg	67,209	517	769.24	50	236	351.14	59
Ulm	116,668	892	764.56	51	397	340.28	63
Forchheim (LK)	112,144	856	763.30	52	126	112.36	238
Tuttlingen (LK)	132,595	1009	760.96	53	1045	788.11	19
Miesbach (LK)	91,112	686	752.92	54	251	275.49	90
Mainz-Bingen (LK)	193,624	1455	751.46	55	726	374.95	45
Tübingen (LK)	207,783	1548	745.01	56	619	297.91	75
Pfaffenhofen a.d.Ilm (LK)	111,023	818	736.78	57	165	148.62	183

Table A.4: Patenting in German regions (continued)

NUTS 3 ('Kreis')	Population (2000)	Patents (1995–2001) – inventor-based			Patents (1995–2001) – applicant-based		
		number	per 100' pop.	rank	number	per 100' pop.	rank
Krefeld	240,890	1763	731.87	58	630	261.53	98
Lindau (LK)	76,972	556	722.34	59	358	465.10	30
Mainz	182,615	1318	721.74	60	737	403.58	40
Reutlingen (LK)	277,333	1971	710.70	61	747	269.35	94
Mannheim	307,230	2180	709.57	62	2211	719.66	21
Fürth	109,985	771	701.00	63	504	458.24	31
Eichstätt (LK)	118,932	828	696.20	64	77	64.74	338
Rastatt (LK)	223,429	1526	682.99	65	817	365.66	54
Main-Kinzig-Kreis (LK)	405,025	2758	680.95	66	1431	353.31	57
Coburg	43,041	291	676.10	67	391	908.44	15
Fürth (LK)	112,983	759	671.78	68	155	137.19	197
Heilbronn (LK)	319,267	2141	670.60	69	576	180.41	153
Main-Spessart (LK)	132,063	885	670.13	70	703	532.32	25
Neu-Ulm (LK)	159,237	1057	663.79	71	585	367.38	51
Weilheim-Schongau (LK)	126,326	825	653.07	72	224	177.32	155
Traunstein (LK)	167,148	1089	651.52	73	642	384.09	42
Düsseldorf	569,085	3670	644.89	74	5729	1006.70	13
Offenbach (LK)	334,003	2126	636.52	75	771	230.84	117
Worms	80,302	507	631.37	76	101	125.78	216
Neuss (LK)	443,220	2795	630.61	77	818	184.56	143
Ravensburg (LK)	267,959	1683	628.08	78	1109	413.87	37
Karlsruhe (LK)	417,992	2601	622.26	79	1171	280.15	87
Rosenheim (LK)	234,811	1455	619.65	80	581	247.43	108
Aichach-Friedberg (LK)	122,564	756	616.82	81	204	166.44	168
Ingolstadt	115,151	709	615.71	82	1022	887.53	17
Calw (LK)	158,627	962	606.45	83	316	199.21	133
Karlsruhe	277,881	1682	605.30	84	1019	366.70	52
Solingen	165,267	999	604.48	85	388	234.77	115
Groß-Gerau (LK)	248,790	1470	590.86	86	837	336.43	64
Coburg (LK)	92,255	539	584.25	87	135	146.33	185
Schwarzwald-Baar-Kreis (LK)	209,976	1214	578.16	88	1068	508.63	28
Wuppertal	367,695	2110	573.85	89	1345	365.79	53
Alb-Donau-Kreis (LK)	185,366	1060	571.84	90	336	181.26	151
Rheingau-Taunus-Kreis (LK)	184,446	1052	570.36	91	206	111.69	239
Baden-Baden	52,678	296	561.90	92	159	301.83	73
Rottweil (LK)	140,751	786	558.43	93	574	407.81	39
Heilbronn	119,416	666	557.71	94	898	751.99	20
Neuburg-Schrobenhausen (LK)	88,798	486	547.31	95	114	128.38	213
Wetteraukreis (LK)	293,201	1585	540.58	96	411	140.18	192
Würzburg	127,409	685	537.64	97	838	657.72	23
Meißen-Radebeul (LK)	153,564	825	537.24	98	368	239.64	112
Erding (LK)	114,686	593	517.06	99	123	107.25	245
Mülheim an der Ruhr	173,401	893	514.99	100	302	174.16	158
Wolfenbüttel (LK)	126,069	643	510.04	101	117	92.81	282
Oberbergischer Kreis (LK)	287,258	1459	507.91	102	1061	369.35	50
Nürnberg	487,135	2438	500.48	103	1833	376.28	43
Würzburg (LK)	158,691	793	499.71	104	186	117.21	228
Ennepe-Ruhr-Kreis (LK)	351,022	1733	493.70	105	1020	290.58	79
Dresden	476,683	2345	491.94	106	1231	258.24	100
Augsburg (LK)	235,622	1159	491.89	107	397	168.49	165
Frankfurt am Main	645,414	3168	490.85	108	8041	1245.87	10
Ostalbkreis (LK)	313,758	1536	489.55	109	582	185.49	142
Lahn-Dill-Kreis (LK)	262,727	1283	488.34	110	1197	455.61	32
Dillingen a.d.Donau (LK)	93,635	457	488.07	111	119	127.09	215
Günzburg (LK)	121,346	586	482.92	112	400	329.64	66
Rhön-Grabfeld (LK)	86,839	418	481.35	113	194	223.40	122
Alzey-Worms (LK)	123,586	593	479.83	114	63	50.98	358

168 *Appendix*

Table A.4: Patenting in German regions (continued)

NUTS 3 ('Kreis')	Population (2000)	Patents (1995–2001) – inventor-based			Patents (1995–2001) – applicant-based		
		number	per 100' pop.	rank	number	per 100' pop.	rank
Biberach (LK)	182,194	872	478.61	115	590	323.83	68
Wiesbaden	269,370	1257	466.64	116	1454	539.78	24
Düren (LK)	267,355	1222	457.07	117	1047	391.61	41
Roth (LK)	123,760	563	454.91	118	178	143.83	187
Helmstedt (LK)	100,331	456	454.50	119	44	43.85	375
Amberg	43,593	196	449.61	120	143	328.03	67
Viersen (LK)	299,910	1345	448.47	121	305	101.70	262
Bamberg	69,025	307	444.77	122	83	120.25	223
Hohenlohekreis (LK)	107,342	476	443.44	123	367	341.90	61
Kelheim (LK)	109,073	483	442.82	124	113	103.60	255
Märkischer Kreis (LK)	458,642	2025	441.52	125	1959	427.13	34
Offenbach	117,126	512	437.14	126	978	835.00	18
Neustadt/Aisch-Bad Windsheim (LK)	98,393	428	434.99	127	101	102.65	258
Olpe (LK)	141,089	611	433.06	128	427	302.65	71
Rhein-Sieg-Kreis (LK)	574,486	2465	429.08	129	1354	235.69	114
Freudenstadt (LK)	120,956	516	426.60	130	452	373.69	46
Mühldorf a.Inn (LK)	108,189	458	423.33	131	322	297.63	76
Hildesheim (LK)	292,670	1228	419.59	132	398	135.99	201
Emmendingen (LK)	150,910	627	415.48	133	367	243.19	111
Augsburg	254,781	1058	415.26	134	718	281.81	85
Limburg-Weilburg (LK)	175,243	723	412.57	135	147	83.88	299
Konstanz (LK)	265,362	1089	410.38	136	748	281.88	84
Rosenheim	58,781	241	410.00	137	168	285.81	83
Amberg-Sulzbach (LK)	108,538	444	409.07	138	157	144.65	186
Verden (LK)	132,528	537	405.20	139	357	269.38	93
Bamberg (LK)	142,065	562	395.59	140	181	127.41	214
Gütersloh (LK)	344,152	1341	389.65	141	1136	330.09	65
Siegen-Wittgenstein (LK)	296,769	1148	386.83	142	724	243.96	110
Neumarkt i.d.OPf. (LK)	125,932	482	382.75	143	228	181.05	152
Münster	264,975	1007	380.04	144	802	302.67	70
Freiburg i.Breisgau	203,779	774	379.82	145	597	292.96	77
Miltenberg (LK)	130,942	496	378.79	146	238	181.76	149
Peine (LK)	131,624	498	378.35	147	143	108.64	241
Bad Kissingen (LK)	109,450	414	378.25	148	113	103.24	256
Chemnitz	261,320	985	376.93	149	648	247.97	106
Waldshut (LK)	164,956	621	376.46	150	264	160.04	172
Mönchengladbach	263,226	981	372.68	151	795	302.02	72
Köln	962,146	3546	368.55	152	1761	183.03	145
Paderborn (LK)	289,136	1061	366.96	153	1040	359.69	55
Neuwied (LK)	184,001	674	366.30	154	495	269.02	95
Odenwaldkreis (LK)	99,477	364	365.91	155	95	95.50	274
Aachen (LK)	306,028	1108	362.06	156	314	102.60	259
Zollernalbkreis (LK)	192,906	695	360.28	157	484	250.90	104
Coesfeld (LK)	213,760	760	355.54	158	228	106.66	248
Breisgau-Hochschwarzwald (LK)	239,658	850	354.67	159	436	181.93	148
Pforzheim	117,192	410	349.85	160	435	371.19	49
Marburg-Biedenkopf (LK)	253,123	883	348.84	161	465	183.71	144
Ilm-Kreis (LK)	122,172	426	348.69	162	282	230.82	118
Garmisch-Partenkirchen (LK)	86,406	299	346.04	163	305	352.98	58
Main-Tauber-Kreis (LK)	137,096	472	344.28	164	341	248.73	105
Kaiserslautern	99,710	343	344.00	165	267	267.78	97
Haßberge (LK)	88,388	303	342.81	166	119	134.63	205
Pinneberg (LK)	290,233	993	342.14	167	251	86.48	293
Gießen (LK)	253,115	863	340.95	168	475	187.66	141
Ostallgäu (LK)	131,143	447	340.85	169	288	219.61	126
Bad Kreuznach (LK)	157,344	536	340.65	170	225	143.00	188
Harburg (LK)	231,244	784	339.04	171	218	94.27	277

Table A.4: Patenting in German regions (continued)

NUTS 3 ('Kreis')	Population (2000)	Patents (1995–2001) – inventor-based			Patents (1995–2001) – applicant-based		
		number	per 100' pop.	rank	number	per 100' pop.	rank
Schwäbisch Hall (LK)	185,274	627	338.42	172	358	193.23	136
Warendorf (LK)	279,524	942	337.00	173	787	281.55	86
Schwandorf (LK)	143,028	475	332.10	174	118	82.50	302
Bonn	300,971	990	328.94	175	2148	713.69	22
Lörrach (LK)	216,643	712	328.65	176	513	236.80	113
Heinsberg (LK)	249,248	817	327.79	177	335	134.40	206
Kempten	61,330	201	327.74	178	159	259.25	99
Schaumburg (LK)	165,747	541	326.40	179	445	268.48	96
Hof	50,979	166	325.62	180	112	219.70	125
Wesel (LK)	473,682	1528	322.58	181	480	101.33	263
Holzminden (LK)	81,711	262	320.64	182	289	353.69	56
Südliche Weinstrasse (LK)	109,247	350	320.37	183	75	68.65	331
Rottal-Inn (LK)	117,989	371	314.44	184	161	136.45	198
Saar-Pfalz-Kreis (LK)	157,492	493	313.03	185	169	107.31	244
Straubing	43,881	137	312.21	186	100	227.89	120
Donnersbergkreis (LK)	78,360	241	307.55	187	59	75.29	319
Germersheim (LK)	123,048	378	307.20	188	114	92.65	283
Soest (LK)	306,270	940	306.92	189	749	244.56	109
Ortenaukreis (LK)	406,867	1247	306.49	190	623	153.12	177
Erftkreis (LK)	453,807	1383	304.76	191	355	78.23	312
Hannover (Region)	1,117,132	3392	303.63	192	2765	247.51	107
Halle (Saale)	251,177	756	300.98	193	195	77.63	314
Ansbach (LK)	182,771	550	300.92	194	217	118.73	225
Weißenburg-Gunzenhausen (LK)	95,079	286	300.80	195	156	164.07	169
Kitzingen (LK)	88,847	266	299.39	196	170	191.34	139
Saale-Holzland-Kreis (LK)	93,520	275	294.05	197	97	103.72	253
Unna (LK)	430,420	1265	293.90	198	600	139.40	193
Sankt Wendel (LK)	95,438	280	293.38	199	64	67.06	334
Göttingen (LK)	265,453	766	288.56	200	563	212.09	128
Recklinghausen (LK)	659,017	1896	287.70	201	1312	199.08	134
Berchtesgadener Land (LK)	99,516	281	282.37	202	152	152.74	178
Bochum	391,979	1106	282.16	203	534	136.23	199
Landshut (LK)	141,510	399	281.96	204	192	135.68	203
Sonneberg (LK)	68,122	192	281.85	205	62	91.01	286
Koblenz	107,902	303	280.81	206	252	233.55	116
Kaufbeuren	41,834	117	279.68	207	63	150.60	181
Straubing-Bogen (LK)	94,829	265	279.45	208	132	139.20	194
Essen	596,841	1662	278.47	209	1531	256.52	101
Segeberg (LK)	248,665	683	274.67	210	290	116.62	229
Kronach (LK)	75,735	208	274.64	211	131	172.97	160
Landshut	58,586	159	271.40	212	25	42.67	378
Ansbach	40,200	109	271.14	213	77	191.54	138
Rhein-Lahn-Kreis (LK)	128,891	349	270.77	214	147	114.05	232
Minden-Lübbecke (LK)	322,388	870	269.86	215	715	221.78	124
Freiberg (LK)	153,881	413	268.39	216	218	141.67	190
Weißeritzkreis (LK)	125,204	335	267.56	217	95	75.88	318
Hagen	204,247	545	266.83	218	220	107.71	242
Bottrop	120,897	322	266.34	219	52	43.01	377
Bielefeld	321,322	852	265.15	220	630	196.07	135
Oberallgäu (LK)	147,115	390	265.10	221	179	121.67	219
Sigmaringen (LK)	133,200	353	265.02	222	229	171.92	162
Herford (LK)	254,286	665	261.52	223	463	182.08	147
Goslar (LK)	156,641	408	260.47	224	244	155.77	175
Steinfurt (LK)	433,789	1121	258.42	225	748	172.43	161
Lichtenfels (LK)	70,898	181	255.30	226	88	124.12	217
Dingolfing-Landau (LK)	90,307	229	253.58	227	102	112.95	235
Salzgitter	112,600	282	250.44	228	153	135.88	202

Table A.4: Patenting in German regions (continued)

NUTS 3 ('Kreis')	Population (2000)	Patents (1995–2001) – inventor-based			Patents (1995–2001) – applicant-based		
		number	per 100' pop.	rank	number	per 100' pop.	rank
Weimar	62,421	156	249.92	229	64	102.53	261
Neckar-Odenwald-Kreis (LK)	149,181	371	248.69	230	180	120.66	222
Osnabrück (LK)	352,455	874	247.97	231	665	188.68	140
Berlin	3,384,146	8390	247.92	232	6496	191.95	137
Stade (LK)	191,235	471	246.29	233	150	78.44	310
Celle (LK)	181,598	447	246.15	234	286	157.49	173
Unterallgäu (LK)	133,278	323	242.35	235	224	168.07	167
Stormarn (LK)	216,460	524	242.08	236	227	104.87	251
Soltau-Fallingbostel (LK)	139,683	338	241.98	237	247	176.83	156
Borken (LK)	357,914	866	241.96	238	561	156.74	174
Kleve (LK)	298,430	717	240.26	239	299	100.19	267
Bayreuth	73,811	177	239.80	240	95	128.71	212
Osnabrück	164,031	393	239.59	241	277	168.87	164
Lippe (LK)	365,022	874	239.44	242	658	180.26	154
Altenkirchen (LK)	137,296	327	238.17	243	223	162.42	170
Hochsauerlandkreis (LK)	282,595	673	238.15	244	491	173.75	159
Herzogtum Lauenburg (LK)	178,645	423	236.78	245	307	171.85	163
Neunkirchen (LK)	147,624	349	236.41	246	158	107.03	247
Höxter (LK)	155,763	365	234.33	247	131	84.10	298
Kaiserslautern (LK)	110,065	256	232.59	248	96	87.22	292
Northeim (LK)	151,515	349	230.34	249	183	120.78	221
Potsdam-Mittelmark (LK)	207,572	472	227.39	250	214	103.10	257
Lübeck	213,365	481	225.44	251	480	224.97	121
Bayreuth (LK)	108,952	245	224.87	252	123	112.89	236
Oberspreewald-Lausitz (LK)	146,737	327	222.85	253	114	77.69	313
Donau-Ries (LK)	129,454	286	220.93	254	147	113.55	233
Duisburg	517,270	1142	220.77	255	481	92.99	281
Hamburg	1,710,271	3760	219.85	256	4660	272.47	91
Hersfeld-Rotenburg (LK)	130,896	286	218.49	257	92	70.28	329
Sächsische Schweiz (LK)	148,056	322	217.49	258	156	105.37	249
Saarlouis (LK)	212,177	461	217.27	259	245	115.47	230
Oberhausen	222,191	479	215.58	260	292	131.42	210
Vechta (LK)	125,497	270	215.14	261	149	118.73	225
Vogelsbergkreis (LK)	118,510	254	214.33	262	115	97.04	272
Potsdam	129,252	277	214.31	263	154	119.15	224
Dortmund	589,249	1250	212.13	264	837	142.05	189
Deggendorf (LK)	115,517	245	212.09	265	238	206.03	129
Oldenburg (LK)	120,094	253	210.67	266	109	90.76	287
Memmingen	40,919	86	210.17	267	91	222.39	123
Greifswald	54,833	115	209.73	268	55	100.30	266
Euskirchen (LK)	188,468	384	203.75	269	203	107.71	242
Osterholz (LK)	109,948	224	203.73	270	53	48.20	364
Osterode am Harz (LK)	85,815	174	202.76	271	115	134.01	207
Merzig-Wadern (LK)	105,851	213	201.23	272	119	112.42	237
Ahrweiler (LK)	129,162	258	199.75	273	121	93.68	278
Stadtverband Saarbrücken (LK)	351,101	697	198.52	274	532	151.52	179
Cottbus	109,762	217	197.70	275	84	76.53	316
Passau (LK)	186,077	366	196.69	276	259	139.19	195
Saalkreis (LK)	81,432	160	196.48	277	18	22.10	420
Diepholz (LK)	210,900	401	190.14	278	287	136.08	200
Herne	175,099	323	184.47	279	148	84.52	297
Neustadt a.d.Waldnaab (LK)	100,809	185	183.52	280	123	122.01	218
Westerwaldkreis (LK)	201,692	367	181.96	281	202	100.15	268
Hameln-Pyrmont (LK)	162,619	292	179.56	282	171	105.15	250
Wunsiedel i.Fichtelgebirge (LK)	86,410	155	179.38	283	134	155.07	176
Oberhavel (LK)	190,463	338	177.46	284	288	151.21	180
Pirmasens (LK)	105,456	186	176.38	285	49	46.46	368

Table A.4: Patenting in German regions (continued)

NUTS 3 ('Kreis')	Population (2000)	Patents (1995–2001) – inventor-based			Patents (1995–2001) – applicant-based		
		number	per 100' pop.	rank	number	per 100' pop.	rank
Magdeburg	233,396	409	175.24	286	309	132.39	209
Kassel	195,322	342	175.10	287	274	140.28	191
Fulda (LK)	217,425	377	173.39	288	223	102.56	260
Rendsburg-Eckernförde (LK)	269,089	465	172.81	289	249	92.53	284
Dessau	84,266	145	172.07	290	54	64.08	339
Stollberg (LK)	94,354	162	171.69	291	67	71.01	327
Kulmbach (LK)	78,757	135	171.41	292	90	114.28	231
Plauen	71,819	123	171.26	293	19	26.46	413
Kiel	232,972	398	170.84	294	343	147.23	184
Saalfeld-Rudolstadt (LK)	133,582	228	170.68	295	177	132.50	208
Suhl	48,711	83	170.39	296	73	149.86	182
Rhein-Hunsrück-Kreis (LK)	105,204	174	165.39	297	85	80.80	307
Hof (LK)	109,365	178	162.76	298	184	168.24	166
Lüneburg (LK)	165,414	268	162.02	299	113	68.31	333
Oldenburg	154,394	250	161.92	300	144	93.27	279
Waldeck-Frankenberg (LK)	170,613	275	161.18	301	235	137.74	196
Havelland (LK)	146,301	235	160.63	302	59	40.33	385
Kamenz (LK)	156,309	251	160.58	303	82	52.46	356
Kassel (LK)	245,810	394	160.29	304	137	55.73	347
Regen (LK)	82,521	131	158.75	305	72	87.25	291
Werra-Meißner-Kreis (LK)	114,466	181	158.13	306	98	85.61	296
Mayen-Koblenz (LK)	210,368	327	155.44	307	218	103.63	254
Plön (LK)	132,427	203	153.29	308	71	53.61	353
Passau	50,341	77	152.96	309	65	129.12	211
Dahme-Spreewald (LK)	158,193	241	152.35	310	77	48.67	362
Erfurt	200,849	303	150.86	311	244	121.48	220
Delmenhorst	76,755	115	149.83	312	35	45.60	371
Bremen	539,617	804	148.99	313	732	135.65	204
Barnim (LK)	168,666	248	147.04	314	75	44.47	374
Leipzig	493,287	721	146.16	315	529	107.24	246
Steinburg (LK)	135,896	198	145.70	316	100	73.59	323
Wesermarsch (LK)	94,058	137	145.65	317	53	56.35	346
Trier-Saarburg (LK)	137,486	199	144.74	318	73	53.10	355
Cham (LK)	130,986	189	144.29	319	124	94.67	276
Döbeln (LK)	78,519	113	143.91	320	77	98.07	270
Zwickau	103,609	147	141.88	321	115	110.99	240
Ostholstein (LK)	201,851	286	141.69	322	95	47.06	367
Mittweida (LK)	138,920	196	141.09	323	104	74.86	320
Freyung-Grafenau (LK)	82,433	116	140.72	324	68	82.49	303
Weimarer Land (LK)	91,617	128	139.71	325	17	18.56	427
Kusel (LK)	78,937	110	139.35	326	24	30.40	404
Tirschenreuth (LK)	80,191	110	137.17	327	44	54.87	349
Schmalkalden-Meiningen (LK)	144,111	194	134.62	328	163	113.11	234
Schwalm-Eder-Kreis (LK)	193,374	260	134.45	329	104	53.78	352
Hildburghausen (LK)	74,002	98	132.43	330	68	91.89	285
Cochem-Zell (LK)	65,567	86	131.16	331	50	76.26	317
Wartburgkreis (LK)	145,215	189	130.15	332	146	100.54	265
Rostock	201,938	262	129.74	333	159	78.74	309
Bitterfeld (LK)	110,683	142	128.29	334	103	93.06	280
Vogtlandkreis (LK)	203,585	259	127.22	335	136	66.80	336
Niederschles. Oberlausitzkreis (LK)	107,057	136	127.04	336	57	53.24	354
Hamm	182,061	228	125.23	337	98	53.83	351
Emsland (LK)	302,006	377	124.83	338	288	95.36	275
Nienburg(Weser) (LK)	126,091	154	122.13	339	94	74.55	321
Zwickauer Land (LK)	135,816	164	120.75	340	101	74.37	322
Trier	98,803	119	120.44	341	117	118.42	227
Bernkastel-Wittlich (LK)	113,768	136	119.54	342	93	81.75	306

Table A.4: Patenting in German regions (continued)

NUTS 3 ('Kreis')	Population (2000)	Patents (1995–2001) – inventor-based			Patents (1995–2001) – applicant-based		
		number	per 100' pop.	rank	number	per 100' pop.	rank
Rotenburg (Wümme) (LK)	160,783	192	119.42	343	87	54.11	350
Gelsenkirchen	280,472	332	118.37	344	241	85.93	295
Lüchow-Dannenberg (LK)	51,989	61	117.33	345	17	32.70	402
Bautzen (LK)	158,464	185	116.75	346	106	66.89	335
Ammerland (LK)	109,864	126	114.69	347	86	78.28	311
Merseburg-Querfurt (LK)	136,200	155	113.80	348	247	181.35	150
Gera	113,920	128	112.36	349	103	90.41	288
Muldentalkreis (LK)	136,515	150	109.88	350	62	45.42	372
Hoyerswerda	51,336	56	109.09	351	8	15.58	429
Chemnitzer Land (LK)	141,800	153	107.90	352	116	81.81	304
Eisenach	44,486	48	107.90	352	28	62.94	340
Mittlerer Erzgebirgskreis (LK)	94,946	101	106.38	354	67	70.57	328
Delitzsch (LK)	128,718	136	105.66	355	93	72.25	326
Riesa-Großenhain (LK)	123,129	130	105.58	356	106	86.09	294
Aue-Schwarzenberg (LK)	141,579	148	104.54	357	83	58.62	344
Elbe-Elster (LK)	132,101	138	104.47	358	52	39.36	387
Greiz (LK)	124,540	129	103.58	359	91	73.07	324
Bremerhaven	121,836	126	103.42	360	109	89.46	289
Jerichower Land (LK)	101,070	104	102.90	361	37	36.61	395
Frankfurt (Oder)	73,058	75	102.66	362	74	101.29	264
Nordhausen (LK)	99,045	99	99.95	363	81	81.78	305
Neubrandenburg	74,040	72	97.24	364	62	83.74	300
Schwerin	102,180	99	96.89	365	106	103.74	252
Neumünster	80,103	77	96.13	366	129	161.04	171
Emden	50,985	49	96.11	367	50	98.07	270
Leipziger Land (LK)	154,320	147	95.26	368	62	40.18	386
Grafschaft Bentheim (LK)	129,417	123	95.04	369	115	88.86	290
Görlitz	62,301	59	94.70	370	26	41.73	382
Oder-Spree (LK)	196,489	186	94.66	371	93	47.33	366
Spree-Neiße (LK)	154,369	146	94.58	372	65	42.11	380
Wilhelmshaven	85,888	81	94.31	373	66	76.84	315
Flensburg	84,414	79	93.59	374	56	66.34	337
Friesland (LK)	100,570	94	93.47	375	56	55.68	348
Löbau-Zittau (LK)	156,426	146	93.33	376	81	51.78	357
Birkenfeld (LK)	90,208	84	93.12	377	75	83.14	301
Daun (LK)	64,374	59	91.65	378	28	43.50	376
Uelzen (LK)	97,272	89	91.50	379	36	37.01	393
Ohre-Kreis (LK)	118,094	105	88.91	380	81	68.59	332
Annaberg (LK)	88,846	78	87.79	381	45	50.65	359
Halberstadt (LK)	79,905	67	83.85	382	36	45.05	373
Gotha (LK)	149,113	125	83.83	383	63	42.25	379
Bad Doberan (LK)	117,162	97	82.79	384	58	49.50	360
Teltow-Fläming (LK)	158,958	130	81.78	385	61	38.37	390
Bitburg-Prüm (LK)	96,376	78	80.93	386	47	48.77	361
Brandenburg a.d. Havel	78,306	62	79.18	387	21	26.82	412
Aschersleben-Staßfurt (LK)	104,510	82	78.46	388	72	68.89	330
Ostvorpommern (LK)	114,861	90	78.36	389	38	33.08	400
Kyffhäuserkreis (LK)	94,835	72	75.92	390	44	46.40	369
Märkisch-Oderland (LK)	187,294	142	75.82	391	49	26.16	414
Dithmarschen (LK)	137,070	103	75.14	392	57	41.58	383
Eichsfeld (LK)	114,439	84	73.40	393	92	80.39	308
Leer (LK)	160,790	114	70.90	394	96	59.71	341
Wernigerode (LK)	96,090	67	69.73	395	27	28.10	410
Weißenfels (LK)	79,383	53	66.76	396	46	57.95	345
Burgenlandkreis (LK)	144,238	96	66.56	397	41	28.43	408
Köthen (LK)	70,978	47	66.22	398	26	36.63	394
Parchim (LK)	109,225	72	65.92	399	45	41.20	384

Table A.4: Patenting in German regions (continued)

NUTS 3 ('Kreis')	Population (2000)	Patents (1995–2001) – inventor-based			Patents (1995–2001) – applicant-based		
		number	per 100' pop.	rank	number	per 100' pop.	rank
Quedlinburg (LK)	79,412	52	65.48	400	26	32.74	401
Bördekreis (LK)	80,951	53	65.47	401	22	27.18	411
Cloppenburg (LK)	148,695	96	64.56	402	72	48.42	363
Aurich (LK)	186,796	120	64.24	403	110	58.89	343
Cuxhaven (LK)	204,312	131	64.12	404	72	35.24	396
Torgau-Oschatz (LK)	102,358	64	62.53	405	29	28.33	409
Wittenberg (LK)	133,362	82	61.49	406	45	33.74	398
Schleswig-Flensburg (LK)	196,955	120	60.93	407	75	38.08	392
Altenburger Land (LK)	114,934	70	60.90	408	55	47.85	365
Sömmerda (LK)	81,541	49	60.09	409	20	24.53	415
Anhalt-Zerbst (LK)	78,249	47	60.06	410	30	38.34	391
Saale-Orla-Kreis (LK)	99,142	57	57.49	411	32	32.28	403
Güstrow (LK)	113,217	62	54.76	412	44	38.86	389
Müritz (LK)	70,003	37	52.85	413	32	45.71	370
Pirmasens	45,419	23	50.64	414	9	19.82	426
Altmarkkreis Salzwedel (LK)	101,533	46	45.31	415	23	22.65	419
Schönebeck (LK)	77,935	35	44.91	416	27	34.64	397
Sangerhausen (LK)	68,851	30	43.57	417	16	23.24	416
Mecklenburg-Strelitz (LK)	88,219	38	43.07	418	19	21.54	422
Uckermark (LK)	153,051	65	42.47	419	31	20.25	424
Wittmund (LK)	57,364	24	41.84	420	24	41.84	381
Nordfriesland (LK)	164,147	63	38.38	421	38	23.15	417
Unstrut-Hainich-Kreis (LK)	120,211	44	36.60	422	40	33.27	399
Nordwestmecklenburg (LK)	121,133	40	33.02	423	36	29.72	406
Stralsund	61,144	20	32.71	424	10	16.35	428
Stendal (LK)	141,679	46	32.47	425	42	29.64	407
Nordvorpommern (LK)	119,079	38	31.91	426	25	20.99	423
Ludwigslust (LK)	132,047	35	26.51	427	29	21.96	421
Prignitz (LK)	96,469	25	25.92	428	22	22.81	418
Mansfelder Land (LK)	108,898	27	24.79	429	22	20.20	425
Ostprignitz-Ruppin (LK)	113,489	27	23.79	430	17	14.98	430
Bernburg (LK)	70,716	12	16.97	431	8	11.31	431
Rügen (LK)	75,848	8	10.55	432	6	7.91	433
Uecker-Randow (LK)	85,801	9	10.49	433	9	10.49	432
Demmin (LK)	95,123	8	8.41	434	5	5.26	434
Landau i.d.Pfalz	40,950	NA	NA	–	NA	NA	–
Zweibrücken	35,650	NA	NA	–	NA	NA	–
Weiden i.d.OPf.	42,965	NA	NA	–	NA	NA	–
Schwabach (LK)	38,070	NA	NA	–	NA	NA	–
Wismar	47,171	NA	NA	–	NA	NA	–

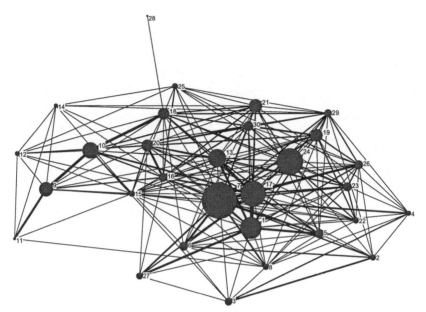

Figure A.2: Map of the knowledge-base of Dresden 1995–1998

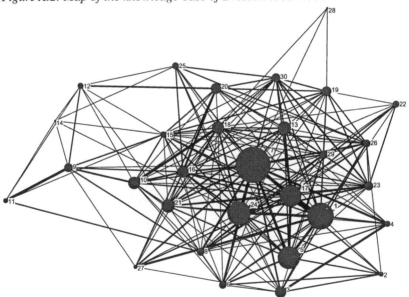

Figure A.3: Map of the knowledge-base of Dresden 1998–2001

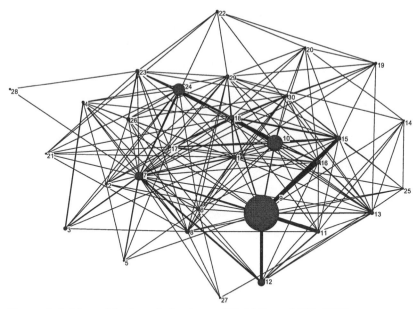

Figure A.4: Map of the knowledge-base of Heidelberg 1995–1998

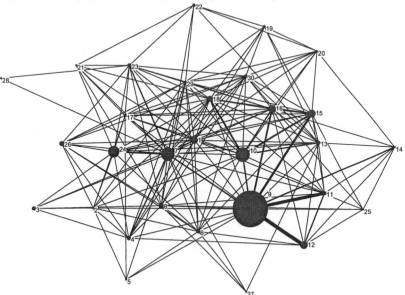

Figure A.5: Map of the knowledge-base of Heidelberg 1998–2001

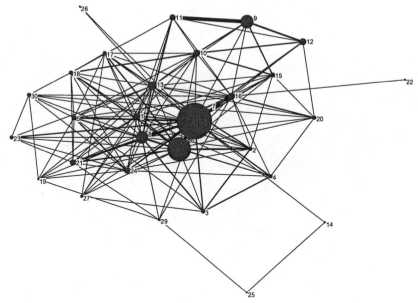

Figure A.6: Map of the knowledge-base of Jena 1995–1998

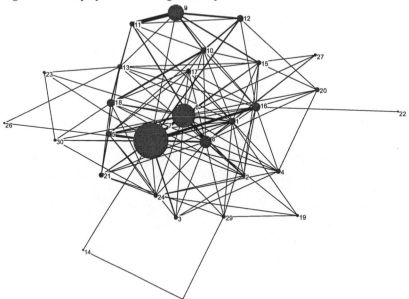

Figure A.7: Map of the knowledge-base of Jena 1998–2001

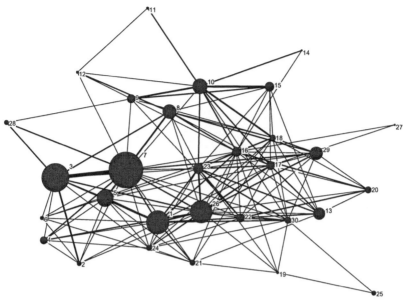

Figure A.8: Map of the knowledge-base of Ulm 1995–1998

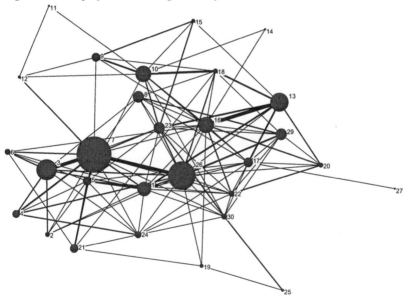

Figure A.9: Map of the knowledge-base of Ulm 1998–2001

Bibliography

Acs, Z. J. (2002), *Innovation and the Growth of Cities*, Cheltenham, UK: Edward Elgar.

Acs, Z. J. and Storey, D. J. (2004), 'Introduction: Entrepreneurship and economic development', *Regional Studies*, **38** (8), 871–877.

Acs, Z. J., Audretsch, D. B. and Feldman, M. P. (1992), 'Real effects of academic research: Comment', *American Economic Review*, **82** (1), 363–367.

—————— (1994), 'R&D spillovers and innovative activity', *Managerial and Decision Economics*, **15**, 131–138.

Aghion, P. and Howitt, P. (1992), 'A model of growth through creative destruction', *Econometrica*, **60** (2), 323–351.

Aharonson, B. S., Baum, J. A. C. and Feldman, M. P. (2004), 'Borrowing from Neighbors: The Location Choice of Entrepreneurs', presented at the International Schumpeter Society Conference 2004, Milan, Italy.

Allen, R. C. (1983), 'Collective invention', *Journal of Economic Behavior and Organization*, **4**, 1–24.

Almeida, P. and Kogut, B. (1999), 'The localization of knowledge and the mobility of engineers in regional networks', *Management Science*, **45** (7), 905–917.

Amin, A. and Thrift, N. (1992), 'Neo-Marshallian nodes in global networks', *International Journal of Urban and Regional Research*, **16**, 571–587.

Amin, A. and Wilkinson, F. (1999), 'Learning, proximity and industrial performance: An introduction', *Cambridge Journal of Economics*, **23** (2), 121–125.

Anselin, L., Varga, A. and Acs, Z. (1997), 'Local geographic spillovers between university research and high technology innovations', *Journal of Urban Economics*, **42**, 422–448.

Arora, A., Fosfuri, A. and Gambardella, A. (2001a), 'Markets for technology and their implications for corporate strategy', *Industrial and Corporate Change*, **10** (2), 419–451.

—————— (2001b), *Markets for Technology: The Economics of Innovation and Corporate Strategy*, Cambridge, Mass: MIT Press.

Arrow, K. J. (1962a), 'The economic implications of learning by doing', *Review of Economic Studies*, **29**, 155–173.

—————— (1962b), 'Economic welfare and the allocation of resources for invention', in Nelson, R. (ed.), *The Rate and Direction of Innovative Activity: Economic and Social Factors*, pp. 609–625, Princeton: Princeton University Press.

Arthur, W. B. (1994), *Increasing Returns and Path Dependence in the Economy*, Ann Arbor, Mich: University of Michigan Press.

Asheim, B. T. (1996), 'Industrial districts as "learning regions": A condition for prosperity?', *European Planning Studies*, **4** (4), 379–400.

—— (2001), 'Learning regions as development coalitions: Partnership as governance in European workfare states?', *Concepts and Transformation*, **6** (1), 73–101.

Asheim, B. T. and Cooke, P. (1998), 'Localised innovation networks in a global economy: A comparative analysis of endogenous and exogenous regional development approaches', *Comparative Social Research*, **17**, 199–240.

Asheim, B. T. and Gertler, M. S. (2004), 'Regional innovation systems and the geographical foundations of innovation', in Fagerberg, J., Mowery, D. C. and Nelson, R. R. (eds.), *Oxford Handbook of Innovation*, Oxford, UK: Oxford University Press.

Asheim, B. T. and Isaksen, A. (2002), 'Regional innovations systems: The integration of local 'sticky' and global 'ubiquitous' knowledge', *Journal of Technology Transfer*, **27** (1), 77–86.

Audretsch, D. B. (1998), 'Agglomeration and the location of innovative activity', *Oxford Review of Economic Policy*, **14** (2), 18–29.

Audretsch, D. B. and Feldman, M. P. (1996a), 'Innovation clusters and the industry life cycle', *Review of Industrial Organization*, **11** (2), 253–273.

—— (1996b), 'R&D spillovers and the geography of innovation and production', *American Economic Review*, **86** (3), 630–640.

Audretsch, D. B. and Fritsch, M. (2002), 'Growth regimes over time and space', *Regional Studies*, **36** (2), 113–124.

Audretsch, D. B. and Keilbach, M. (2002), 'The Mobility of Economic Agents as Conduits of Knowledge Spillovers', presented at the workshop on 'The Role of Labour Mobility and Informal Networks for Knowledge Transfer', Max-Planck Institute, Jena, 5–7 December, 2002.

Audretsch, D. B. and Thurik, R. A. (2000), 'Capitalism and democracy in the 21st century: from the managed to the entrepreneurial economy', *Journal of Evolutionary Economics*, **10**, 17–34.

Bade, F. J. and Nerlinger, E. A. (2000), 'The spatial distribution of new technology-based firms: Empirical results for West-Germany', *Papers in Regional Science*, **79**, 155–176.

Bala, V. and Goyal, S. (1998), 'Learning from neighbors', *Review of Economic Studies*, **65** (224), 595–621.

Balassa, B. (1965), 'Trade liberalisation and revealed comparative advantage', *The Manchester School of Economic and Social Studies*, **33**, 99–123.

Balconi, M., Breschi, S. and Lissoni, F. (2004), 'Networks of inventors and the role of academia: An exploration of Italian patent data', *Research Policy*, **33**, 127–145.

Balzat, M. and Hanusch, H. (2004), 'Recent trends in the research on national innovation systems', *Journal of Evolutionary Economics*, **14** (2), 197–210.

Baptista, R. and Swann, P. (1998), 'Do firms in clusters innovate more?', *Research Policy*, **27**, 525–540.

Bathelt, H. (2003), 'In Good Faith? The "Distanced Neighbor" Paradox: "Overembedded" and "Under-Socialized" Economic Relations in Leipzig's Media Industry', presented at the DRUID Summer Conference 2003, Copenhagen/Elsinore June 12-14, 2003.

Bathelt, H., Malmberg, A. and Maskell, P. (2004), 'Clusters and knowledge: Local buzz, global pipelines and the process of knowledge creation', *Progress in Human Geography*, **28** (1), 31–56.

Bhidé, A. V. (2000), *The Origin and Evolution of New Businesses*, Oxford: Oxford University Press.

Blanc, H. and Sierra, C. (1999), 'The internationalisation of R&D by multinationals: a trade-off between external and internal proximity', *Cambridge Journal of Economics*, **23** (2), 187–206.

Bluestone, B. and Harrison, B. (1982), *The Deindustrialization of America: Plant Closings, Community Abandonment, and the Dismantling of Basic Industry*, New York: Basic Books.

BMBF (2002a), 'Förderkatalog des BMBF/BMWA, Internetdatenbank, Abfrage am 5.12.2002, Bundesministerium für Bildung und Forschung', Http://oas2.ip.kp.dlr.de/foekat/foekat/foekat.

——— (2002b), *Spinoff-Gründungen aus der öffentlichen Forschung in Deutschland*, Bonn: Bundesministerium für Bildung und Forschung.

Borgatti, S., Everett, M. and Freeman, L. (2002), *Ucinet for Windows: Software for Social Network Analysis*, Harvard: Analytic Technologies.

Borys, B. and Jemison, D. B. (1989), 'Hybrid arrangements as strategic alliances: Theoretical issues in organizational combinations', *Academy of Management Review*, **14**, 234–249.

Boschma, R. (2005), 'Proximity and innovation: A critical assessment', *Regional Studies*, **39** (1), 61–74.

Bott, H. (2000), 'Der Geist, der durch die Luft fliegt', *Spiegel*, **2000** (18), 96–100.

Boucke, C., Cantner, U. and Hanusch, H. (1994), '"Technopolises" as a policy goal: A morphological study of the Wissenschaftsstadt Ulm', *Technovation*, **14** (6), 407–418.

Braczyk, H.-J., Cooke, P. and Heidenreich, M. (1998), *Regional Innovation Systems: The Role of Governances in a Globalized World*, London: UCL Press.

Breschi, S. and Lissoni, F. (2001a), 'Knowledge spillovers and local innovation systems: A critical survey', *Industrial and Corporate Change*, **10** (4), 975–1005.

——— (2001b), 'Localised knowledge spillovers vs. innovative milieux: Knowledge "tacitness" reconsidered', *Papers in Regional Science*, **80**, 255–273.

——— (2003), 'Mobility and Social Networks: Localised Knowledge Spillovers Revisited', CESPRI Working Paper, No. 142, March 2003.

Breschi, S. and Malerba, F. (1997), 'Sectoral innovation systems: Technological regimes, Schumpeterian dynamics, and spatial boundaries', in Edquist, C. (ed.), *Systems of Innovation: Technologies, Institutions and Organizations*, pp. 130–156, London: Pinter.

——— (2001), 'The geography of innovation and economic clustering: Some introductory notes', *Industrial and Corporate Change*, **10** (4), 817–833.

Bresnahan, T., Gambardella, A. and Saxenian, A. (2001), '"Old Economy" inputs for "New Economy" outcomes: Cluster formation in the new Silicon Valleys', *Industrial and Corporate Change*, **10** (4), 835–860.

Brusoni, S., Principe, A. and Pavitt, K. (2001), 'Knowledge specialization, organizational coupling, and the boundaries of the firm: Why do firms know more than they make?', *Administrative Science Quarterly*, **46** (4), 597–621.

Bundesamt für Bauwesen und Raumordnung (2000), *INKAR – Indikatoren und Karten zur Raumentwicklung CD-ROM – Ausgabe zu Berichte Band 8*, Bonn: Bundesamt für Bauwesen und Raumordnung.

Butts, C. and Carley, K. (2001), 'Multivariate Methods for Interstructural Analysis', CASOS working paper, Carnegie Mellon University.

Callon, M. (1992), 'The dynamics of techno-economic networks', in Coombs, R., Saviotti, P. and Walsh, V. (eds.), *Technological Change and Company Strategies: Economic and Sociological Perspectives*, London: Academic Press.

Camagni, R. (1991), 'Local milieu, uncertainty and innovation networks: Towards a new dynamic theory of economic space', in Camagni, R. (ed.), *Innovation Networks, Spatial Perspectives*, London, New York: Belhaven Press.

———— (1995a), 'The concept of innovative milieu and its relevance for public policies in European lagging regions', *Papers in Regional Science*, **74**, 317–340.

———— (1995b), 'Global network and local milieu: Towards a theory of economic space', in Conti, G., Malecki, E. and Oinas, P. (eds.), *The Industrial Enterprise and its Environment: Spatial Perspectives*, Avebury: Aldershot.

Cameron, A. C. and Trivedi, P. K. (1998), *Regression Analysis of Count Data*, Cambridge, Mass: Cambridge University Press.

Cantner, U. and Graf, H. (2003a), 'Cooperation and Specialization in German Technology Regions', Jenaer Schriften zur Wirtschaftswissenschaft, FSU Jena, 04/2003.

———— (2003b), 'Innovationssysteme und kollektive Innovationsprozesse', in Cantner, U., Helm, R. and Meckl, R. (eds.), *Strukturen und Strategien in einem Innovationssystem: Das Beispiel Jena*, pp. 21–44, Sternenfels: Verlag Wissenschaft & Praxis.

———— (2004), 'Cooperation and specialization in German technology regions', *Journal of Evolutionary Economics*, **14** (5), 543–562.

———— (2006), 'The network of innovators in Jena: An application of social network analysis', *Research Policy*, **35** (4), 463–480.

Cantner, U., Helm, R. and Meckl, R. (2003), *Strukturen und Strategien in einem Innovationssystem: Das Beispiel Jena*, Sternenfels: Verlag Wissenschaft & Praxis.

Cantwell, J. A. and Iammarino, S. (1998), 'MNCs, technological innovation and regional systems in the EU: Some evidence in the Italian case', *International Journal of the Economics of Business*, **5** (3), 383–408.

———— (2000), 'Multinational corporations and the location of technological innovation in the UK regions', *Regional Studies*, **34** (4), 317–322.

———— (2001), 'EU regions and multinational corporations: Change, stability and strengthening of technological comparative advantages', *Industrial and Corporate Change*, **10** (4), 1007–1037.

Cantwell, J. A. and Janne, O. (1999), 'Technological globalisation and innovative centres: The role of corporate technological leadership and locational hierarchy', *Research Policy*, **28**, 119–144.

Cantwell, J. A. and Santangelo, G. D. (2002), 'The new geography of corporate research in information and communications technology (ICT)', *Journal of Evolutionary Economics*, **12** (1–2), 163–197.

Carlsson, B. (ed.) (1995), *Technological Systems and Economic Performance: The Case of Factory Automation*, Dordrecht: Kluwer.

Carlsson, B. and Stankiewicz, R. (1991), 'On the nature, function and composition of technological systems', *Journal of Evolutionary Economics*, **1** (2), 93–118.

Cesaroni, F., Gambardella, A., Garcia-Fontes, W. and Mariani, M. (2001), 'The Chemical Sectoral System. Firms, Markets, Institutions and the Processes of Knowledge Creation and Diffusion', Essy working paper.

Chapman, K. and Walker, D. (1987), *Industrial Location: Principles and Policies*, Oxford and New York: Basil Blackwell.

Christaller, W. (1933), *Die zentralen Orte in Süddeutschland*, Jena: Fischer.

Cimoli, M. and della Giusta, M. (1998), 'The Nature of Technological Change and its Main Implications on National and Local Systems of Innovation', IIASA Interim Report IR-98-029/June.

Cohen, W. M. and Klepper, S. (1996), 'A reprise of size and R&D', *Economic Journal*, **106**, 925–951.

Cohen, W. M. and Levinthal, D. A. (1990), 'Absorptive capacity: A new perspective on learning and innovation', *Administrative Science Quarterly*, **35**, 128–152.

Cohen, W. M., Nelson, R. R. and Walsh, J. P. (2000), 'Protecting their Intellectual Assets: Appropriability Conditions and why U.S. Manufacturing Firms Patent (or not)', NBER Working Paper No. W7552.

Combs, J. G. and Ketchen, D. J. (1999), 'Explaining inter-firm co-operation and performance: Toward a reconciliation of predictions from the resource-based view and organizational economics', *Strategic Management Journal*, **20**, 867–888.

Cooke, P. (1998), 'Introduction: Origins of the concept', in Braczyk, H.-J., Cooke, P. and Heidenreich, M. (eds.), *Regional Innovation Systems: The Role of Governances in a Globalized World*, pp. 2–25, London: UCL Press.

—— (2001), 'Regional innovation systems, clusters, and the knowledge economy', *Industrial and Corporate Change*, **10** (4), 945–974.

Cooke, P. and Morgan, K. (1998), *The Associational Economy: Firms, Regions and Innovation*, Oxford: Oxford University Press.

Cooper, A. C. and Folta, T. B. (2000), 'Entrepreneurship and high-technology clusters', in Sexton, D. L. and Landström, H. (eds.), *The Blackwell Handbook of Entrepreneurship*, pp. 348–367, Oxford: Blackwell.

Cooper, D. P. (2001), 'Innovation and reciprocal externalities: Information transmission via job mobility', *Journal of Economic Behavior and Organization*, **45** (4), 403–425.

Cowan, R. (2004), 'Network Models of Innovation and Knowledge Diffusion', MERIT-infonomics Research Memorandum series 2004-016.

Cowan, R., David, P. and Foray, D. (2000), 'The explicit economics of knowledge codification and tacitness', *Industrial and Corporate Change*, **9** (2), 211–254.

Cowan, R. and Jonard, N. (2003), 'The dynamics of collective invention', *Journal of Economic Behavior and Organization*, **52** (4), 513–532.

—— (2004), 'Network structure and the diffusion of knowledge', *Journal of Economic Dynamics and Control*, **28** (8), 1557–1575.

Czarnitzki, D. and Fier, A. (2003), 'Publicly Funded R&D Collaborations and Patent Outcome in Germany', ZEW Discussion paper No. 03-24.

Dasgupta, P. and Stiglitz, J. E. (1980), 'Industrial structure and the nature of innovative activity', *Economic Journal*, **90**, 266–293.

D'Aspremont, C. and Jacquemin, A. (1988), 'Cooperative and noncooperative R&D in duopoly with spillovers', *American Economic Review*, **78** (5), 1133–1137.

David, P. A., Hall, B. H. and Toole, A. A. (2000), 'Is public R&D a complement or substitute for private R&D? A review of the econometric evidence', *Research Policy*, **29** (4–5), 497–529.

de Laat, B. (1996), 'Scripts for the Future: Technology Foresight, Strategic Evaluation and Socio-Technical Networks – The Confrontation of Script-Based Scenarios', Ph.D. thesis, University of Amsterdam.

Dearden, L., Machin, S. and Reed, H. (1997), 'Intergenerational mobility in Britain', *Economic Journal*, **107** (440), 47–66.

DeBresson, C. and Amesse, F. (1991), 'Networks of innovators: A review and introduction to the issue', *Research Policy*, **20** (5), 363–379.

Di Gregorio, D. and Shane, S. (2003), 'Why do some universities generate more start-ups than others?', *Research Policy*, **32** (2), 209–227.

Dohse, D. (2000), 'Technology policy and the regions. The case of the BioRegio contest', *Research Policy*, **29** (9), 1111–1133.

Dosi, G. (1984), *Technical Change and Industrial Transformation*, London: Macmillan.
——— (1988a), 'The nature of the innovative process', in Dosi, G., Freeman, C., Nelson, R., Silverberg, G. and Soete, L. (eds.), *Technical Change and Economic Theory*, pp. 221–238, London: Pinter.
——— (1988b), 'Sources, procedure and microeconomic effects of innovation', *Journal of Economic Literature*, **26** (3), 1120–1171.

Dosi, G. and Malerba, F. (1996), *Organization and Strategy in the Evolution of the Enterprise*, London: MacMillan.

DPMA (Deutsches Patent- und Markenamt) (2001), *PATOS Text, CD-ROM*, München: Wila-Verlag.

Drewello, H. and Wurzel, U. G. (2002), 'Humankapital und innovative regionale Netzwerke - Theoretischer Hintergrund und empirische Untersuchungsergebnisse', DIW, Materialien, 12.

Dumais, G., Ellison, G. and Glaeser, E. L. (2002), 'Geographic concentration as a dynamic process', *Review of Economics and Statistics*, **84** (2), 193–204.

Duranton, G. and Puga, D. (2000), 'Diversity and specialization in cities: Why, where and when does it matter?', *Urban Studies*, **37** (3), 533–555.
——— (2001), 'Nursery cities: Urban diversity, process innovation, and the life cycle of products', *American Economic Review*, **91** (5), 1454–1477.

Edquist, C. (1997), 'Systems of innovation approaches – their emergence and characteristics', in Edquist, C. (ed.), *Systems of Innovation: Technologies, Institutions and Organizations*, pp. 1–35, London: Pinter.
——— (2001), 'The Systems of Innovation Approach and Innovation Policy: An Account of the State of the Art', Presented at DRUID Conference, Aalborg, June 12–15, 2001.
——— (2004), 'Systems of innovation – perspectives and challenges', in Fagerberg, J., Mowery, D. C. and Nelson, R. R. (eds.), *Oxford Handbook of Innovation*, Oxford, UK: Oxford University Press.

Edquist, C. and Johnson, B. (1997), 'Institutions and organisations in systems of innovation', in Edquist, C. (ed.), *Systems of Innovation: Technologies, Institutions and Organizations*, pp. 41–63, London: Pinter.

Eisenhardt, K. M. and Schoonhoven, C. B. (1996), 'Resource-based view of strategic alliance formation: strategic and social effects in entrepreneurial firms', *Organization*

Science, **7** (2), 136–150.

Ellison, G. and Glaeser, E. L. (1997), 'Geographic concentration in U.S. manufacturing industries: A dartboard approach', *Journal of Political Economy*, **105** (5), 889–927.

—— (1999), 'The geographic concentration of industry: Does natural advantage explain agglomeration?', *American Economic Review*, **89** (2), 311–316.

Engländer, O. (1926), 'Kritisches und Positives zu einer allgemeinen reinen Lehre vom Standort', *Zeitschrift für Volkswirtschaft und Sozialpolitik*, **Neue Folge 5**.

Fehr, E. and Gächter, S. (2000), 'Fairness and retaliation: The economics of reciprocity', *Journal of Economic Perspectives*, **14** (3), 159–181.

Feldman, M. P. (1994), *The Geography of Innovation*, Dordrecht: Kluwer.

—— (1999), 'The new economics of innovation, spillovers and agglomeration: A review of empirical studies', *Economics of Innovation and New Technology*, **8** (1–2), 5–25.

—— (2001), 'Where science comes to life: University bioscience, commercial spin-offs, and regional economic development', *Journal of Comparative Policy Analysis: Research and Practice*, **2**, 345–361.

Feldman, M. P. and Audretsch, D. B. (1999), 'Innovation in cities: Science-based diversity, specialization and localized competition', *European Economic Review*, **43** (2), 409–429.

Fleming, L., King III, C. and Juda, A. (2004), 'Small Worlds and Innovation', Harvard Business School, mimeo.

Florida, R. (1995), 'Toward the learning region', *Futures*, **27**, 527–536.

Fornahl, D. and Graf, H. (2003), 'Standortfaktoren und Gründungsaktivitäten in Jena', in Cantner, U., Helm, R. and Meckl, R. (eds.), *Strukturen und Strategien in einem Innovationssystem: Das Beispiel Jena*, pp. 97–123, Sternenfels: Verlag Wissenschaft & Praxis.

Franco, A. M. and Filson, D. (2000), 'Knowledge Diffusion through Employee Mobility', Federal Reserve Bank of Minneapolis, Staff Report 272.

Freeman, C. (1987), *Technology and Economic Performance: Lessons from Japan*, London: Pinter.

—— (1995), 'The "National System of Innovation" in historical perspective', *Cambridge Journal of Economics*, **19** (1), 5–24.

—— (2002), 'Continental, national and sub-national innovation systems – complementarity and economic growth', *Research Policy*, **31**, 191–211.

Freeman, C., Clark, H. and Soete, L. (1982), *Unemployment and Technical Innovation. A Study of Long Waves and Economic Development*, London: F. Pinter.

Fritsch, M. and Niese, M. (1999), 'Betriebsgründungen in den westdeutschen Raumordnungsregionen von 1983-97', Freiberger Diskussionpapier Nr. 20, Technische Universität Freiberg.

Fujita, M. and Ishii, R. (1998), 'Global location behavior and organizational dynamics of Japanese electronics firms and their impact on regional economies', in Chandler, A., Hagström, P. and Sölvell, O. (eds.), *The Dynamic Firm: The Role of Technology, Strategy, Organization and Regions*, pp. 343–383, Oxford: Oxford University Press.

Fujita, M., Krugman, P. R. and Venables, A. J. (1999), *The Spatial Economy: Cities, Regions and International Trade*, Cambridge, Mass: MIT Press.

Fujita, M. and Thisse, J.-F. (2002), *Economics of Agglomeration*, Cambridge University

Press.

Gaspar, J. and Glaeser, E. L. (1998), 'Information technology and the future of cities', *Journal of Urban Economics*, **43**, 136–156.

Geroski, P. (1995), 'Markets for technology – knowledge, innovation and appropriability', in Stoneman, P. (ed.), *Handbook of the Economics of Innovation and Technological Change*, pp. 90–131, Oxford: Blackwell Publishers.

Gertler, M. (1997), 'The invention of regional culture', in Lee, R. and Wills, J. (eds.), *Geographies of Economies*, pp. 47–58, London: Edward Arnold.

Gertler, M. S. and Wolfe, D. A. (2004), 'Ontario's regional innovation system: The evolution of knowledge-based institutional assets', in Cooke, P., Heidenreich, M. and Braczyk, H. (eds.), *Regional Innovation Systems (second edition)*, London: Routledge.

Glaeser, E. L., Kallal, H. D., Scheinkman, J. A. and Shleifer, A. (1992), 'Growth in cities', *Journal of Political Economy*, **100** (6), 1126–1152.

Gompers, P., Lerner, J. and Scharfstein, D. (2003), 'Entrepreneurial Spawning: Public Corporations and the Genesis of New Ventures, 1986-1999', Harvard NOM Working Paper No. 03-37; MIT Sloan Working Paper No. 4317-03 (June 2003).

Granovetter, M. (1973), 'The strength of weak ties', *American Journal of Sociology*, **78**, 1360–1380.

――――― (1983), 'The strength of weak ties: A network theory revisited', *Sociological Theory*, **1**, 203–233.

Granovetter, M. S. (1985), 'Economic action and social structure. The problem of embeddedness', *American Journal of Sociology*, **91** (3), 481–510.

Gray, M., Golob, E., Markusen, A. and Park, S. O. (1998), 'New industrial cities? The four faces of Silicon Valley', *Review of Radical Political Economics*, **30**, 1–28.

Greif, S. (1998), *Patentatlas Deutschland: Die räumliche Struktur der Erfindungstätigkeit*, München: Deutsches Patentamt.

Griliches, Z. (1990), 'Patent statistics as economic indicators: A survey', *Journal of Economic Literature*, **28**, 1661–1707.

――――― (1992), 'The search for R&D spillovers', *Scandinavian Journal of Economics*, **94** (Supplement), 29–47.

Grupp, H. (1994), 'The measurement of technical performance of innovations by technometrics and its impact on established technology indicators', *Research Policy*, **23** (2), 175–193.

Hagedoorn, J. (1993), 'Understanding the rationale of strategic technology partnering: Inter-organizational modes of cooperation and sectoral differences', *Strategic Management Journal*, **14**, 371–385.

――――― (2002), 'Inter-firm R&D partnerships: An overview of major trends and patterns since 1960', *Research Policy*, **31** (4), 477–492.

Hamel, G. (1991), 'Competition for competence and inter-partner learning within international strategic alliances', *Strategic Management Journal*, **12**, 83–103.

Harabi, N. (2002), 'The impact of vertical R&D cooperation on firm innovation: An empirical investigation', *Economics of Innovation and New Technology*, **11** (2), 93–108.

Henderson, V., Kuncoro, A. and Turner, M. (1995), 'Industrial development in cities', *Journal of Political Economy*, **103** (5), 1067–1090.

Hendry, C., Brown, J. and Defillippi, R. (2000), 'Regional clustering of high technology-based firms: Opto-electronics in three countries', *Regional Studies*, **34** (2), 129–144.

Hubert, L. J. (1987), *Assignment Methods in Combinatorial Data Analysis*, New York and Basel: Marcel Dekker, INC.

Huffman, D. and Quigley, J. M. (2002), 'The role of the university in attracting high tech entrepreneurship: A Silicon Valley tale', *Annals of Regional Science*, **36** (3), 403–419.

Hull, R., Walsh, V., Green, K. and McMeekin, A. (1999), 'The techno-economic: Perspectives for analysis and intervention', *Journal of Technology Transfer*, **24** (2–3), 185–195.

Hymer, S. (1979), 'The multinational corporation and the international division of labor', in Cohen, R. B., Felton, N., Nkosi, M. and van Liere, J. (eds.), *The Multinational Corporation: A Radical Approach*, pp. 140–163, Cambridge: Cambridge University Press.

Isard, W. (1956), *Location and Space-Economy*, Wiley.

Jacobs, J. (1969), *The Economy of Cities*, New York: Random House.

Jaffe, A. B. (1986), 'Technological opportunity and spillovers of R&D: Evidence from firms' patents, profits, and market value', *American Economic Review*, **76** (5), 984–1001.

––––––– (1989), 'Real effects of academic research', *American Economic Review*, **79**, 957–970.

Jaffe, A. B., Trajtenberg, M. and Henderson, R. (1993), 'Geographic localization of knowledge spillovers as evidenced by patent citations', *Quarterly Journal of Economics*, **108** (3), 577–598.

Johnson, A. (2001), 'Functions in Innovation System Approaches', Paper presented at DRUID's Nelson and Winter Conference, Aalborg, June 2001.

Johnson, B., Lorenz, E. and Lundvall, B.-A. (2002), 'Why all this fuss about codified and tacit knowledge?', *Industrial and Corporate Change*, **11** (2), 245–262.

Johnson, D. K. N. and Mareva, M. (2002), 'It's a Small(er) World: The Role of Geography and Networks in Biotechnology Innovation', Wellesley College Working Paper 2002-01.

Kamien, M. I., Muller, E. and Zang, I. (1992), 'Research joint ventures and R&D cartels', *American Economic Review*, **82** (5), 1293–1306.

Katz, M. L. and Ordover, J. A. (1990), 'R&D cooperation and competition', *Brookings Papers: Microeconomics*, pp. 137–191.

Keeble, D. and Wilkinson, F. (1999), 'Collective learning and knowledge development in the evolution of regional clusters of high technology SMEs in Europe', *Regional Studies*, **33** (4), 295–303.

Kelly, K. (1998), *New Rules for the New Economy*, London: Fourth Estate.

Kempe, W. (1998), 'Veränderung der Bevölkerungsstruktur Deutschlands bis 2040: Abnehmende Bevölkerungszahl bei wachsender überalterung', *IWH, Wirtschaft im Wandel*, **1998** (5), 3–8.

Klepper, S. (1996), 'Entry, exit, growth, and innovation over the product life cycle', *American Economic Review*, **86** (3), 562–583.

––––––– (2001a), 'Employee startups in high-tech industries', *Industrial and Corporate*

Change, **10**, 639–674.

—— (2001b), 'The Evolution of the U.S. Automobile Industry and Detroit as its Capital', Carnegie Mellon University, Mimeo.

Klepper, S. and Sleeper, S. (2002), 'Entry by Spinoffs', Papers on Economics and Evolution, Nr. 2002-07.

Kline, S. and Rosenberg, N. (1986), 'An overview of innovation', in Landau, R. and Rosenberg, N. (eds.), *The Positive Sum Strategy*, pp. 275–305, Washington: National Academy Press.

Kodde, D. A. and Ritzen, J. M. M. (1988), 'Direct and indirect effects of parental education level on the demand for higher education', *Journal of Human Resources*, **23** (3), 356–371.

Kogut, B. (1989), 'The stability of joint ventures: Reciprocity and competitive rivalry', *Journal of Industrial Economics*, **38** (2), 183–198.

Kogut, B. and Zander, U. (1992), 'Knowledge of the firm, combinative capabilities, and the replication of technology', *Organization Science*, **3** (3), 383–397.

Koschatzky, K. and Zenker, A. (1999), 'Innovative Regionen in Ostdeutschland – Merkmale, Defizite, Potentiale', Fraunhofer Institut für Systemtechnik und Innovationsforschung, Arbeitspapier Regionalforschung Nr. 17.

Krackhardt, D. (1987), 'QAP partialling as a test of spuriousness', *Social Networks*, **9**, 171–186.

—— (1988), 'Predicting with networks: Nonparametric multiple regression analysis of dyadic data', *Social Networks*, **10**, 359–381.

Krugman, P. (1991a), *Geography and Trade*, Cambridge, Mass: MIT Press.

—— (1991b), 'Increasing returns and economic geography', *Journal of Political Economy*, **99**, 483–499.

Lambooy, J. (2003), 'The Role of Intermediate Structures and Regional Context for the Evolution of Knowledge Networks and Structural Change', MPI Jena, Papers on Economics & Evolution, No. 0309.

Länger, A. (2003), 'Die Entwicklung der feinmechanisch-optischen Industrie in Jena ab 1846', in Cantner, U., Helm, R. and Meckl, R. (eds.), *Strukturen und Strategien in einem Innovationssystem: Das Beispiel Jena*, pp. 267–289, Sternenfels: Verlag Wissenschaft & Praxis.

Lanjouw, J. O. and Schankerman, M. (2004), 'Patent quality and research productivity: measuring innovation with multiple indicators', *Economic Journal*, **114**, 441–465.

Latouche, D. (1998), 'Do regions make a difference? The case of science and technology policies in Quebec', in Braczyk, H.-J., Cooke, P. and Heidenreich, M. (eds.), *Regional Innovation Systems: The Role of Governances in a Globalized World*, London: UCL Press.

Laursen, K. (1998), 'Revealed Comparative Advantage and the Alternatives as Measures of International Specialisation', DRUID Working Paper No. 98-30.

Lawson, C. (1999), 'Towards a competence theory of the region', *Cambridge Journal of Economics*, **23** (2), 151–166.

Lawson, C. and Lorenz, E. (1999), 'Collective learning, tacit knowledge and regional innovative capacity', *Regional Studies*, **33** (4), 305–317.

Lazerson, M. H. and Lorenzoni, G. (1999), 'The firms that feed industrial districts: A return to the Italian source', *Industrial and Corporate Change*, **8** (2), 235–266.

Levin, R. C., Klevorick, A. K., Nelson, R. R. and Winter, S. G. (1987), 'Appropriating the returns from industrial research and development', *Brookings Papers on Economic Activity*, **3**, 783–831.

Leyshon, A. and Thrift, N. J. (1997), *Money/Space: Geographies of Monetary Transformation*, London: Routledge.

Lindholm Dahlstrand, A. (1999), 'Technology-based SMEs in the Göteborg region: Their origin and interaction with universities and large firms', *Regional Studies*, **33** (4), 379–389.

List, F. (1841), *Das Nationale System der Politischen ökonomie, Nachdruck der List Gesellschaft E.V. [1959]*, Basel: Kyklos-Verlag.

Longhi, C. (1999), 'Networks, collective learning and technology development in innovative high technology regions: The case of Sophia-Antipolis', *Regional Studies*, **33** (4), 333–342.

Lorenzen, M. and Mahnke, V. (2002), 'Global Strategy and the Acquisition of Local Knowledge: How MNCs Enter Regional Knowledge Clusters', DRUID Working Paper No 02-08.

Lösch, A. (1941), *The Economics of Location*, Yale University Press.

Lucas, R. E. J. (1988), 'On the mechanics of economic development', *Journal of Monetary Economics*, **22**, 3–42.

Lundvall, B.-A. (1985), *Product Innovation and User-Producer Interaction*, Aalborg: Aalborg University Press.

——— (1988), 'Innovation as an interactive process: From user-producer interaction to the national systems of innovation', in Dosi, G., Freeman, C., Nelson, R., Silverberg, G. and Soete, L. (eds.), *Technical change and Economic Theory*, pp. 349–369, London: Pinter.

Lundvall, B.-A. (ed.) (1992), *National Systems of Innovation: Towards a Theory of Innovation and Interactive Learning*, London: Pinter Publishers.

Lundvall, B.-A. and Johnson, B. (1994), 'The learning economy', *Journal of Industry Studies*, **1**, 23–42.

Lundvall, B.-A., Johnson, B., Andersen, E. S. and Dalum, B. (2002), 'National systems of production, innovation and competence building', *Research Policy*, **31**, 213–231.

Lundvall, B.-A. and Maskell, P. (2000), 'Nation states and economic development – from national systems of production to national systems of knowledge creation and learning', in Clark, G. L., Feldman, M. P. and Gertler, M. S. (eds.), *The Oxford Handbook of Economic Geography*, pp. 353–372, Oxford: Oxford University Press.

Malecki, E. (1980), 'Dimensions of R&D location in the United States', *Research Policy*, **9**, 2–22.

Malerba, F. (2002), 'Sectoral systems of innovation and production', *Research Policy*, **31**, 247–264.

——— (2004), 'Sectoral systems: How and why innovation differs across sectors', in Fagerberg, J., Mowery, D. C. and Nelson, R. R. (eds.), *Oxford Handbook of Innovation*, Oxford, UK: Oxford University Press.

Malmberg, A. and Maskell, P. (1997), 'Towards an explanation of regional specialization and industry agglomeration', *European Planning Studies*, **5** (1), 25–41.

——— (2002), 'The elusive concept of localization economies: towards a knowledge-based theory of spatial clustering', *Environment and Planning A*, **34** (3), 429–449.

Mansfield, E., Schwartz, M. and Wagner, S. (1981), 'Imitation costs and patents: An empirical study', *Economic Journal*, **91**, 907–918.

Mare, R. (1980), 'Social background and school continuation decisions', *Journal of the American Statistical Association*, **75**, 295–305.

Markusen, A. (1996), 'Sticky places in slippery space: A typology of industrial districts', *Economic Geography*, **72** (3), 293–313.

—— (1999), 'Fuzzy concepts, scanty evidence, policy distance: The case for rigour and policy relevance in critical regional studies', *Regional Studies*, **33** (9), 869–884.

Marshall, A. (1947), *Principles of Economics: An Introductory Volume*, London: Macmillan, first published 1890.

Martin, R. E. and Justis, R. T. (1993), 'Franchising, liquidity constraints and entry', *Applied Economics*, **25**, 1269–1277.

Maskell, P. (2001), 'Towards a knowledge-based theory of the geographical cluster', *Industrial and Corporate Change*, **10** (4), 921–943.

Maskell, P. and Lorenzen, M. (2004), 'The cluster as market organization', *Urban Studies*, **41** (5–6), 991–1009.

Maskell, P. and Malmberg, A. (1999), 'Localised learning and industrial competitiveness', *Cambridge Journal of Economics*, **23** (2), 167–185.

McKelvey, M. and Orsenigo, L. (2001), 'Pharmaceuticals as a Sectoral Innovation System', Paper presented at the EMAEE Conference Vienna 13–15th September 2001.

Metcalfe, J. S. (1995), 'The economic foundations of technology policy: Equilibrium and evolutionary perspectives', in Stoneman, P. (ed.), *Handbook of the Economics of Innovation and Technological Change*, Oxford: Blackwell.

Mohnen, P. (1996), 'R&D externalities and productivity growth', *STI Review*, **18**, 39–66.

Morgan, K. (1997), 'The learning region: Institutions, innovation and regional renewal', *Regional Studies*, **31**, 491–504.

Morone, P. and Taylor, R. (2004), 'Knowledge diffusion dynamics and network properties of face-to-face interactions', *Journal of Evolutionary Economics*, **14** (3), 327–351.

Mowery, D. and Rosenberg, N. (1979), 'The Influence of market demand upon innovation: A critical review of some recent empirical studies', *Research Policy*, **8**, 103–153.

Mowery, D. C., Oxley, J. E. and Silverman, B. S. (1998), 'Technology overlap and interfirm cooperation: Implications for the resource-based view of the firm', *Research Policy*, **27** (5), 507–523.

Nelson, R. R. (1987), *Understanding Technical Change as an Evolutionary Process*, Amsterdam: Elsevier.

—— (1990), 'What is Public and What is Private About Technology?', University of California Center for Research in Management, CCC Working Paper, no. 90-9, September 1990.

Nelson, R. R. (ed.) (1993), *National Innovation Systems: A Comparative Analysis*, New York: Oxford University Press.

Nelson, R. R. and Mowery, D. (eds.) (1999), *Sources of Industrial Leadership: Studies of Seven Industries*, Cambridge: Cambridge University Press.

Nelson, R. R. and Winter, S. G. (1982), *An Evolutionary Theory of Economic Change*, Cambridge, Mass: Belknap Press.

Oakey, R., Rothwell, R. and Cooper, S. (1988), *The Management of Innovation in High-Technology Small Firms: Innovation and Regional Development in Britain and the United States*, London: Pinter.

OECD (1992), *Technology and the Economy: The Key Relationships*, Paris: Organisation for Economic Cooperation and Development.

—— (2001), *Cities and Regions in the New Learning Economy*, Paris: OECD.

Owen-Smith, J., Riccaboni, M., Pammolli, F. and Powell, W. W. (2002), 'A comparison of U.S. and European university-industry relations in the life sciences', *Management Science*, **48** (1), 24–43.

Palander, T. (1935), *Beiträge zur Standortheorie*, Almqvist and Wicksell.

Palmberg, C., Leppälahti, A., Lemola, T. and Toivonen, H. (1999), 'Towards a Better Understanding of Innovation and Industrial Renewal in Finland – a New Perspective', Vol. 41 of Working Papers, VTT Group for Technology Studies, Espoo.

Patel, P. and Pavitt, K. (1991), 'Europe's technological performance', in Freeman, C., Sharp, M. and Walker, W. (eds.), *Technology and the Future of Europe: Global Competition and the Environment in the 1990s*, London: Pinter.

Patel, P. and Vega, M. (1999), 'Patterns of internationalization of corporate technology: Location vs. home country advantages', *Research Policy*, **28**, 145–155.

Pavitt, K. (1988), 'Uses and abuses of patent statistics', in Van Raan, A. (ed.), *Handbook of Quantitative Studies of Science and Technology*, Amsterdam: North Holland.

—— (1991), 'What makes basic research economically useful?', *Research Policy*, **20** (2), 109–120.

Penrose, E. T. (1959), *The Theory of the Growth of the Firm*, New York: Wiley.

Polany, M. (1967), *The Tacit Dimension*, New York: Doubleday Anchor.

Porter, M. E. (1990), *The Competitive Advantages of Nations*, London: Macmillan.

—— (1998), 'Clusters and the new economics of competition', *Harvard Business Review Nov-Dec*, pp. 77–90.

—— (2000), 'Location, competition, and economic development: Local clusters in a global economy', *Economic Development Quarterly*, **14** (1), 15–34.

Porter, M. E. and Stern, S. (2004), 'Ranking national innovative capacity: Findings from the national innovative capacity index', in Porter, M. E., Sala-i-Martin, X., Lopez-Carlos, A. and Schwab, K. (eds.), *The Global Competitiveness Report 2003-2004*, pp. 91–116.

Potts, J. (2000), *The New Evolutionary Microeconomics: Complexity, Competence, and Adaptive Behaviour*, Cheltenham: Edward Elgar.

Powell, W. W. (1990), 'Neither market nor hierarchy: Network forms of organization', *Research in Organizational Behavior*, **12**, 295–336.

—— (1998), 'Learning from collaboration: Knowledge and networks in the biotechnology and pharmaceutical industries', *California Management Review*, **40** (3), 228–240.

Powell, W. W., Koput, K. W. and Smith-Doerr, L. (1996), 'Interorganizational collaboration and the locus of innovation: Networks of learning in biotechnology', *Administrative Science Quarterly*, **41** (1), 116–145.

Powell, W. W., Koput, K. W., Smith-Doerr, L. and Owen-Smith, J. (1999), 'Network po-

sition and firm performance: Organizational returns to collaboration in the biotechnology industry', in Andrews, S. B. and Knoke, D. (eds.), *Research in the Sociology
of Organizations*, pp. 129–159, Greenwich, CT: JAI Press.

Pred, A. (1976), 'The interurban transmission of growth in advanced economies:
Empirical findings versus regional-planning assumptions', *Regional Studies*, **10**,
151–171.

Predöhl, A. (1925), 'Das Standortproblem in der Wirtschaftslehre', *Weltwirtschaftliches
Archiv*, **21**, 294–331.

Prognos (2004), 'Zukunftsatlas 2004', http://www.prognos.de/zukunftsatlas/.

Pyka, A. (2002), 'Innovation networks in economics – from the incentive based to
the knowledge based approaches', *European Journal of Innovation Management*, **5**,
152–163.

Pyke, F., Becattini, G. and Sengenberger, W. (eds.) (1990), *Industrial Districts and
Interfirm Cooperation in Italy*, Geneva: International Institute for Labour Studies.

Quigley, J. M. (1998), 'Urban diversity and economic growth', *Journal of Economic
Perspectives*, **12** (2), 127–138.

Reinganum, J. F. (1989), 'The timing of innovation: Research, development, and
diffusion', in Schmalensee, R. and Willig, R. D. (eds.), *Handbook of Industrial
Organization, Vol. 1*, pp. 849–908, Amsterdam: Elsevier.

Ritschl, H. (1927), 'Reine und historische Dynamik des Standortes der Erzeu-
gungszweige', *Schmollers Jahrbuch*, **51**, 813–870.

Romer, P. M. (1986), 'Increasing returns and long run growth', *Journal of Political
Economy*, **94**, 1002–1037.

——— (1990), 'Endogenous technical change', *Journal of Political Economy*, **98**, 71–
102.

Rosenberg, N. (1982), *Inside the Black Box: Technology and Economics*, Cambridge:
Cambridge University Press.

Saviotti, P., de Looze, M.-A., Nesta, L. and Maupertius, M.-A. (2003), 'Knowledge
dynamics and the mergers of firms in the biotechnology based sectors', *International
Journal of Biotechnology*, **5** (3/4), 371–401.

Saviotti, P. P. (1996), *Technological Evolution, Variety and the Economy*, Cheltenham:
Edward Elgar.

——— (2004), 'The knowledge-base of the firm in biotechnology based sectors:
Properties and performance', *Revista Brasileira de Inovação*, **3** (1), 129–166.

Saxenian, A. (1994), *Regional Advantage*, Cambridge: Harvard University Press.

Saxenian, A. and Hsu, J.-Y. (2001), 'The Silicon Valley – Hsinchu connection: Technical communities and industrial upgrading', *Industrial and Corporate Change*, **10** (4),
893–920.

Schmookler, J. (1962), 'Economic sources of inventive activity', *Journal of Economic
History*, **22** (1), 1–20.

Schrader, S. (1991), 'Informal technology transfer between firms: Cooperation through
information trading', *Research Policy*, **20**, 153–170.

Schumpeter, J. A. (1912), *Theorie der wirtschaftlichen Entwicklung, 5.Auflage (1935)*,
Berlin: Duncker & Humblot.

——— (1942), *Capitalism, Socialism and Democracy*, London: Unwin, reprint (1987).

Shane, S. A. (1996), 'Hybrid organizational arrangements and their implications for firm growth and survival: A study of new franchisors', *Academy of Management Journal*, **39**, 216–234.

Singh, J. (2003), 'Social Networks as Drivers of Knowledge Diffusion', Harvard University, Mimeo.

—— (2004), 'Collaboration Networks as Determinants of Knowledge Diffusion Patterns', Harvard University, Mimeo.

Soete, L. (1981), 'A general test of technological gap trade theory', *Weltwirtschaftliches Archiv*, **117**, 638–666.

Sorenson, O. (2003), 'Social networks and industrial geography', *Journal of Evolutionary Economics*, **13**, 513–527.

—— (2004), 'Social networks, informational complexity and industrial geography', in Fornahl, D., Zellner, C. and Audretsch, D. B. (eds.), *The Role of Labour Mobility and Informal Networks for Knowledge Transfer*, Dordrecht: Kluwer.

Statistische Ämter des Bundes und der Länder (2002), 'Statistik Regional - Daten und Informationen, CD-ROM - Ausgabe', .

Steinmueller, W. E. (2001), 'The Software Sectoral Innovation System: Open Source Software and the Alternatives', Essy working paper.

Storper, M. and Venables, A. J. (2004), 'Buzz: Face-to-face contact and the urban economy', *Journal of Economic Geography*, **4** (4), 351–370.

Teece, D. (1992), 'Competition, cooperation, and innovation: Organizational arrangements for regimes of rapid technological progress', *Journal of Economic Behavior and Organization*, **18** (1), 1–25.

—— (1996), 'Firm organization, industrial structure, and technological innovation', *Journal of Economic Behavior and Organization*, **31**, 193–224.

Tether, B. S. and Metcalfe, J. S. (2001), 'Innovation Systems & Services. Investigating "Systems of Innovation" in the Service Sectors – an Overview', Essy working paper.

Torre, A. and Gilly, J. P. (2000), 'On the analytical dimension of proximity dynamics', *Regional Studies*, **34** (2), 169–180.

Uzzi, B. (1997), 'Social structure and competition in interfirm networks: the paradox of embeddedness', *Administrative Science Quarterly*, **42** (1), 35–67.

van Oort, F. (2003), 'Knowledge Spillovers and Agglomeration Economies: An Empirical Analysis of Geographical and Sectoral Composition Effects Determining Economic Growth Externalities', Paper presented at the 3rd EMAEE Conference Augsburg, April 9–12 2003.

von Hippel, E. (1987), 'Cooperation between rivals: Informal know-how trading', *Research Policy*, **16**, 291–302.

—— (1994), 'Sticky information and the locus of problem-solving: implications for innovation', *Management Science*, **40** (4), 429–439.

von Thünen, J. H. (1826), *Der isolierte Staat in Beziehung auf Landwirtschaft und Nationalökonomie*, Hamburg.

Walter, R. (2000), 'Die Ressource "Wissen" und ihre Nutzung: Ernst Abbe und der Jenaer Aufschwung um 1900', in Kodalle, K. M. (ed.), *Angst vor der Moderne*, pp. 11–23, Würzburg: Königshausen & Neumann.

Wassermann, S. and Faust, K. (1994), *Social Network Analysis: Methods and Applications*, Cambridge: Cambridge University Press.

Watts, D. J. and Strogatz, S. H. (1998), 'Collective dynamics of "small-world" networks', *Nature*, **393** (4), 440–442.

Weber, A. (1909), *Theory of the Location of Industries*, Chicago: University of Chicago Press.

Winter, S. G. (1984), 'Schumpeterian competition in alternative technological regimes', *Journal of Economic Behavior and Organization*, **5** (3-4), 287–320.

Zander, U. and Kogut, B. (1995), 'Knowledge and the speed of the transfer and imitation of organizational capabilities: An empirical test', *Organization Science*, **6**, 76–91.

Zucker, L., Darby, M. and Armstrong, J. (1998a), 'Geographically localised knowledge: Spillovers or markets?', *Economic Inquiry*, **36**, 65–86.

Zucker, L. G., Darby, M. R. and Brewer, M. B. (1998b), 'Intellectual human capital and the birth of U.S. biotechnology enterprises', *American Economic Review*, **88** (1), 290–306.

Index